HANDBOOK OF COMMONLY PRESCRIBED DRUGS

Tenth Edition

G. John DiGregorio, M.D., Ph.D.
Professor of Pharmacology and Medicine
Medical College of Pennsylvania and
Hahnemann University
Philadelphia, Pennsylvania

Edward J. Barbieri, Ph.D.
Associate Professor of Pharmacology
Medical College of Pennsylvania and
Hahnemann University
Philadelphia, Pennsylvania

1995

HANDBOOK OF COMMONLY PRESCRIBED DRUGS

Tenth Edition

ISBN 0-942447-15-8

The **HANDBOOK OF COMMONLY PRESCRIBED DRUGS, Tenth Edition**, attempts to present the most common trade names and adult doses, and should be used only as a guideline to these; it should not be considered as an official therapeutic document. If there is a discrepancy in therapeutic category, preparations, and dosages, the reader is advised to obtain official and more complete information from the pharmaceutical manufacturer.

The Authors or Publisher are not responsible for typographical errors within the contents of this booklet.

PREFACE

The **Tenth Edition** of the **HANDBOOK OF COMMONLY PRESCRIBED DRUGS** includes new therapeutic agents and new dosage forms. Listed below are a few of the new individual therapeutic agents that have been added to this edition:

Aprotinin (TRASYLOL) — a prophylactic hemostatic used to reduce perioperative blood loss in patients undergoing coronary artery bypass surgery

Budesonide (RHINOCORT) and Fluticasone Propionate (FLONASE) — intranasal corticosteroids for the management of symptoms of perennial allergic rhinitis

Calcipotriene (DOVONEX) — a topical vitamin D_3 analog for the treatment of psoriasis

Diclofenac Potassium (CATAFLAM) — an NSAID for use in arthritides and pain

Didanosine (VIDEX) — an oral antiviral drug for use in patients with advanced HIV infection

Famciclovir (FAMVIR) — another oral antiviral drug for use in patients with acute *Herpes zoster*

Felbamate (FELBATROL) and Gabapentin (NEURONTIN) — two new antiepileptic agents

Fluvastatin Sodium (LESCOL) — an HMG-CoA reductase inhibitor for use as a hypolipemic drug

Ganciclovir Sodium (CYTOVENE) — a parenteral antiviral drug for use against CMV infections

Granisetron Hydrochloride (KYTRIL) — an antiemetic used during chemotherapy

Mivacurium Chloride (MIVACRON) — a new neuromuscular blocking agent

Pegaspargase (ONCASPAR) — an antineoplastic agent (a modified form of asparaginase) for use in patients with acute lymphoblastic leukemia

Risperidone (RISPERDAL) — an antipsychotic agent

Salmeterol (SEREVENT) — a long-acting selective β_2-adrenergic agonist for bronchial asthma

Tacrolimus (PROGRAF) — an immunosuppressant for liver rejection prophylaxis

Venlafaxine (EFFEXOR) — an antidepressant structurally unrelated to other drugs within this group

During the past year, some drugs have received approval for new indications. Some of these products, for which new indications are now included in the text, are:

Captopril (CAPOTEN) — approved for use in diabetic nephropathy and in left ventricular dysfunction after a myocardial infarction

Cefuroxime Axetil (CEFTIN) — approved for use in the treatment of acute and chronic bacterial bronchitis

Doxepin Hydrochloride (ZONALON) — a topical cream of this compound has been approved for use as an antihistamine

Fluconazole (DIFLUCAN) — approved for use in the treatment of vaginal and esophageal candidiasis

Megestrol Acetate (MEGACE) — an oral suspension of this progestin has been approved as an appetite stimulant in patients with AIDS

Pamidronate Disodium (AREDIA) — approved for treatment of Paget's Disease

Pilocarpine HCl (SALAGEN) — an oral form of this cholinomimetic has been approved for patients with severe xerostomia due to radiation treatments

Quinapril Hydrochloride (ACCUPRIL) — approved for treatment of heart failure

A number of new dosage forms of existing drugs were marketed in the United States. We have included a number of these in this edition; for example:

Colestipol Hydrochloride (COLESTID) — tablets of this hypolipemic drug

Fentanyl Citrate (FENTANYL ORALET) — a lozenge form of this opioid analgesic

Glipizide (GLUCOTROL XL) — extended-release tablets of this hypoglycemic drug

Naproxen Sodium (ALEVE) — this NSAID has been approved for OTC use and is marketed as 220 mg tablets

Nicardipine Hydrochloride (CARDENE I.V.) — an injectable form of this antihypertensive drug is now available

Testosterone (TESTODERM) — transdermal preparations of this androgenic drug

Due to a number of requests from physicians, physician assistants, medical residents, medical students, and students in other allied health fields, we have added a section on PRESCRIPTION WRITING, which had been eliminated several years ago.

This booklet is intended to provide medical personnel with a concise reference source for drug names, the preparations available, and common dosages in adults in a tabular format. The pocket size of the handbook has been exceptionally popular (with over 550,000 copies in circulation of over the 10 years of publication). The size of the book continues to increase due to new drugs, new dosage forms, and new indications becoming available each year. Despite the increased size, we will continue to maintain this design so that it can be placed in a jacket or laboratory coat pocket and carried throughout the hospital or used in the office, emergency room, and classroom.

The **HANDBOOK OF COMMONLY PRESCRIBED DRUGS, Tenth Edition**, attempts to present the most common trade names and adult dosages, and should be used only as a guideline to these; it should not be considered as an official therapeutic document. If there is a discrepancy in therapeutic category, preparations, and dosages, the reader is advised to obtain official and more complete information from the pharmaceutical manufacturer.

As always, we are most grateful for your continued interest and support.

G. John DiGregorio, M.D., Ph.D.
Edward J. Barbieri, Ph.D.

TABLE OF CONTENTS

THERAPEUTIC CATEGORY LISTING[a]

[a]   This section lists, by Therapeutic Category, drugs found in the **SELECTED INDIVIDUAL DRUG PREPARATIONS** (pp. 25 to 166) and the **SELECTED COMBINATION DRUG PREPARATIONS** (pp. 167 to 209) sections only. Refer to the **INDEX** for a more complete listing of drugs.

Drug names in UPPER CASE represent TRADE NAMES; the TRADE NAMES without generic names preceeding them are COMBINATION PRODUCTS.

4

5

6

ANTIINFLAMMATORY AGENTS, BOWEL

ANTIINFLAMMATORY AGENTS, SYSTEMIC

11

13

16

17

DRUGS	PAGE	DRUGS	PAGE

22

SELECTED

INDIVIDUAL

DRUG

PREPARATIONS

GENERIC NAME	COMMON TRADE NAMES	THERAPEUTIC CATEGORY	PREPARATIONS	COMMON ADULT DOSAGE
Acebutolol Hydrochloride	SECTRAL	Antihypertensive, Antiarrhythmic	Cpsl: 200, 400 mg	**Hypertension:** Initially, 400 mg once daily po. An optimal response is usually achieved with 400 - 800 mg daily. **Ventricular Arrhythmias:** Initially, 200 mg bid po; increase dosage gradually until an optimal clinical response is obtained, generally at 600 - 1200 mg daily.
Acetaminophen	ANACIN, ASPIRIN FREE	Non-Opioid Analgesic, Antipyretic	Cplt, Tab & Gelcap: 500 mg	1000 mg tid or qid po.
	BAYER SELECT HEADACHE		Cplt: 500 mg	1000 mg tid or qid po.
	JUNIOR STRENGTH FEVERALL		Rectal Suppos: 325 mg	Insert two 325 mg suppositories rectally q 4 - 6 h.
	PANADOL, MAXIMUM STRENGTH		Cplt & Tab: 500 mg	1000 mg q 4 h po.
	TYLENOL, REGULAR STRENGTH		Cplt & Tab: 325 mg	325 - 650 mg tid or qid po.
	TYLENOL, EXTRA-STRENGTH		Cplt, Tab & Gelcap: 500 mg Liquid: 500 mg/15 mL (7% alcohol)	1000 mg tid or qid po. 30 mL (1000 mg) q 4 - 6 h po.
Acetazolamide	DIAMOX	Diuretic, Antiepileptic, Anti-Glaucoma Agent	Tab: 125, 250 mg Inj: 500 mg	**Diuresis in CHF:** 250 - 375 mg once daily in the morning po or IV. Best results occur when given on alternate days, or for 2 days alternating with a day of rest. **Drug-induced Edema:** 250 - 375 mg once daily po or IV for 1 or 2 days. **Epilepsy:** 8 - 30 mg/kg/day in divided doses po (optimum range: 375 to 1000 mg daily). **Glaucoma:** 250 - 1000 mg per day usually in divided doses po.
	DIAMOX SEQUELS	Anti-Glaucoma Agent	Sustained-Rel. Cpsl: 500 mg	**Glaucoma:** 500 mg bid po.

26

Drug	Brand	Class	Forms	Dosage
Acetic Acid	VOSOL	Antibacterial, Antifungal	Otic Solution: 2%	Carefully remove all cerumen and debris. Insert a wick saturated with the solution into the ear canal. Keep in for at least 24 h and keep moist by adding 3 - 5 drops of solution q 4 - 6 h.
Acetohexamide	DYMELOR	Hypoglycemic	Tab: 250, 500 mg	250 - 1500 mg once daily po.
Acetylcysteine Sodium	MUCOMYST	Mucolytic	Solution: 10, 20%	Nebulization (tracheostomy, mask or mouth piece): 3 - 5 mL (of 20% solution) or 6 - 10 mL (of 10% solution) tid to qid. Direct Instillation: 1 - 2 mL (of 10 or 20% solution) q 1 - 4 h.
Acyclovir	ZOVIRAX	Antiviral	Oint: 5%	Apply sufficient quantity to adequately cover all lesions q 3 h, 6 times daily for 7 days.
			Cpsl: 200 mg Susp: 200 mg/5 mL Tab: 400, 800 mg	*Herpes simplex:* Initial Genital Herpes: 200 mg q 4 h (5 times daily) po for 10 days. Chronic Suppressive Therapy for Recurrent Disease: 400 mg bid po for up to 1 year. *Herpes zoster,* Acute Treatment: 800 mg q 4 h (5 times daily) po for 7 to 10 days. Chickenpox: 20 mg/kg (not to exceed 800 mg) qid po for 5 days.
Acyclovir Sodium	ZOVIRAX	Antiviral	Powd for Inj: 500, 1000 mg	Mucosal and Cutaneous *Herpes simplex* Infections in Immunocompromised Patients: 5 mg/kg infused IV at a constant rate over 1 h, q 8 h (15 mg/kg/day) for 7 days. *Herpes simplex* Encephalitis: 10 mg/kg infused IV at a constant rate over at least 1 h, q 8 h for 10 days. *Varicella zoster* in Immunocompromised Patients: 10 mg/kg infused IV at a constant rate over at 1 h, q 8 h for 7 days.

27

GENERIC NAME	COMMON TRADE NAMES	THERAPEUTIC CATEGORY	PREPARATIONS	COMMON ADULT DOSAGE
Adenosine	ADENOCARD	Antiarrhythmic	Inj: 6 mg/2 mL	Initial dose is 6 mg (rapid IV bolus given over a 1 - 2 second period). If the first dose does not stop the arrhythmia within 1 - 2 minutes, 12 mg should be given (by rapid IV bolus). The 12 mg dose may be repeated a second time if required.
Albuterol	PROVENTIL, VENTOLIN	Bronchodilator	**Aerosol**: 90 μg/spray	2 inhalations q 4 - 6 h.
Albuterol Sulfate	PROVENTIL, VENTOLIN NEBULES	Bronchodilator	**Solution for Inhalation**: 0.083% (1 mg/mL, equal to 0.83 mg/mL of albuterol base)	2.5 mg tid - qid by nebulization. This solution requires no dilution prior to administration.
	PROVENTIL, VENTOLIN		**Solution for Inhalation**: 0.5% (6 mg/mL, equal to 5 mg/mL of albuterol base)	2.5 mg tid - qid by nebulization. Dilute 0.5 mL of the 0.5% solution with 2.5 mL of sterile normal saline before administration.
			Syrup: 2 mg (of albuterol base)/5 mL **Tab**: 2, 4 mg (of albuterol base)	2 - 4 mg tid or qid po. For those who do not respond to 2 mg qid, the dose may be cautiously increased stepwise, but not to exceed 8 mg qid as tolerated.
	PROVENTIL REPETABS		**Extended-Release Tab**: 4 mg (of albuterol base)	4 - 8 mg q 12 h po.
	VENTOLIN ROTACAPS		**Cpsl for Inhalation**: 200 μg	200 μg inhaled q 4 - 6 h using a Rotahaler inhalation device.
Alclometasone Dipropionate	ACLOVATE	Corticosteroid	**Cream & Oint**: 0.05%	Apply a thin film to affected skin areas bid to tid; massage gently until the medication disappears.
Alfentanil Hydrochloride (C-II)	ALFENTA	Opioid Analgesic	Inj: 500 μg/mL	**Duration of Anesthesia:** **Under 30 min:** 8 - 20 μg/kg IV, followed by increments of 3 - 5 μg/kg IV. **30 - 60 min:** 20 - 50 μg/kg IV, followed by increments of 5 - 15 μg/kg IV.

28

Generic	Brand	Class	Preparations	Dosage
Allopurinol	ZYLOPRIM	Antigout Agent	Tab: 100, 300 mg	Mild Gout: 200 - 300 mg daily po. Moderately Severe Gout: 400 - 600 mg daily po.
Alprazolam (C-IV)	XANAX	Antianxiety Agent	Tab: 0.25, 0.5, 1, 2 mg	0.25 - 0.5 mg tid po.
Alteplase, Recombinant	ACTIVASE	Thrombolytic	Powd for Inj: 20, 50, 100 mg	Acute Myocardial Infarction: 100 mg IV given as: 60 mg in the first hour (of which 6 - 10 mg is given as an IV bolus over the first 1 to 2 min), 20 mg over the second hour and 20 mg over the third hour. Pulmonary Embolism: 100 mg by IV infusion over 2 hours.
Altretamine	HEXALEN	Antineoplastic	Cpsl: 50 mg	260 mg/m^2/day po in 4 divided doses after meals and hs. Administer either for 14 or 21 consecutive days in a 28 day cycle.
Aluminum Hydroxide Gel	ALTERNAGEL	Antacid	Liquid: 600 mg/5 mL	5 - 10 mL po, prn, between meals & hs.
	ALU-CAP ALU-TAB		Cpsl: 475 mg Tab: 600 mg	3 capsules tid po. 3 tablets tid po.
	AMPHOJEL		Susp: 320 mg/5 mL Tab: 300, 600 mg	10 mL (640 mg) 5 or 6 times daily po, between meals & hs. 600 mg 5 or 6 times daily po, between meals & hs.
Amantadine Hydrochloride	SYMMETREL	Antiparkinsonian, Antiviral	Cpsl: 100 mg Syrup: 50 mg/5 mL	Parkinsonism: 100 mg bid po. Influenza Virus: 200 mg once daily po or 100 mg bid po.
Ambenonium Chloride	MYTELASE	Cholinomimetic	Tab: 10 mg	5 - 25 mg tid to qid po. Start with 5 mg and gradually increase dosage.
Amcinonide	CYCLOCORT	Corticosteroid	Cream & Oint: 0.1% Lotion: 0.1%	Apply to affected areas bid to tid. Rub into affected areas bid.
Amikacin Sulfate	AMIKIN	Antibacterial	Inj (per mL): 100, 500 mg	15 mg/kg/day IM or IV divided in 2 or 3 equal doses at equal intervals.

GENERIC NAME	COMMON TRADE NAMES	THERAPEUTIC CATEGORY	PREPARATIONS	COMMON ADULT DOSAGE
Amiloride Hydrochloride	MIDAMOR	Diuretic	**Tab:** 5 mg	5 mg once daily po with food. The dosage may be increased to 10 mg daily if needed.
Aminocaproic Acid	AMICAR	Hemostatic	**Syrup:** 250 mg/mL **Tab:** 500 mg **Inj:** 250 mg/mL	5 g po during the first hour, followed by 1 to 1.25 g po per hour for about 8 h or until bleeding has been controlled. 4 - 5 g by IV infusion during the first hour, followed by a continuing infusion at the rate of 1 g/h in 50 mL of diluent for about 8 h or until bleeding has been controlled.
Aminoglutethimide	CYTANDREN	Adrenal Steroid Inhibitor	**Tab:** 250 mg	250 mg qid po, preferably at 6 hour intervals.
Aminophylline		Bronchodilator	**Liquid:** 105 mg/5 mL **Tab:** 100, 200 mg **Inj:** 250 mg/10 mL **Suppos:** 250, 500 mg	See Oral Aminophylline Doses Table, p. 219. See Oral Aminophylline Doses Table, p. 219. See IV Aminophylline Doses Table, p. 220. 500 mg daily or bid rectally.
Amiodarone Hydrochloride	CORDARONE	Antiarrhythmic	**Tab:** 200 mg	**Loading Doses:** 800 - 1600 mg/day po for 1 to 3 weeks (sometimes longer) until therapeutic response occurs. Administer in divided doses with meals if daily dose ≥ 1000 mg, or when gastrointestinal upset occurs. For life-threatening arrhthmias, administer loading doses in a hospital. **Dosage Adjustment and Daily Maintenance Dose:** For approximately 1 month, 600 - 800 mg po; then 400 mg daily po.

Drug	Brand Names	Class	Forms	Dosage
Amitriptyline Hydrochloride	ELAVIL, ENDEP	Antidepressant	Tab: 10, 25, 50, 75, 100, 150 mg	**Outpatients:** Initially, 25 mg tid po; may be increased to 50 mg tid po if necessary. The usual maintenance dose is 50 - 100 mg daily po. **Hospitalized Patients:** Initially, these patients may require up to 100 mg daily po; may be increased to 200 mg daily if necessary. The usual maintenance dose is 50 - 100 mg daily po. **Adolescent Patients:** 10 mg tid po, with 20 mg hs, may be satisfactory.
	ELAVIL		Inj: 10 mg/mL	Initially, 20 - 30 mg qid IM. Amitriptyline tablets should replace the injection as soon as possible.
Amlodipine Besylate	NORVASC	Antihypertensive, Antianginal	Tab: 2.5, 5, 10 mg	**Hypertension:** 2.5 - 5 mg once daily po. **Angina:** 5 - 10 mg once daily po.
Amobarbital Sodium	AMYTAL SODIUM	Sedative / Hypnotic	Powd for Inj: 250, 500 mg	**Sedation:** 30 - 50 mg bid - tid IM or IV. **Hypnosis:** 65 - 200 mg IM or IV.
Amoxapine	ASENDIN	Antidepressant	Tab: 25, 50, 100, 150 mg	Initially, 50 mg bid or tid po. Depending upon tolerance, dosage may be increased to 100 mg bid or tid po by the end of the first week. When an effective dosage is established, the drug may be given in a single dose (not to exceed 300 mg) hs.
Amoxicillin	AMOXIL	Antibacterial	Cpsl: 250, 500 mg Chewable Tab: 125, 250 mg Powd for Susp (per 5 mL): 125, 250 mg	**Infections of the Lower Respiratory Tract:** 500 mg q 8 h po. **Gonorrheal Infections, Acute Uncomplicated:** 3 grams as a single oral dose. **Other Susceptible Infections:** 250 - 500 mg q 8 h po.
	POLYMOX, TRIMOX, WYMOX		Cpsl: 250, 500 mg Powd for Susp (per 5 mL): 125, 250 mg	Same dosages as for AMOXIL above.

GENERIC NAME	COMMON TRADE NAMES	THERAPEUTIC CATEGORY	PREPARATIONS	COMMON ADULT DOSAGE
Amphetamine Sulfate (C-II)		CNS Stimulant, Anorexiant	Tab: 5, 10 mg	**Narcolepsy:** Start with 10 mg daily po; raise dosage in increments of 10 mg daily at weekly intervals. **Exogenous Obesity:** 5 - 10 mg once daily to tid 30 - 60 minutes ac po.
Amphotericin B	FUNGIZONE INTRAVENOUS	Antifungal	**Powd for Inj:** 50 mg	Initially, 0.25 mg/kg/day by slow IV infusion (given over 6 h); dose may be increased gradually as tolerance permits.
	FUNGIZONE		Cream, Lotion & Oint: 3%	Apply topically bid - qid.
Ampicillin Anhydrous	OMNIPEN	Antibacterial	**Cpsl:** 250, 500 mg **Powd for Susp (per 5 mL):** 125, 250 mg	**Respiratory Tract and Soft Tissue Infections:** 250 mg q 6 h po. **Genitourinary or Gastrointestinal Tract Infections other than Gonorrhea:** 500 mg q 6 h po. **Gonorrhea:** 3.5 g administered as a single po dose with 1.0 g of probenecid.
Ampicillin Sodium	OMNIPEN-N, POLYCILLIN-N	Antibacterial	**Powd for Inj:** 125, 250, 500 mg; 1, 2 g	**Respiratory Tract and Soft Tissue Infections:** **Under 40 kg:** 25 - 50 mg/kg/day in equally divided doses at 6 - 8 h intervals IM or IV. **Over 40 kg:** 250 - 500 mg q 6 h IM or IV. **Genitourinary or Gastrointestinal Tract Infections including Gonorrhea in Females:** **Under 40 kg:** 50 mg/kg/day in equally divided doses at 6 - 8 h intervals IM or IV. **Over 40 kg:** 500 mg q 6 h IM or IV. **Urethritis in Males due to *N. gonorrhoeae*:** Two doses of 500 mg Each IM or IV at an interval of 8 - 12 h. Repeat if necessary. **Bacterial Meningitis:** 150 - 200 mg/kg/day in equally divided doses q 3 - 4 h. Treatment may be initiated with IV drip and continued with IM injections. **Septicemia:** 150 - 200 mg/kg/day. Start with IV administration for at least 3 days and continue with IM injections q 3 - 4 h.

32

Ampicillin Trihydrate	POLYCILLIN	Antibacterial	**Cpsl:** 250, 500 mg **Powd for Susp (per 5 mL):** 125, 250, 500 mg	Same dosages as for OMNIPEN above.
	PRINCIPEN		**Cpsl:** 250, 500 mg **Powd for Susp (per 5 mL):** 125, 250 mg	Same dosages as for OMNIPEN above.
Aminone Lactate	INOCOR	Inotropic Agent	**Inj:** 5 mg/mL	0.75 mg/kg IV bolus (over 2 - 3 minutes), then 5 - 10 µg/kg/min by IV infusion.
Amyl Nitrite		Antianginal	**Inhalant Cpsl:** 0.3 mL	Crush the capsule and wave under the nose; 1 - 6 inhalations from 1 capsule are usually sufficient. May repeat in 3 - 5 minutes.
Anistreplase	EMINASE	Thrombolytic	**Powd for Inj:** 30 units	30 units IV (over 2 to 5 minutes).
Anthralin	ANTHRA-DERM DRITHOCREME	Anti-Psoriasis Agent	**Oint:** 0.1, 0.25, 0.5, 1.0% **Cream:** 0.1, 0.25, 0.5, 1.0%	Begin with the 0.1% concentration and after at least 1 week gradually increase until the desired effect is obtained. Apply a thin layer to psoriatic areas once daily; rub in gently.
	DRITHO-SCALP		**Cream:** 0.25, 0.5%	Begin with the 0.25% concentration; apply to to the psoriatic lesions only once daily and rub in well. After at least 1 week, may increase dosage with the 0.5% strength.
Aprotinin	TRASYLOL	Hemostatic	**Inj:** 10,000 KIU (kallikrein Inhibitor Units)/mL (equivalent to 1.4 mg/mL)	Two dosage regimens (A and B) are suggested. Regimen A appears to be more effective in patients given aspirin preoperatively. The experience with Regimen B (reduced dosage) is limited (see table below).

Dosage Regimen	IV Test Dose (given at least 10 minutes before the loading dose is administered)	IV Loading Dose (given slowly over 20 - 30 minutes after induction of anesthesia but prior to sternotomy)	IV Pump Prime Dose	Constant IV Infusion Dose (continued until surgery is complete and patient leaves the operating room)
A	1 mL (10,000 KIU)	200 mL (2 million KIU)	200 mL (2 million KIU)	50 mL/h (500,000 KIU/h)
B	1 mL (10,000 KIU)	100 mL (1 million KIU)	100 mL (1 million KIU)	25 mL/h (250,000 KIU/h)

33

GENERIC NAME	COMMON TRADE NAMES	THERAPEUTIC CATEGORY	PREPARATIONS	COMMON ADULT DOSAGE
Asparaginase	ELSPAR	Antineoplastic	Powd for Inj: 10,000 IUnits	200 IU/kg/day IV (over a 30 minute period) for 28 days.
Aspirin	BAYER CHILDREN'S ASPIRIN BAYER ENTERIC ASPIRIN	Non-Opioid Analgesic, Antipyretic, Antiinflammatory	Chewable Tab: 81 mg Enteric Coated Tab: 81 mg Enteric Coated Cplt: 325 mg	Usual Dosage: 325 - 650 mg q 4 h po, prn. Analgesic or Antiinflammatory: the OTC maximum dosage is 4000 mg per day po in divided doses.
	BAYER ASPIRIN BAYER ASPIRIN, MAXIMUM		Cplt & Tab: 325 mg Cplt & Tab: 500 mg	Transient Ischemic Attacks in Men: 1300 mg daily po in divided doses (650 mg bid or 325 mg qid).
	ECOTRIN		Enteric Coated Tab & Cplt: 325 mg Enteric Coated Tab: 325, 500 mg	
	NORWICH ENTERIC SAFETY COATED APIRIN			
	ST. JOSEPH ADULT CHEWABLE ASPIRIN		Chewable Cplt: 81 mg	
Astemizole	HISMANAL	Antihistamine	Tab: 10 mg	10 mg once daily po.
Atenolol	TENORMIN	Antihypertensive, Antianginal, Post-MI Drug	Tab: 25, 50, 100 mg	Hypertension & Angina: Initially, 50 mg once daily po; dosage may be increased to 100 mg daily if necessary. Acute Myocardial Infarction: In patients who tolerate the full IV dose (10 mg), give 50 mg po 10 minutes after the last IV dose, followed by 50 mg po 12 h later. Thereafter, 100 mg daily po or 50 mg bid po for 6 - 9 days or until discharged from the hospital.
	TENORMIN I.V.	Post-MI Drug	Inj: 5 mg/10 mL	Acute Myocardial Infarction: 5 mg IV (over 5 to 10 minutes), followed by 5 mg IV 10 minutes later.
Atovaquone	MEPRON	Antiprotozoal	Tab: 250 mg	750 mg tid po with food for 21 days.

Generic	Brand	Class	Forms	Dosage
Atracurium Besylate	TRACRIUM INJECTION	Neuromuscular Blocker	Inj: 10 mg/mL	0.4 - 0.5 mg/kg IV bolus when used alone; 0.25 - 0.35 mg/kg IV bolus when used under steady state with certain general anesthetics. Doses of 0.08 - 0.10 mg/kg for maintenance during prolonged surgery.
Atropine Sulfate	ISOPTO ATROPINE ATROPISOL	Anticholinergic	Tab: 0.4, 0.6 mg Inj: 0.05 to 1.0 mg/mL	0.4 - 0.6 mg po. 0.4 - 0.6 mg IV, IM or SC.
		Mydriatic - Cycloplegic	Ophth Solution: 0.5, 1% Ophth Solution: 2%	1 - 2 drops in eye(s) up to qid.
	ATROPINE SULFATE S.O.P.		Ophth Oint: 0.5, 1%	Apply to eye(s) up to bid.
Attapulgite	DIASORB	Antidiarrheal	Liquid: 750 mg/5 mL Tab: 750 mg	20 mL or 4 tablets (3000 mg) po at the first sign of diarrhea, and repeat after each subsequent bowel movement. Maximum: 60 mL or 12 tablets per 24 hours.
	DONNAGEL		Liquid: 600 mg/15 mL Chewable Tab: 600 mg	30 mL or 2 chewable tablets (1200 mg) po at the first sign of diarrhea and after each subsequent loose bowel movement. Maximum: 7 doses per 24 hours.
	KAOPECTATE		Liquid: 600 mg/15 mL Chewable Tab: 300 mg	30 mL or 4 chewable tablets (1200 mg) po at the first sign of diarrhea and after each subsequent loose bowel movement. Maximum: 7 doses per 24 hours.
			Cplt: 750 mg	2 caplets (1500 mg) po at the first sign of diarrhea and after each subsequent loose bowel movement. Maximum: 12 caplets per 24 hours.
	PAREPECTOLIN		Liquid: 600 mg/15 mL	30 mL po after each bowel movement, up to 7 times daily.
	RHEABAN		Cplt: 750 mg	2 caplets po after the initial bowel movement, and 2 caplets after each subsequent bowel movement. Max: 12 caplets per 24 hours.

GENERIC NAME	COMMON TRADE NAMES	THERAPEUTIC CATEGORY	PREPARATIONS	COMMON ADULT DOSAGE
Auranofin	RIDAURA	Antirheumatic	Cpsl: 3 mg	3 mg bid po or 6 mg daily po.
Aurothioglucose	SOLGANAL	Antiarthritic	Inj: 50 mg/mL	First dose: 10 mg IM; second and third doses: 25 mg IM; fourth and subsequent doses: 50 mg IM. The interval between doses is 1 week. The 50 mg dose is continued at weekly intervals until 0.8 - 1.0 g has been given. If the patient has improved and shows no sign of toxicity, the 50 mg dose may be continued for many months longer, at 3 - 4 week intervals.
Azatadine Maleate	OPTIMINE	Antihistamine	Tab: 1 mg	1 - 2 mg bid po.
Azathioprine	IMURAN	Immunosuppressant	Tab: 50 mg	Renal Homotransplantation: Initial dose is usually 3 - 5 mg/kg daily po or IV, beginning at the time of transplant. Usually given as a single daily dose. Therapy is often initiated with the IV administration of the sodium salt and continued with the tablets after the postoperative period. Dose reduction to maintenance levels of 1 - 3 mg/kg is usually possible.
Azathioprine Sodium	IMURAN	Immunosuppressant	Powd for Inj: 100 mg	Rheumatoid Arthritis: Initially, 1 mg/kg (50 to 100 mg) as a single daily dose or on a bid schedule. May increase dose at 6 - 8 weeks and therafter by steps at 4-week intervals. Dose increments should be 0.5 mg/kg daily, up to a maximum dose of 2.5 mg/kg/day.
Azithromycin Dihydrate	ZITHROMAX	Antibacterial	Cpsl: 250 mg	Usual Dosage: 500 mg po as a single dose on the first day followed by 250 mg once daily on days 2 through 5. Non-gonococcal Urethritis and Cervicitis due to C. trachomatis: 1 g po as a single dose.

Drug	Brand	Category	Dosage Form	Dosage
Aztreonam	AZACTAM	Antibacterial	**Powd for Inj:** 0.5, 1, 2 g **Inj (per 100 mL):** 0.5, 1, 2 g	**Urinary Tract Infections:** 0.5 - 1.0 g q 8 or 12 h by IV infusion or IM. **Moderately Severe Systemic Infections:** 1 - 2 g q 8 or 12 h by IV infusion. **Severe Systemic or Life-Threatening Infections:** 2 g q 6 or 8 h by IV infusion.
Bacampicillin Hydrochloride	SPECTROBID	Antibacterial	**Tab:** 400 mg **Powd for Susp:** 125 mg/5 mL	**Upper Respiratory Tract Infections, Urinary Tract Infections, Skin and Skin Structure Infections:** 400 mg q 12 h po. **Lower Respiratory Tract Infections and Severe Infections:** 800 mg q 12 h po. **Gonorrhea, Acute Uncomplicated:** 1.6 g (plus 1 g of probenecid) as a single dose po.
Bacitracin		Antibacterial	**Ophth Oint:** 500 units/g **Oint:** 500 units/g	Apply to affected eye(s) 1 or more times daily. Apply topically to the affected areas 1 - 3 times daily.
Baclofen	LIORESAL	Skeletal Muscle Relaxant	**Tab:** 10, 20 mg	5 mg tid po for 3 days; increase by 5 mg tid every 3 days (maximum 80 mg daily (20 mg qid)) until optimum effect is achieved.
Beclomethasone Dipropionate	BECLOVENT, VANCERIL BECONASE, VANCENASE BECONASE AQ, VANCENASE AQ	Corticosteroid	**Aerosol:** 42 μg/spray **Nasal Aerosol:** 42 μg/spray **Nasal Spray:** 0.042% (42 μg/spray)	2 inhalations tid to qid. 1 spray in each nostril bid - qid. 1 or 2 inhalations in each nostril bid.
Benazepril Hydrochloride	LOTENSIN	Antihypertensive	**Tab:** 5, 10, 20, 40 mg	Initially, 10 mg once daily po. Maintenance dosage is 20 - 40 mg daily as a single dose or in two equally divided doses.

GENERIC NAME	COMMON TRADE NAMES	THERAPEUTIC CATEGORY	PREPARATIONS	COMMON ADULT DOSAGE
Bendroflumethiazide	NATURETIN	Diuretic, Antihypertensive	Tab: 5, 10 mg	**Diuresis:** 5 mg once daily po, preferably given in the morning. To initiate therapy, doses up to 20 mg may be given once daily or divided into two doses. For maintenance, 2.5 - 5 mg once daily should suffice. **Hypertension:** Initially, 5 - 20 mg daily po. Maintenance doses range from 2.5 - 15 mg daily.
Benzocaine	AMERICAINE	Local Anesthetic	Oint & Spray: 20%	Apply liberally to affected areas not more than tid to qid.
			Liquid, Solution & Gel: 20%	Apply to oral membranes prn.
	AMERICAINE OTIC		Otic Sol: 20%	Instill 4 - 5 drops in the ear canal, then insert a cotton pledget into the meatus. May repeat q 1 - 2 h prn.
	ANBESOL MAXIMUM STRENGTH		Liquid & Gel: 20%	Apply topically to the affected area on or around the lips, or within the mouth.
Benzoyl Peroxide	BENOXYL	Anti-acne Agent	Lotion: 10%	Cleanse affected area. Apply topically once or twice daily.
	BENZAC, BENZAGEL, PANOXYL		Gel: 5, 10%	Cleanse affected area. Apply topically once or twice daily.
	BENZAC W. PANOXYL AQ		Water Base Gel: 2.5, 5, 10%	Cleanse affected area. Apply topically once or twice daily.
	BENZAC W WASH		Liquid: 5, 10%	Wash face with product once or twice daily.
	DESQUAM-X		Gel: 2.5, 5, 10%	Cleanse affected areas. Rub gently into all affected areas once or twice daily.
			Water Base Gel: 5, 10%	Wash affected areas with product once or twice daily. Rinse well.
	PANOXYL		Bar: 5, 10%	Wash entire area with fingertips for 1 or 2 minutes bid to tid. Rinse well.

Benzphetamine Hydrochloride (C-III)	DIDREX	Anorexiant	**Tab:** 50 mg	Initially, 25 - 50 mg once daily po with subsequent increase to tid according to the response. A single daily dose is preferably given in mid-morning or mid-afternoon.
Benzquinamide Hydrochloride	EMETE-CON	Antiemetic	**Powd for Inj:** 50 mg (as the base)	**IM:** 50 mg (0.5 - 1.0 mg/kg); may repeat in 1 hour with subsequent doses q 3 - 4 h prn. **IV:** 25 mg (0.2 - 0.4 mg/kg as a single dose) administered slowly (1 mL per 0.5 - 1 min). Subsequent doses should be given IM.
Benzthiazide	EXNA	Diuretic, Antihypertensive	**Tab:** 50 mg	**Diuresis:** Initially, 50 - 200 mg daily po for several days, or until dry weight is attained. With 100 mg or more daily, it is preferable to administer in two doses following AM & PM meals. For maintenance, 50 - 150 mg daily po depending on patient's response. **Hypertension:** Initially, 50 - 100 mg daily po as a single dose or in two divided doses. For maintenance, adjust according to the patient's response. Max: 50 mg qid po.
Benztropine Mesylate	COGENTIN	Antiparkinsonian	**Tab:** 0.5, 1, 2 mg **Inj:** 1 mg/mL	0.5 - 2 mg daily or bid po. 0.5 - 2 mg daily or bid IM.
Bepridil Hydrochloride	VASCOR	Antianginal	**Tab:** 200, 300, 400 mg	200 mg once daily po. After 10 days, the dosage may be raised; most patients are maintained at 300 mg daily.
Betamethasone	CELESTONE	Corticosteroid	**Tab:** 0.6 mg **Syrup:** 0.6 mg/5mL	0.6 - 7.2 mg per day po.
Betamethasone Benzoate	UTICORT	Corticosteroid	**Cream, Lotion & Gel:** 0.025%	Apply topically 2 - 4 times daily.

GENERIC NAME	COMMON TRADE NAMES	THERAPEUTIC CATEGORY	PREPARATIONS	COMMON ADULT DOSAGE
Betamethasone Dipropionate, Regular	DIPROSONE, MAXIVATE	Corticosteroid	Cream & Oint: 0.05% (in a standard vehicle)	Apply a thin film to affected areas once or twice daily.
	DIPROSONE		Lotion: 0.05%	Massage a few drops into affected areas bid.
			Topical Aerosol: 0.1%	Apply sparingly to affected skin areas tid.
Betamethasone Dipropionate, Augmented	DIPROLENE	Corticosteroid	Gel & Oint: 0.05% (in an optimized vehicle)	Apply a thin film to affected areas once or twice daily.
			Lotion: 0.05%	Massage a few drops into affected areas once or twice daily.
	DIPROLENE AF		Cream: 0.05%	Apply a thin film to affected areas once or twice daily.
Betamethasone Valerate	VALISONE	Corticosteroid	Cream: 0.1%	Apply topically 1 - 3 times daily.
			Lotion & Oint: 0.1%	Apply topically 1 - 3 times daily.
	VALISONE REDUCED STRENGTH		Cream: 0.01%	Apply a thin film to affected areas 1 - 3 times daily.
Betaxolol Hydrochloride	BETOPTIC BETOPTIC S	Anti-Glaucoma Agent	Ophth Solution: 0.5% Ophth Suspension: 0.25%	1 - 2 drops into affected eye(s) bid. 1 - 2 drops into affected eye(s) bid.
	KERLONE	Antihypertensive	Tab: 10, 20 mg	10 mg once daily po. If the desired response is not achieved, the dose can be doubled in 7 to 14 days.
Bethanechol Chloride	URECHOLINE	Cholinomimetic	Tab: 5, 10, 25, 50 mg Inj: 5 mg/mL	10 - 50 mg tid or qid po. 2.5 - 5 mg tid or qid SC.
Biperiden Hydrochloride	AKINETON	Antiparkinsonian	Tab: 2 mg	2 mg tid - qid po.
Biperiden Lactate	AKINETON	Antiparkinsonian	Inj: 5 mg/mL	2 mg q 30 minutes IM or IV, not to exceed 4 doses in 24 hours.

40

Generic	Brand	Class	Form	Dosage
Bisacodyl	DULCOLAX	Irritant Laxative	**Tab:** 5 mg **Suppos:** 10 mg	10 - 15 mg po once daily. 1 rectally once daily.
	FLEET BISACODYL ENEMA		**Rectal Suspension:** 10 mg/30 mL	Administer 30 mL rectally.
Bismuth Subsalicylate	PEPTO-BISMOL	Antidiarrheal	**Chewable Tab:** 262 mg **Cplt:** 262 mg **Liquid:** 262 mg/15 mL	2 tablets or caplets (or 30 mL of Liquid) po; repeat every 30 - 60 minutes prn, to a maximum of 8 doses in a 24 hour period.
	PEPTO-BISMOL MAXIMUM STRENGTH		**Liquid:** 525 mg/15 mL	30 mL po; repeat every 60 minutes prn, to a maximum of 4 doses in a 24 hour period.
Bisoprolol Fumarate	ZEBETA	Antihypertensive	**Tab:** 5, 10 mg	Initially 5 mg once daily po. The dose may be increased to 10 mg once daily and then to 20 mg once daily, if necessary.
Bitolterol Mesylate	TORNALATE	Bronchodilator	**Aerosol:** 370 µg/spray	**Acute Relief:** 2 inhalations at an interval of at least 1 - 3 minutes, followed by a third prn. **Prophylaxis:** 2 inhalations q 8 h.
			Solution for Inhalation: 0.2% (2.0 mg/mL)	**Intermittent Aerosol Flow Nebulizer (Patient Activated Nebulizer):** 0.25 to 0.75 mL (0.5 to 1.5 mg) over 10 - 15 minutes tid. **Continuous Aerosol Flow Nebulizer:** 0.75 to 1.75 mL (1.5 to 3.5 mg) over 10 - 15 minutes tid.
Bleomycin Sulfate	BLENOXANE	Antineoplastic	**Powd for Inj:** 15 units	0.25 - 0.50 units/kg IV, IM or SC once or twice weekly.

GENERIC NAME	COMMON TRADE NAMES	THERAPEUTIC CATEGORY	PREPARATIONS	COMMON ADULT DOSAGE
Bretylium Tosylate	BRETYLOL	Antiarrhythmic	Inj: 50 mg/mL	**Life-Threatening Ventricular Arrhythmias:** Administer undiluted at 5 mg/kg by rapid IV. If the arrhythmia persists, the dosage may be increased to 10 mg/kg and repeated as necessary. **Other Ventricular Arrhythmias:** **IV:** Administer a diluted solution at 5 - 10 mg/kg by IV infusion over a period greater than 8 minutes. For maintenance, the same dosage may be administered q 6 h. **IM:** Administer undiluted at 5 - 10 mg/kg. Subsequent doses may be given at 1 - 2 hour intervals if the arrhythmia persists.
Bromocriptine Mesylate	PARLODEL	Antiparkinsonian	**Tab:** 2.5 mg **Cpsl:** 5 mg	Initially, 1.25 mg po bid with meals. If necessary, the dosage may be increased every 14 - 28 days by 2.5 mg per day.
Brompheniramine Maleate	DIMETANE	Antihistamine	**Elixir:** 2 mg/5 mL (3% alcohol) **Extended-Rel. Tab:** 8 mg **Extended-Rel. Tab:** 12 mg	10 mL (4 mg) q 4 - 6 h po. 8 mg q 8 - 12 h po. 12 mg q 12 h po.
	DIMETAPP ALLERGY		**Tab:** 4 mg	4 mg q 4 - 6 h po.
Buclizine Hydrochloride	BUCLADIN-S	Antiemetic, Antivertigo Agent	**Chewable Tab:** 50 mg	**Nausea:** 50 mg daily or bid po. **Motion Sickness:** 50 mg po taken at least 30 minutes before beginning travel. For extended travel, repeat in 4 - 6 h.
Budesonide	RHINOCORT	Corticosteroid	**Aerosol:** 32 μg/spray	256 μg daily, given as either 2 sprays in each nostril in the morning and evening or 4 sprays in each nostril in the morning.
Bumetanide	BUMEX	Diuretic	**Tab:** 0.5, 1, 2 mg **Inj:** 0.25 mg/mL	0.5 - 2 mg daily po. 0.5 - 1 mg IV (over 1 - 2 minutes) or IM; if necessary, repeat at 2 - 3 h intervals, not to exceed 10 mg/day.

Drug	Brand	Form	Classification	Dosage
Buprenorphine Hydrochloride (C-V)	BUPRENEX	Inj: 0.3 mg/mL	Opioid Analgesic	0.3 mg by deep IM or slow IV (over at least 2 minutes) at up to 6-hour intervals. Repeat once, if required, in 30 - 60 minutes.
Bupropion Hydrochloride	WELLBUTRIN	Tab: 75, 100 mg	Antidepressant	100 mg bid po. Dosage may be increased to 100 mg tid po no sooner than 3 days after beginning therapy.
Buspirone Hydrochloride	BUSPAR	Tab: 5, 10 mg	Antianxiety Agent	5 mg tid po. Dosage may be increased 5 mg daily at 2 to 3 day intervals. Maximum: 60 mg per day.
Busulfan	MYLERAN	Tab: 2 mg	Antineoplastic	Daily dosage range is 4 - 8 mg po. Dosing on a weight basis is approximately 60 μg/kg daily or 1.8 mg/m² daily.
Butabarbital Sodium (C-III)	BUTISOL SODIUM	Elixir: 30 mg/5 mL (7% alcohol) Tab: 15, 30, 50, 100 mg	Sedative / Hypnotic	Preoperative Sedation: 50 - 100 mg po, 60 to 90 minutes before surgery. Daytime Sedation: 15 - 30 mg tid to qid po. Bedtime Hypnosis: 50 - 100 mg hs po.
Butamben Picrate	BUTESIN PICRATE	Oint: 1%	Local Anesthetic	Spread thinly on painful or denuded lesions of the skin, if these are small. Apply a loose bandage to protect the clothing.
Butoconazole Nitrate	FEMSTAT	Vaginal Cream: 2%	Antifungal	Non-Pregnant Patients: 1 applicatorful intra-vaginally hs for 3 days. Treatment can be extended for another 3 days if necessary. Pregnant Patients (2nd & 3rd trimesters only): 1 applicatorful intravaginally hs for 6 days.
Butorphanol Tartrate	STADOL	Inj (per mL): 1, 2 mg	Opioid Analgesic	IM: 2 mg. May be repeated q 3 - 4 h prn. IV: 1 mg. May be repeated q 3 - 4 h prn.
	STADOL NS	Nasal Spray: 10 mg/mL		1 spray in one nostril. If pain is not relieved in 60 - 90 minutes, an additional 1 spray may be given. The initial 2 dose sequence may be repeated in 3 - 4 h prn.

43

GENERIC NAME	COMMON TRADE NAMES	THERAPEUTIC CATEGORY	PREPARATIONS	COMMON ADULT DOSAGE
Caffeine	NO DOZ NO DOZ MAXIMUM STRENGTH	CNS Stimulant	Tab: 100 mg Cplt: 200 mg	100 - 200 mg q 3 - 4 h po prn. 100 - 200 mg q 3 - 4 h po prn.
Calcifediol	CALDEROL	Vitamin D Analog	Cpsl: 20, 50 µg	300 - 350 µg weekly po, administered on a daily or alternate-day schedule. Most patients respond to doses of 50 - 100 µg daily or 100 - 200 µg on alternate days.
Calcipotriene	DOVONEX	Anti-Psoriasis Agent	Oint: 0.005%	Apply a thin layer to the affected skin bid and rub in gently and completely.
Calcitonin-Human	CIBACALCIN	Antiosteoporotic, Hypocalcemic	Powd for Inj: 0.5 mg	0.5 mg daily SC. Some respond to 0.25 mg daily SC or 0.5 mg 2 or 3 times weekly SC.
Calcitonin-Salmon	CALCIMAR, MIACALCIN	Antiosteoporotic, Hypocalcemic	Inj: 200 IUnits/mL	**Paget's Disease:** 100 IUnits daily SC or IM. In many patients, 50 IUnits daily or every other day SC or IM is satisfactory. **Hypercalcemia:** Initially, 4 IUnits/kg q 12 h SC or IM. After 1 or 2 days the dosage may be increased to 8 IUnits/kg q 12 h SC or IM. **Postmenopausal Osteoporosis:** 100 IUnits daily SC or IM with calcium supplementation.
Calcitriol	CALCIJEX	Vitamin D Analog	Inj (per mL): 1, 2 µg	Initially, 0.5 µg IV 3 times weekly, approx. every other day. The dosage may be increased by 0.25 - 0.5 µg at 2 - 4 week intervals. Most patients respond to doses between 0.5 and 3 µg IV 3 times weekly.
	ROCALTROL		Cpsl: 0.25, 0.5 µg	**Dialysis Patients:** 0.25 µg daily po. Dosage may be increased by 0.25 µg per day at 4 to 8 week intervals. Most patients respond to doses between 0.5 and 1 µg daily.

44

Calcium Carbonate	DICARBOSIL	Antacid	**Chewable Tab:** 500 mg	Chew or let dissolve slowly in the mouth, 500 to 1000 mg prn.
	CALTRATE 600	Calcium Supplement	**Tab:** 3.0 g	3 - 6 g daily po.
	MAALOX	Antacid	**Cplt:** 1000 mg	1000 mg po prn.
	OS-CAL 500	Calcium Supplement	**Tab:** 500 mg	500 mg bid or tid po with meals.
	TUMS TUMS E-X TUMS ULTRA	Antacid	**Chewable Tab:** 500 mg **Chewable Tab:** 750 mg **Chewable Tab:** 1000 mg	Chew and swallow 500 - 1000 mg prn. Chew and swallow 750 - 1500 mg prn. Chew and swallow 1000 mg prn.
Calcium Glubionate	NEO-CALGLUCON	Calcium Supplement	**Syrup:** 1.8 g/5 mL	**Dietary Supplement:** 15 mL tid po.
Calcium Gluconate		Calcium Supplement	**Tab:** 500, 650, 1000 mg	500 - 2000 mg bid to qid po.
Calcium Polycarbophil	MITROLAN	Bulk Laxative	**Chewable Tab:** 500 mg	Chew and swallow 2 tablets qid or prn. A full glass of liquid (8 oz.) should be taken with each dose.
	FIBERCON		**Tab:** 625 mg	Swallow 2 tablets up to qid. A full glass of liquid (8 oz.) should be taken with each dose.
	FIBERALL		**Chewable Tab:** 1000 mg	Chew and swallow 1 tablet 1 - 4 times daily. A full glass of liquid (8 oz.) should be taken with each dose.
Capsaicin	ZOSTRIX ZOSTRIX-HP	Analgesic, Topical	**Cream:** 0.025% **Cream:** 0.075%	Apply to affected area tid or qid. Apply to affected area tid or qid.

GENERIC NAME	COMMON TRADE NAMES	THERAPEUTIC CATEGORY	PREPARATIONS	COMMON ADULT DOSAGE
Captopril	CAPOTEN	Antihypertensive, Heart Failure Drug, Post-MI Drug	**Tab:** 12.5, 25, 50, 100 mg	**Hypertension:** Initially, 25 mg bid or tid po. Dosage may be increased after 1 - 2 weeks to 50 mg bid or tid. **Diabetic Nephropathy:** 25 mg tid po. **Heart Failure:** Initially, 25 mg tid po. After a dose of 50 mg tid is reached, further increases in dosage should be delayed for at least 2 weeks. Most patients have a satisfactory response at 50 or 100 mg tid. **Left Ventricular Dysfunction after an MI:** Initiate therapy as early as 3 days following an MI. After a single 6.25 mg po dose, give 12.5 mg tid, then increase to 25 mg tid during the next several days and to a target of 50 mg tid over the next several weeks.
Carbachol	ISOPTO CARBACHOL	Anti-Glaucoma Agent	**Ophth Solution:** 0.75, 1.5, 2.25, 3%	1 - 2 drops into eye(s) up to tid.
Carbamazepine	TEGRETOL	Antiepileptic	**Susp:** 100 mg/5 mL **Chewable Tab:** 100 mg **Tab:** 200 mg	**Initial:** 100 mg qid po (Susp.) or 200 mg bid po (Tabs). Increase at weekly intervals by adding up to 200 mg per day using a tid or qid regimen. Maximum: 1000 mg daily (ages 12 to 15); 1200 mg daily (ages over 15). **Maintenance:** Adjust to minimum effective levels; usually 800 - 1200 mg daily po.
Carbenicillin Indanyl Sodium	GEOCILLIN	Antibacterial	**Tab:** 382 mg	**Urinary Tract Infections:** *E. coli, Proteus* species, and *Enterobacter:* 382 - 764 mg qid po. *Pseudomonas and Enterococcus:* 764 mg qid po. **Prostatitis:** 764 mg qid po.
Carboplatin	PARAPLATIN	Antineoplastic	**Powd for Inj:** 50, 150, 450 mg	360 mg/m^2 on day 1 every 4 weeks IV. Single intermittent doses should not be repeated until the neutrophil count is at least 2,000 and the platelet count is at least 100,000.

Carisoprodol	SOMA	Skeletal Muscle Relaxant	**Tab:** 350 mg	350 mg tid and hs po.
Carmustine	BiCNU	Antineoplastic	**Powd for Inj:** 100 mg	150 - 200 mg/m² IV q 6 weeks (given as a single dose or divided into daily injections on 2 successive days). A repeat course of drug should not be given until the leukocyte count is above 4,000/mm³ and platelet count is above 100,000/mm³.
Carteolol Hydrochloride	CARTROL	Antihypertensive	**Tab:** 2.5, 5 mg	Initially, 2.5 mg once daily po. Dosage may be gradually increased to 5 mg and 10 mg daily po.
	OCUPRESS	Anti-Glaucoma Agent	**Ophth Solution:** 1%	1 drop into affected eye(s) bid.
Cascara Sagrada		Irritant Laxative	**Tab:** 325 mg	325 mg po hs.
Castor Oil (Plain)		Irritant Laxative	**Liquid:** (pure)	15 - 30 mL po.
Castor Oil, Emulsified	NEOLOID	Irritant Laxative	**Liquid:** 36.4% w/w	30 - 60 mL po.
	FLEET FLAVORED CASTOR OIL EMULSION		**Liquid:** 67% v/v (10 mL of castor oil/15 mL)	**Laxative:** 45 mL po. **Purgative:** 90 mL po.
Cefaclor	CECLOR	Antibacterial	**Powd for Susp (per 5 mL):** 125, 187, 250, 375 mg **Cpsl:** 250, 500 mg	250 mg q 8 h po. For more severe infections (e.g., pneumonia) or those caused by less susceptible organisms, the doses may be doubled.
Cefadroxil Monohydrate	DURICEF	Antibacterial	**Powd for Susp (per 5 mL):** 125, 250, 500 mg **Cpsl:** 500 mg **Tab:** 1 g	**Urinary Tract Infections: Lower, Uncomplicated:** 1 - 2 g daily po in single or divided doses (bid). **Other:** 2 g daily po in divided doses (bid). **Skin and Skin Structure Infections:** 1 g daily po in single or divided doses (bid). **Pharyngitis and Tonsillitis:** 1 g daily po in single or divided doses (bid) for 10 days.
	ULTRACEF	Antibacterial	**Powd for Susp (per 5 mL):** 125, 250 mg **Cpsl:** 500 mg **Tab:** 1 g	

47

GENERIC NAME	COMMON TRADE NAMES	THERAPEUTIC CATEGORY	PREPARATIONS	COMMON ADULT DOSAGE
Cefamandole Nafate	MANDOL	Antibacterial	Powd for Inj: 1, 2 g	**Usual Dosage Range:** 500 mg - 1 g q 4 - 8 h IM or IV. In life-threatening infections or infections caused by less susceptible organisms, up to 2 g q 4 h may be needed. **Skin Structure Infections & Uncomplicated Pneumonia:** 500 mg q 6 h IM or IV. **Urinary Tract Infections:** 500 mg - 1 g q 8 h IM or IV.
Cefazolin Sodium	ANCEF	Antibacterial	Powd for Inj: 500, 1000 mg	**Moderate to Severe Infections:** 500 - 1000 mg q 6 - 8 h IM or IV. **Mild Infections caused by susceptible Gram Positive Cocci:** 250 - 500 mg q 8 h IM or IV. **Urinary Tract Infections, Acute, Uncomplicated:** 1000 mg q 12 h IM or IV. **Pneumococcal Pneumonia:** 500 mg q 12 h IM or IV. **Severe, Life-Threatening Infections (e.g., Septicemia):** 1 - 1.5 g q 6 h IM or IV.
Cefixime	SUPRAX	Antibacterial	Tab: 200, 400 mg Powd for Susp: 100 mg/5 mL	**Usual Dosage:** 400 mg once daily or 200 mg q 12 h po. **Gonorrhea, Uncomplicated:** 400 mg once daily po.
Cefmetazole Sodium	ZEFAZONE	Antibacterial	Powd for Inj: 1, 2 g	**Usual Dosage:** 2 g q 6 - 12 h IV for 5 - 14 days. **Urinary Tract Infections:** 2 g q 12 h IV. **Other Sites:** For mild to moderate infections, 2 g q 8 h IV; for severe to life-threatening infections, 2 g q 6 h IV.

48

Cefonicid Sodium	MONOCID	Antibacterial	Powd for Inj: 0.5, 1 g	**Usual Dosage:** 1 g daily IV or deep IM. **Urinary Tract Infections:** 0.5 g q 24 h IV or deep IM. **Mild to Moderate Infections:** 1 g q 24 h IV or deep IM. **Severe or Life-Threatening Infections:** 2 g q 24 h IV or deep IM in different large muscle masses.
Cefoperazone Sodium	CEFOBID	Antibacterial	Powd for Inj: 1, 2 g	2 - 4 g daily in equally divided doses q 12 h IM or IV. In severe infections or infections caused by less susceptible organisms, the daily dosage may be increased.
Cefotaxime Sodium	CLAFORAN	Antibacterial	Powd for Inj: 0.5, 1, 2 g Inj (per 50 mL): 1, 2 g	**Gonorrhea:** 1 g IM. **Uncomplicated Infections:** 1 g q 12 h IM or IV. **Moderate to Severe Infections:** 1 - 2 g q 8 h IM or IV. **Infections Commonly Needing Antibiotics in Higher Dosage (e.g., Septicemia):** 2 g q 6 - 8 h IV. **Life-Threatening Infections:** 2 g q 4 h IV.
Cefotetan Disodium	CEFOTAN	Antibacterial	Powd for Inj: 1, 2 g	**Urinary Tract Infections:** 500 mg q 12 h IM or IV; or 1 - 2 g q 12 - 24 h IM or IV. **Other Sites:** 1 - 2 g q 12 h for 5 - 10 days IM or IV. **Severe Infections:** 2 g q 12 h IV. **Life-Threatening Infections:** 3 g q 12 h IV.
Cefoxitin Sodium	MEFOXIN	Antibacterial	Inj (per 50 mL): 1, 2 g Powd for Inj: 1, 2 g	**Uncomplicated Infections (e.g., Pneumonia, Urinary Tract or Cutaneous Infections:** 1 g q 6 - 8 h IV or 2 g q 6 - 8 h IV. **Moderate to Severe Infections:** 1 g q 4 h IV or 2 g q 6 - 8 h IV. **Infections Commonly Needing Higher Dosage (e.g., Gas Gangrene):** 2 g q 4 h IV or 3 g q 6 h IV.

49

GENERIC NAME	COMMON TRADE NAMES	THERAPEUTIC CATEGORY	PREPARATIONS	COMMON ADULT DOSAGE
Cefpodoxime Proxetil	VANTIN	Antibacterial	Gran for Susp (per 5 mL): 50, 100 mg Tab: 100, 200 mg	**Pharyngitis & Tonsillitis:** 100 mg q 12 h for 10 days. **Urinary Tract Infections, Uncomplicated:** 100 mg q 12 h po for 7 days. **Pneumonia:** 200 mg q 12 h po for 14 days. **Bacterial Exacerbation of Chronic Bronchitis:** 200 mg q 12 h po for 10 days. **Skin & Skin Structure Infections:** 400 mg q 12 h po for 7 - 14 days. **Gonococcal Infections:** 200 mg po as a single dose.
Cefprozil	CEFZIL	Antibacterial	Powd for Susp (per 5 mL): 125, 250 mg Tab: 250, 500 mg	**Upper Respiratory Tract Infections:** 500 mg q 24 h po for 10 days. **Lower Respiratory Tract Infections:** 500 mg q 12 h po for 10 days. **Skin & Skin Structure Infections:** 250 mg q 12 h po for 10 days or 500 mg q 12 - 24 h po for 10 days.
Ceftazidime	FORTAZ, TAZIDIME	Antibacterial	Powd for Inj: 0.5, 1, 2 g	**Usual Dosage:** 1 g q 8 - 12 h IV or IM. **Urinary Tract Infections:** **Uncomplicated:** 250 mg q 12 h IV or IM. **Complicated:** 500 mg q 8 - 12 h IV or IM. **Bone & Joint Infections:** 2 g q 12 h IV. **Pneumonia, Skin & Skin Structure Infections:** 500 mg - 1 g q 8 h IV or IM. **Meningitis, Serious Gynecologic & Intra-Abdominal Infections, and Severe Life-Threatening Infections:** 2 g q 8 h IV.
Ceftazidime Sodium	FORTAZ	Antibacterial	Inj (per 50 mL): 1, 2 g	Same dosages as for FORTAZ above.

Ceftizoxime Sodium	CEFIZOX	Antibacterial	Inj (per 20, 50, or 100 mL): 1, 2 g	**Usual Dosage:** 1 - 2 g q q 8 - 12 h IM or IV. Urinary Tract Infections: 500 mg q 12 h IM or IV. **Pelvic Inflammatory Disease:** 2 g q q 8 h IV. Other Sites: 1 g q 8 - 12 h IM or IV. **Severe or Refractory Infections:** 1 g q q 8 h IM or IV; or 2 g q q 8 - 12 h IM (divided dose in different large muscle masses) or IV. **Life-Threatening Infections:** 3 - 4 g q q 8 h IV.
Ceftriaxone Sodium	ROCEPHIN	Antibacterial	Powd for Inj: 250, 500 mg; 1, 2 g	**Usual Dosage:** 1 - 2 g once daily (or in equally divided doses bid) IM or IV. **Gonorrhea:** 250 mg IM, one dose. **Meningitis:** 100 mg/kg/day in divided doses q 12 h IM or IV, with or without a loading dose of 75 mg/kg.
Cefuroxime Axetil	CEFTIN	Antibacterial	Tab: 125, 250, 500 mg	**Usual Dosage:** 250 mg bid po for 10 days. **Urinary Tract Infections, Uncomplicated:** 125 - 250 mg bid po for 7 - 10 days. **Acute Bacterial Exacerbations of Chronic Bronchitis and Secondary Bacterial Infections of Acute Bronchitis:** 250 - 500 mg bid po for 10 days. **Skin or Skin Struct. Infections, Uncomplicated:** 250 - 500 mg bid po for 10 days. **Gonorrhea, Uncomplicated:** 1 g po as a single dose.
Cefuroxime Sodium	KEFUROX, ZINACEF	Antibacterial	Powd for Inj: 0.75, 1.5 g	**Usual Dosage:** 750 mg - 1.5 g q q 8 h for 5 - 10 days IM or IV. **Bone & Joint Infections:** 1.5 g q q 8 h IM or IV. **Life-Threatening Infections or Infections due to Less Susceptible Organisms:** 1.5 g q q 6 h IV **Meningitis:** Up to 3.0 g q q 8 h IM or IV. **Gonorrhea:** 1.5 g IM, single dose given at 2 different sites with 1.0 g of probenecid po.

GENERIC NAME	COMMON TRADE NAMES	THERAPEUTIC CATEGORY	PREPARATIONS	COMMON ADULT DOSAGE
Cephalexin	KEFLEX	Antibacterial	Powd for Susp (per 5 mL): 125, 250 mg Cpsl: 250, 500 mg	Usual Dosage: 250 mg q 6 h po. Streptococcal Pharyngitis, Skin and Skin Structure Infections and Cystitis: 500 mg may be used q 12 h po. For cystitis, continue therapy for 7 - 14 days.
Cephalexin Hydrochloride	KEFTAB	Antibacterial	Tab: 250, 500 mg	Same dosage as for KEFLEX above.
Cephalothin Sodium	KEFLIN NEUTRAL	Antibacterial	Powd for Inj: 1, 2 g	Usual Dosage: 500 mg - 1 g q 4 - 6 h IV or deep IM. Life-Threatening Infections: Up to 2 g q 4 h IV or deep IM.
Cephapirin Sodium	CEFADYL	Antibacterial	Powd for Inj: 0.5, 1, 2, 4 g	Usual Dosage: 500 mg - 1 g q 4 - 6 h IV or IM. Serious or Life-Threatening Infections: Up to 12 g daily IV or IM. Use IV for high doses.
Cephradine	VELOSEF	Antibacterial	Powd for Susp (per 5 mL): 125, 250 mg Cpsl: 250, 500 mg	Respiratory Tract, Skin and Skin Structure Infections: 250 mg q 6 h po or 500 mg q 12 h po. Lobar Pneumonia: 500 mg q 6 h po or 1 g q 12 h po. Urinary Tract Infections: 500 mg q 12 h po. In more serious urinary tract infections (including prostatitis), 500 mg q 6 h po or 1 g q 12 h po.
Chloral Hydrate (C-IV)		Sedative - Hypnotic	Cpsl: 500 mg Syrup: 500 mg/5 mL	Sedative: 250 mg tid po. pc. Hypnotic: 500 mg - 1 g po, 15 - 30 minutes before bedtime or 30 min. before surgery.
Chlorambucil	LEUKERAN	Antineoplastic	Tab: 2 mg	0.1 - 0.2 mg/kg daily po for 3 - 6 weeks.

Generic	Brand	Classification	Dosage Form	Dosage
Chloramphenicol	CHLOROMYCETIN	Antibacterial	Cpsl: 250 mg Otic Solution: 0.5% Powd for Ophth Solution: 25 mg [with diluent] Ophth Oint: 1% Topical Cream: 1%	50 mg/kg/day in divided doses at 6 h intervals po. 2 - 3 drops into affected ear(s) tid. 2 drops in the affected eye(s) q 3 h. Continue administration day & night for 48 h, after which the dosing interval may be increased. Apply to affected eye(s) q 3 h day & night for 48 h, as above. Apply to infected area tid or qid.
Chloramphenicol Sodium Succinate	CHLOROMYCETIN SODIUM SUCCINATE	Antibacterial	Powd for Inj: 100 mg/mL (when reconstituted)	50 mg/kg/day in divided doses at 6 h intervals IV.
Chlordiazepoxide (C-IV)	LIBRITABS	Antianxiety Agent	Tab: 5, 10, 25 mg	5 - 25 mg tid or qid po.
Chlordiazepoxide Hydrochloride (C-IV)	LIBRIUM	Antianxiety Agent	Cpsl: 5, 10, 25 mg Powd for Inj: 100 mg	5 - 25 mg tid or qid po. 50 - 100 mg IM or IV initially; then 25 - 50 mg tid or qid, if necessary.
Chlormezanone	TRANCOPAL	Antianxiety Agent	Cplt: 100, 200 mg	100 - 200 mg tid or qid po.
Chloroquine Hydrochloride	ARALEN HCL	Antimalarial	Inj: 50 mg salt (= to 40 mg of chloroquine base)/mL	160 - 200 mg of chloroquine base IM initially; repeat in 6 h if necessary.
Chloroquine Phosphate	ARALEN PHOSPHATE	Antimalarial	Tab: 500 mg salt (= to 300 mg of chloroquine base)	Suppression: 300 mg of chloroquine base once weekly po, on the same day each week. Acute Attacks: Initially, 600 mg of chloroquine base po, followed by 300 mg after 6 - 8 h and a single dose of 300 mg on each of two consecutive days.
Chlorothiazide	DIURIL	Diuretic, Antihypertensive	Susp: 250 mg/5 mL (0.5% alcohol) Tab: 250, 500 mg	Diuresis: 0.5 - 1.0 g once daily or bid po. Hypertension: 0.5 - 1.0 g po as a single dose or in divided doses.
Chlorothiazide Sodium	DIURIL	Diuretic	Powd for Inj: 500 mg	0.5 - 1.0 g once daily or bid IV.
Chlorotrianisene	TACE	Estrogen, Antineoplastic	Cpsl: 12, 25 mg	12 - 25 mg daily po.

GENERIC NAME	COMMON TRADE NAMES	THERAPEUTIC CATEGORY	PREPARATIONS	COMMON ADULT DOSAGE
Chlorphenesin Carbamate	MAOLATE	Skeletal Muscle Relaxant	Tab: 400 mg	Initially, 800 mg tid po until the desired effect is obtained; then 400 mg qid po.
Chlorpheniramine Maleate	CHLOR-TRIMETON	Antihistamine	Syrup: 2 mg/5 mL (7% alcohol) Tab: 4 mg Timed-Rel. Tab: 8, 12 mg Inj: 10 mg/mL	10 mL (4 mg) q 4 - 6 h po. 4 mg q 4 - 6 h po. 8 - 12 mg q 12 h po. 10 - 20 mg IM, SC, or IV.
	TELDRIN		Timed-Rel. Cpsl: 12 mg	12 mg bid po (in the AM and in the PM).
Chlorpromazine	THORAZINE	Antiemetic	Suppos: 25, 100 mg	50 - 100 mg rectally q 6 - 8 h.
Chlorpromazine Hydrochloride	THORAZINE	Antipsychotic, Antiemetic	Syrup: 10 mg/5 mL Liquid Conc: 30, 100 mg/mL Tab: 10, 25, 50, 100, 200 mg Sustained-Rel. Cpsl: 30, 75, 150, 200, 300 mg	**Psychoses (Hospitalized Patients, Less Acutely Disturbed):** 25 mg tid po. Increase gradually until the effective dose is reached, usually 400 mg daily. **Psychoses (Outpatients):** **Usual Dosage:** 10 mg tid or qid po; or 25 mg bid to tid po. **More Severe Cases:** 25 mg tid po. After 1 to 2 days, daily dosage may be raised by 20 - 50 mg at semiweekly intervals until patient becomes calm and cooperative. **Prompt Control of Severe Symptoms:** 25 mg IM. If necessary, repeat in 1 h. Subsequent doses should be oral. 25 - 50 mg tid. **Nausea & Vomiting:** 10 - 25 mg q 4 - 6 h po. **Presurgical Apprehension:** 25 - 50 mg po 2 - 3 h before the operation. **Intractable Hiccups:** 25 - 50 mg tid or qid po. If symptoms persist for 2 - 3 days, use injection [see dosage below].

54

Psychoses (Hospitalized Patients, Acutely Disturbed or Manic): 25 mg IM. If necessary, give additional 25 - 50 mg in 1 h. Increase subsequent IM doses gradually over several days (up to 400 mg q 4 - 6 h in severe cases) until patient is controlled.

Psychoses (Outpatients; Prompt Control of Severe Symptoms): 25 mg IM. If necessary, repeat in 1 h. Subsequent doses should be oral, 25 - 50 mg tid.

Nausea & Vomiting:

Usual Dosage: 25 mg IM. If no hypotension occurs, 25 - 50 mg q 3 - 4 h prn, until vomiting stops; then switch to oral dosage (above).

During Surgery: 12.5 mg IM. Repeat in 30 min, if necessary and if no hypotension occurs. May give 2 mg IV per fractional injection at 2 min. intervals. Dilute to 1 mg/mL and do not exceed 25 mg.

Presurgical Apprehension: 12.5 - 25 mg IM 1 to 2 h before the operation.

Intractable Hiccups: If symptoms persist for 2 or 3 days after oral dosing, give 25 - 50 mg IM. Should symptoms persist, use slow IV infusion with patient flat in bed: 25 - 50 mg in 500 - 1000 mL of saline.

Inj: 25 mg/mL

Chlorpropamide — DIABINESE — Hypoglycemic — Tab: 100, 250 mg

Initial: 250 mg daily po. After 5 - 7 days, dosage may be adjusted upward or downward by increments of not more than 50 - 125 mg at intervals of 3 - 5 days. **Maintenance:** 100 - 250 mg daily po.

Chlortetracycline — AUREOMYCIN — Antibacterial — Oint: 3%

Apply to affected areas tid prn.

55

GENERIC NAME	COMMON TRADE NAMES	THERAPEUTIC CATEGORY	PREPARATIONS	COMMON ADULT DOSAGE
Chlorthalidone	HYGROTON	Diuretic, Antihypertensive	Tab: 25, 50, 100 mg	**Edema:** Initially, 50 - 100 mg daily po or 100 mg on alternate days. Maintenance doses may be lower than initial doses. **Hypertension:** Initially, 25 mg daily po. May increase the dosage to 50 mg daily po and then to 100 mg daily po if necessary.
	THALITONE		Tab: 15, 25 mg	**Edema:** Initially, 30 - 60 mg daily po or 60 mg on alternate days. Maintenance doses may be lower than initial doses. **Hypertension:** Initially, 15 mg daily po. May increase the dosage to 30 mg daily po and then to 45 - 50 mg daily po if necessary.
Chlorzoxazone	PARAFLEX PARAFON FORTE DSC	Skeletal Muscle Relaxant	Cplt: 250 mg Cplt: 500 mg	250 mg tid or qid po. 500 mg tid or qid po.
Cholestyramine	QUESTRAN	Hypolipidemic	Powder: 4 g drug/9 g powder	9 g 1 - 6 times daily po.
	QUESTRAN LIGHT		Powder: 4 g drug/5 g powder	5 g 1 - 6 times daily po.
Ciclopirox Olamine	LOPROX	Antifungal	Cream & Lotion: 1%	Gently massage into affected and surrounding skin areas bid, in the AM and PM.
Cimetidine	TAGAMET	Histamine H$_2$-Blocker, Anti-Ulcer Agent	Liquid: 300 mg/5 mL (2.8% alcohol) Tab: 200, 300, 400, 800 mg	**Duodenal Ulcer:** **Active:** 800 mg hs po; or 300 mg qid po with meals & hs; or 400 mg bid po in the AM and PM. **Maintenance:** 400 mg hs po. **Active Benign Gastric Ulcer:** 800 mg hs po; or 300 mg qid po with meals & hs. **Erosive Gastroesophageal Reflux Disease:** 800 mg bid po; or 400 mg qid po for 12 weeks. **Pathological Hypersecretory Conditions:** 300 mg qid po with meals & hs.

Cinoxacin	CINOBAC	Urinary Anti-infective	Cpsl: 250, 500 mg	500 mg bid or 250 mg qid po for 7 - 14 days.
Ciprofloxacin	CIPRO I.V.	Antibacterial	Inj: 200, 400 mg	**Urinary Tract Infections:** 200 mg q 12 h by IV infusion (over 60 minutes). For severe or complicated UTI, double the dose. **Lower Respiratory Tract, Bone & Joint, and Skin & Skin Structure Infections:** 400 mg q 12 h by IV infusion (over 60 minutes).
Ciprofloxacin Hydrochloride	CIPRO	Antibacterial	Tab: 250, 500, 750 mg	**Urinary Tract Infections:** 250 - 500 mg q 12 h po. **Lower Respiratory Tract, Bone & Joint, and Skin & Skin Structure Infections:** 500 - 750 mg q 12 h po.
	CILOXAN	Antibacterial	Ophth Solution: 0.3%	**Corneal Ulcers:** 2 drops in affected eye(s) q 15 min. for the 1st 6 hours, then 2 drops q 30 min. for the rest of the 1st day. Second day: 2 drops q 1 h; 3rd - 14th day: 2 drops q 4 h. **Conjunctivitis:** 1 - 2 drops in affected eye(s) q 2 h while awake for 2 days, then 1 - 2 drops q 4 h while awake for the next 5 days.
Cisapride	PROPULSID	GI Stimulant	Tab: 10, 20 mg	Initially, 10 mg qid po, at least 15 min ac & hs. May increase to 20 mg qid po.
Cisplatin	PLATINOL PLATINOL AQ	Antineoplastic	Powd for Inj: 10, 50 mg Inj: 1 mg/mL	**Metastatic Testicular Tumors:** 20 mg/m² IV daily for 5 days. **Metastatic Ovarian Tumors:** 100 mg/m₂ IV once every 4 weeks. **Advanced Bladder Cancer:** 50 - 70 mg/m₂ IV q 3 - 4 weeks.

Inj: 300 mg/2 mL

Pathological Hypersecretory Conditions or Intractable Ulcers: 300 mg q 6 - 8 h IM or IV (infused over 15 - 20 minutes). For a Continuous IV Infusion: 37.5 mg/h (900 mg daily); may be preceded by a 150 mg loading dose by IV infusion (over 15 - 20 minutes).

GENERIC NAME	COMMON TRADE NAMES	THERAPEUTIC CATEGORY	PREPARATIONS	COMMON ADULT DOSAGE
Clarithromycin	BIAXIN	Antibacterial	**Granules for Susp (per 5 mL):** 125, 250 mg **Tab:** 250, 500 mg	250 - 500 mg q 12 h po for 7 - 14 days. 250 - 500 mg q 12 h po for 7 - 14 days.
Clemastine Fumarate	TAVIST	Antihistamine	**Syrup:** 0.67 mg/5 mL (5.5% alcohol)	**Allergic Rhinitis:** 10 mL bid po. **Urticaria and Angioedema:** 20 mL bid po.
	TAVIST-1 TAVIST		**Tab:** 1.34 mg **Tab:** 2.68 mg	1.34 - 2.68 mg bid or tid po. 2.68 mg bid or tid po.
Clidinium Bromide	QUARZAN	Anticholinergic	**Cpsl:** 2.5, 5 mg	2.5 - 5 mg tid or qid po ac & hs.
Clindamycin Hydrochloride	CLEOCIN HCL	Antibacterial	**Cpsl:** 75, 150, 300 mg	**Serious Infections:** 150 - 300 mg q 6 h po. **More Severe Infections:** 300 - 450 mg q 6 h po.
Clindamycin Palmitate HCl	CLEOCIN PEDIATRIC	Antibacterial	**Powd for Susp:** 75 mg/5 mL	Same dosages as for CLEOCIN above.
Clindamycin Phosphate	CLEOCIN PHOSPHATE	Antibacterial	**Inj:** 150 mg/mL	**Serious Infections:** 600 - 1200 mg/day IV or IM in 2, 3 or 4 equal doses. **More Severe Infections:** 1200 - 2700 mg/day IV or IM in 2, 3 or 4 equal doses. **Life-Threatening Infections:** Up to 4800 mg/day IV.
	CLEOCIN	Antibacterial	**Vaginal Cream:** 2%	Insert 1 applicatorful intravaginally, preferably hs, for 7 consecutive days.
	CLEOCIN-T	Anti-Acne Agent	**Topical Solution, Gel &:** **Lotion:** 10 mg/mL	Apply a thin film to affected areas bid.
Clioquinol	VIOFORM	Antifungal, Antibacterial	**Cream & Oint:** 3%	Apply to the affected area tid or qid.
Clobetasol Propionate	TEMOVATE	Corticosteroid	**Cream, Oint & Gel:** 0.05% **Scalp Application:** 0.05%	Apply topically to affected area bid. Apply to affected scalp areas bid.

Clocortolone Pivalate	CLODERM	Corticosteroid	**Cream:** 0.1%	Apply sparingly to the affected area tid. Rub in gently.
Clofazimine	LAMPRENE	Leprostatic	**Cpsl:** 50, 100 mg	100 mg daily with meals po.
Clofibrate	ATROMID-S	Hypolipidemic	**Cpsl:** 500 mg	500 mg qid po.
Clomiphene Citrate	CLOMID, SEROPHENE	Ovulation Stimulant	**Tab:** 50 mg	50 mg daily for 5 days po.
Clomipramine Hydrochloride	ANAFRANIL	Antidepressant	**Cpsl:** 25, 50, 75 mg	Initiate with 25 mg daily po with meals and gradually increase, as tolerated, to 100 mg a day during the first 2 weeks. Thereafter, the dosage may be increased gradually over the next several weeks, up to a maximum of 250 mg daily. After titration, the total daily dose may be given once daily hs.
Clonazepam (C-IV)	KLONOPIN	Antiepileptic	**Tab:** 0.5, 1, 2 mg	Initially, 0.5 mg tid po. Dosage may be increased in increments of 0.5 - 1 mg every 3 days; maximum 20 mg per day.
Clonidine	CATAPRES-TTS	Antihypertensive	**Transdermal:** rate = 0.1, 0.2, 0.3 mg/24 hr	Apply to hairless area of intact skin on the upper arm or torso, once every 7 days.
Clonidine Hydrochloride	CATAPRES	Antihypertensive	**Tab:** 0.1, 0.2, 0.3 mg	Initially, 0.1 mg bid po (AM and hs). Further increments of 0.1 mg may be made until the desired response is achieved.
Clorazepate Dipotassium (C-IV)	TRANXENE	Antianxiety Agent, Antiepileptic	**Tab:** 3.75, 7.5, 15 mg	**Anxiety:** 15 - 60 mg daily in divided doses po; or 15 mg hs po. **Epilepsy:** The maximum recommended initial dose is 7.5 mg tid po. Dosage should be increased no more than 7.5 mg every week and should not exceed 90 mg per day.
	TRANXENE-SD	Antianxiety Agent	**Gradual-Rel. Tab:** 11.25, 22.5 mg	**Anxiety:** 11.25 or 22.5 mg as a single po dose q 24 h. Used as an alternative for patients stabilized on TRANXENE.

59

GENERIC NAME	COMMON TRADE NAMES	THERAPEUTIC CATEGORY	PREPARATIONS	COMMON ADULT DOSAGE
Clotrimazole	LOTRIMIN	Antifungal	Cream, Lotion & Solution: 1%	Massage into affected and surrounding skin areas bid, AM and PM.
	MYCELEX		Cream & Solution: 1%	Same dosage as for LOTRIMIN above.
			Troche: 10 mg	**Treatment:** Slowly dissolve 1 in the mouth 5 times daily for 14 consecutive days. **Prophylaxis:** Slowly dissolve 1 in the mouth 3 times daily for the duration of therapy.
	MYCELEX-G		Vaginal Cream: 1%	One applicatorful daily intravaginally for 7 to 14 consecutive days.
			Vaginal Tab: 500 mg	Insert 1 tablet intravaginally once only hs.
	GYNE-LOTRIMIN, MYCELEX-7		Vaginal Cream: 1%	One applicatorful daily intravaginally for 7 consecutive days.
			Vaginal Insert: 100 mg	Place 1 insert daily intravaginally for 7 consecutive days.
Cloxacillin Sodium	TEGOPEN	Antibacterial	Powd for Solution: 125 mg/5 mL	**Mild to Moderate Infections:** 250 mg q 6 h po. **Severe Infections:** 500 mg q 6 h po.
Clozapine	CLOZARIL	Antipsychotic	Tab: 25, 100 mg	25 mg once or twice daily po; then, increase daily by 25 - 50 mg/day (if well-tolerated) to a max. of 300 - 450 mg/day by the end of 2 weeks. Subsequent dosage increments should be made no more than 1 - 2 times a week in increments not to exceed 100 mg.
Cocaine Hydrochloride (C-II)		Local Anesthetic	Topical Solution: 4, 10%	1 - 4% applied topically.
Codeine Phosphate (C-II)		Opioid Analgesic	Inj (per mL): 30, 60 mg	15 - 60 mg q 4 - 6 h IM, SC or IV.
Codeine Sulfate (C-II)		Opioid Analgesic, Antitussive	Tab: 15, 30, 60 mg	**Analgesia:** 15 - 60 mg q 4 - 6 h po. **Antitussive:** 10 - 20 mg q 4 - 6 h po.

Colchicine		Antigout Agent	**Tab:** 0.5, 0.6 mg	**Acute:** 1.0 - 1.2 mg po stat; then 0.5 - 1.2 mg q 1 - 2 h po, until pain is relieved, or nausea, vomiting or diarrhea occurs. **Prophylaxis:** 0.5 or 0.6 mg daily for 3 - 4 days a week.
			Inj: 1 mg/2 mL	**Acute:** 2 mg stat IV; then 0.5 mg q 6 h IV up to a maximum of 4 mg in 24 h. **Prophylaxis:** 0.5 - 1 mg once daily or bid IV.
Colestipol Hydrochloride	COLESTID	Hypolipidemic	**Tab:** 1 g	Initially, 2 g once or twice daily po. Dosage increases of 2 g once or twice daily po should occur at 1 - 2 month intervals. Dosage range: 2 - 16 g/day given once daily or in divided doses.
			Granules for Oral Susp: 5 g packettes and 300, 500 g bottles (Unflavored); 7.5 g packettes and 450 g bottles (Orange Flavor)	Initially, 5 g daily or bid po with a daily increment of 5 g at 1 - 2 month intervals. Usual dose: 5 - 30 g/day po given once daily or in divided doses.
Colistimethate Sodium	COLY-MYCIN M PARENTERAL	Antibacterial	**Powd for Inj:** 150 mg	2.5 - 5 mg/kg/day in 2 - 4 divided doses IM or IV.
Colistin Sulfate	COLY-MYCIN S FOR ORAL SUSPENSION	Antibacterial	**Powd for Susp:** 25 mg/5 mL	5 - 15 mg/kg/day given in 3 divided doses po.
Cromolyn Sodium	GASTROCROM	Antiallergic	**Cpsl:** 100 mg	200 mg qid po, 30 minutes ac & hs.
	INTAL	Antiasthmatic	**Solution for Nebulization:** 20 mg/2 mL **Inhaler:** 800 μg/spray **Cpsl (for Inhalation):** 20 mg	20 mg qid nebulized. 2 sprays qid inhaled. 20 mg qid inhaled.
	NASALCROM	Antiallergic	**Nasal Solution:** 40 mg/mL	1 spray in each nostril 3 - 6 times daily.
Crotamiton	EURAX	Scabicide	**Cream & Lotion:** 10%	Massage into the skin from the chin to the toes including folds and creases. Re-apply 24 hours later. A cleansing bath should be taken 48 h after the last application.

61

GENERIC NAME	COMMON TRADE NAMES	THERAPEUTIC CATEGORY	PREPARATIONS	COMMON ADULT DOSAGE
Cyclizine Hydrochloride	MAREZINE	Antiemetic	**Tab:** 50 mg	50 mg q 4 - 6 h po, staring 30 minutes prior to travel.
Cyclobenzaprine Hydrochloride	FLEXERIL	Skeletal Muscle Relaxant	**Tab:** 10 mg	10 mg tid po.
Cyclophosphamide	CYTOXAN	Antineoplastic	**Tab:** 25, 50 mg **Powd for Inj:** 100, 200, 500 mg; 1, 2 g	1 - 5 mg/kg/day po. 40 - 50 mg/kg IV in divided doses over a period of 2 - 5 days; or 10 - 15 mg/kg IV q 7 - 10 days; or 3 - 5 mg/kg IV twice weekly.
Cyclosporine	SANDIMMUNE	Immunosuppressant	**Cpsl:** 25, 100 mg **Solution:** 100 mg/mL (12.5% alcohol) **Inj:** 50 mg/mL	15 mg/kg, 4 to 12 hours prior to transplantation. Continue dose postoperatively for 1 - 2 weeks, then taper by 5% per week to a maintenance level of 5 - 10 mg/kg/day. 5 - 6 mg/kg/day IV, 4 to 12 hours prior to transplantation. Give as a dilute solution (50 mg in 20 to 100 mL) and administer as a slow infusion over 2 - 6 hrs. Continue this single dose postoperatively until patient can tolerate oral dosage forms.
Cyproheptadine Hydrochloride	PERIACTIN	Antihistamine, Antipruritic	**Syrup:** 2 mg/5 mL (5% alcohol) **Tab:** 4 mg	4 mg tid po.
Cytarabine	CYTOSAR-U	Antineoplastic	**Powd for Inj:** 100, 500 mg; 1, 2 g	100 mg/m²/day by continuous IV infusion or 100 mg/m² IV q 12 h.
Dacarbazine	DTIC-DOME	Antineoplastic	**Powd for Inj:** 100, 200 mg	**Malignant Melanoma:** 2 - 4.5 mg/kg/day IV for 10 days; may repeat q 4 weeks. Alternate dosage: 250 mg/m²/day IV for 5 days; may repeat q 3 weeks. **Hodgkin's Disease:** 150 mg/m²/day IV for 5 days, in combination with other effective drugs; may repeat q 4 weeks. Alternate dosage: 375 mg/m² on day 1, in combination with other drugs: repeat q 15 days.

Dactinomycin	COSMEGEN	Antineoplastic	Powd for Inj: 500 μg	500 μg/day IV for 5 days.
Danazol	DANOCRINE	Gonadotropin Inhibitor	Cpsl: 50, 100, 200 mg	**Endometriosis:** 100 - 200 mg bid po (mild disease) or 400 mg bid po (moderate to severe cases). Continue therapy for 3 - 6 months. **Fibrotic Breast Disease:** 50 - 200 mg bid po. Therapy should begin during menstruation. **Hereditary Angioedema:** 200 mg bid or tid po. After a favorable initial response, determine continuing dosage by reducing the dosage by 50% or less at intervals of 1 - 3 months or longer. If an attack occurs, increase dosage by up to 200 mg/day.
Dantrolene Sodium	DANTRIUM	Skeletal Muscle Relaxant	Cpsl: 25, 50, 100 mg	**Chronic Spasticity:** 25 mg once daily po; increase to 25 mg bid, tid, or qid and then by increments of 25 mg up to as high as 100 mg bid, tid, or qid if necessary. **Malignant Hyperthermia:** **Preoperatively:** 4 - 8 mg/kg/day po in 3 - 4 divided doses for 1 or 2 days prior to surgery, with the last dose given approx. 3 - 4 h before scheduled surgery. **Post Crisis Follow Up:** 4 - 8 mg/kg/day po in 4 divided doses for 1 - 3 days.
	DANTRIUM INTRAVENOUS		Powd for Inj: 20 mg	**Malignant Hyperthermia:** **Acute Therapy:** Administer by continuous rapid IV push beginning at a minimum dose of 1 mg/kg, and continuing until the symptoms subside or the maximum cumulative dose of 10 mg/kg has been reached. **Preoperatively:** 2.5 mg/kg IV starting approx. 1.25 hours before anticipated anesthesia and infused over 1 h. **Post Crisis Follow Up:** Individualize, starting with 1 mg/kg IV.

63

GENERIC NAME	COMMON TRADE NAMES	THERAPEUTIC CATEGORY	PREPARATIONS	COMMON ADULT DOSAGE
Dapsone	DAPSONE USP	Leprostatic	Tab: 25, 100 mg	100 mg daily po alone or in combination with other leprostatic drugs.
Demeclocycline Hydrochloride	DECLOMYCIN	Antibacterial	Tab: 150, 300 mg	150 mg qid po or 300 mg bid po.
Desipramine Hydrochloride	NORPRAMIN	Antidepressant	Tab: 10, 25, 50, 75, 100, 150 mg	100 - 200 mg daily po in a single dose or in divided doses.
Desmopressin Acetate	DDAVP NASAL SPRAY	Posterior Pituitary Hormone, Anti-Enuretic Agent	Nasal Spray: 0.1 mg/mL (delivers 0.1 mL (10 µg) per spray)	**Central Cranial Diabetes Insipidus:** 0.1 - 0.4 mL daily as a single dose or in 2 - 3 divided doses intranasally.
	DDAVP RHINAL TUBE		Nasal Solution: 0.1 mg/mL (with rhinal tube applicators)	**Primary Nocturnal Enuresis:** 0.2 mL intra-nasally hs. Dosage adjustment up to 0.4 mL may be made if necessary.
	DDAVP INJECTION		Inj: 4.0 µg/mL	Diabetes Insipidus: 1 - 2 µg bid SC or IV.
	STIMATE	Posterior Pituitary Hormone	Nasal Spray: 1.5 mg/mL (delivers 0.1 mL (150 µg) per spray)	**Hemophilia A and von Willebrand's Disease (Type I):** 1 spray per nostril (300 µg) in patients weighing ≥ 50 kg; 1 spray only in patients weighing < 50 kg.
Desonide	DESOWEN	Corticosteroid	Cream, Oint & Lotion: 0.05%	Apply to the affected areas bid to tid.
	TRIDESILON	Corticosteroid	Cream & Oint: 0.05%	Apply to the affected areas bid to qid.
Desoximetasone	TOPICORT	Corticosteroid	Cream: 0.05, 0.25% Oint: 0.25% Gel: 0.05%	Apply a thin film to the affected areas bid. Rub in gently.
Dexamethasone	DECADRON	Corticosteroid	Elixir: 0.5 mg/5 mL (5% alcohol) Tab: 0.25, 0.5, 0.75, 1.5 4, 6 mg	Initial dosage varies from 0.75 - 9 mg daily po, depending on the disease being treated. This should be maintained or adjusted until the patient's response is satisfactory.
	DECASPRAY		Topical Aerosol: 0.04%	Spray each 4 square inch of affected area for 1 or 2 seconds tid or qid.

64

Drug	Brand	Class	Form	Dosage
	MAXIDEX		Ophth Susp: 0.1%	1 - 2 drops in affected eye(s). In severe disease, may use hourly; taper to discontinuation as the inflammation subsides. In mild disease, may use up to 4 - 6 times daily.
Dexamethasone Acetate	DECADRON-LA	Corticosteroid	Inj: 8 mg/mL	Intramuscular Inj: 8 - 16 mg q 1 - 3 weeks. Intralesional Inj: 0.8 - 1.6 mg per inj. site. Intra-articular & Soft Tissue Inj: 4 - 16 mg q 1 - 3 weeks.
Dexamethasone Sodium Phosphate	DECADRON PHOSPHATE	Corticosteroid	Inj: 4 mg/mL Inj: 24 mg/mL [for IV use only]	IV and IM Inj: Initial dosage varies from 0.5 - 9 mg daily depending on the disease being treated. This dosage should be maintained or adjusted until the patient's response is satisfactory. Intra-articular, Intralesional, and Soft Tissue Injection: Varies from 0.2 - 6 mg given from once q 3 - 5 days to once q 2 - 3 weeks.
	DECADRON PHOSPHATE, MAXIDEX		Ophth Solution: 0.1%	Eye: 1 - 2 drops into eye(s) q 1 h during the day & q 2 h at night, initially. When a favorable response occurs, reduce to 1 drop into eye(s) q 4 h. Later, 1 drop tid - qid. Ear: 3 - 4 drops into aural canal bid - tid. When a favorable response occurs, reduce dosage gradually and eventually discontinue.
	DECADRON PHOSPHATE, MAXIDEX		Ophth Oint: 0.05%	Apply to eye(s) tid or qid. When a favorable response occurs, reduce daily applications to 2, and later to 1 as maintenance therapy.
			Topical Cream: 0.1%	Apply a thin film to affected area tid or qid.
	DECADRON PHOSPHATE RESPIHALER		Aerosol: 84 µg/spray	3 inhalations tid or qid (Maximum: 3 inhalations per dose, 12 per day).
	DEXACORT TURBINAIRE		Nasal Aerosol: 84 µg/spray	2 sprays in each nostril bid or tid.

GENERIC NAME	COMMON TRADE NAMES	THERAPEUTIC CATEGORY	PREPARATIONS	COMMON ADULT DOSAGE
Dexchlorpheniramine Maleate	POLARAMINE	Antihistamine	**Syrup:** 2 mg/5 mL (6% alcohol) **Tab:** 2 mg **Repeat Action Tab:** 4, 6 mg	5 mL (2 mg) q 4 - 6 h po. 2 mg q 4 - 6 h po. 4 or 6 mg po hs or q 8 - 10 h during the day.
Dextroamphetamine Sulfate (C-II)	DEXEDRINE	CNS Stimulant	**Tab:** 5 mg **Sustained-Rel. Cpsl:** 5, 10, 15 mg	**Narcolepsy:** 5 - 60 mg per day in divided doses, depending on the patient response.
Dextromethorphan Hydrobromide	HOLD DM, SUCRETS COUGH CONTROL	Antitussive	**Lozenge:** 5 mg	Dissolve 2 lozenges in the mouth q 4 h prn.
	ROBITUSSIN COUGH CALMERS		**Lozenge:** 5 mg	Dissolve 2 - 4 lozenges in the mouth q 4 h prn.
	VICKS PEDIATRIC FORMULA 44 COUGH MEDICINE		**Liquid:** 5 mg/5 mL	30 mL q 6 - 8 h po.
	ST. JOSEPH COUGH SUPPRESSANT		**Syrup:** 7.5 mg/5 mL	15 mg q 4 - 8 h po.
	ROBITUSSIN PEDIATRIC COUGH SUPPRESSANT		**Liquid:** 7.5 mg/5 mL	20 mL q 6 - 8 h po.
	BENYLIN ADULT FORMULA		**Liquid:** 15 mg/5 mL	30 mg q 6 - 8 h po, not to exceed 4 doses in 24 h.
	PERTUSSIN ES		**Syrup:** 15 mg/5 mL (9.5% alcohol)	5 mL (15 mg) q 4 h po or 10 mL (30 mg) q 6 - 8 h po.
	ROBITUSSIN MAXIMUM STRENGTH COUGH SUPPRESSANT		**Liquid:** 15 mg/5 mL	10 mL (30 mg) q 6 - 8 h po.
	VICKS FORMULA 44 COUGH MEDICINE		**Liquid:** 15 mg/5 mL (10% alcohol)	10 mL q 6 - 8 h po.

Generic	Brand	Class	Forms	Dosage
	DRIXORAL COUGH LIQUID CAPS		Cpsl: 30 mg	30 mg q 6 - 8 h po.
Dextromethorphan Polistirex	DELSYM	Antitussive	Syrup: equal to 30 mg of dextromethorphan HBr/5 mL	10 mL (60 mg) q 12 h po.
Dezocine	DALGAN	Opioid Analgesic	Inj (per mL): 5, 10, 15 mg	IM: 5 - 20 mg q 3 - 6 h. IV: 2.5 - 10 mg q 2 - 4 h.
Diazepam (C-IV)	VALIUM	Antianxiety Agent, Anticonvulsant, Skel. Muscle Relax.	Tab: 2, 5, 10 mg	**Anxiety & Adjunct in Convulsive Disorders:** 2 - 10 mg bid to qid po. **Muscle Spasms:** 2 - 10 mg tid to qid po.
			Inj: 5 mg/mL	**Anxiety (Moderate):** 2 - 5 mg IM or IV. Repeat in 3 - 4 h, if necessary. **Anxiety (Severe) and Muscle Spasms:** 5 - 10 mg IM or IV. Repeat in 3 - 4 h, if necessary. **Preoperative Medication:** 10 mg IM (preferred route) before surgery. **Status Epilepticus and Severe Recurrent Convulsive Seizures:** 5 - 10 mg IV. Repeat at 10 - 15 minute intervals, if necessary, up to a maximum dose of 30 mg. **Acute Alcohol Withdrawal:** Initially 10 mg IM or IV, then 5 - 10 mg in 3 - 4 h, if needed. **Endoscopic Procedures:** Titrate IV dosage to desired sedative response. Generally 10 mg or less is adequate, but up to 20 mg IV may be given.
	VALRELEASE	Antianxiety Agent, Skel. Muscle Relax.	Slow-Release Cpsl: 15 mg	15 - 30 mg once daily po.
Diazoxide	PROGLYCEM	Hyperglycemic Agent	Susp: 50 mg/mL Cpsl: 50 mg	3 - 8 mg/kg po, divided into 2 or 3 equal doses q 8 - 12 h.
	HYPERSTAT I.V.	Antihypertensive	Inj: 300 mg/20 mL	1 - 3 mg/kg IV repeated at intervals of 5 - 15 minutes (max.: 150 mg in a single injection).

GENERIC NAME	COMMON TRADE NAMES	THERAPEUTIC CATEGORY	PREPARATIONS	COMMON ADULT DOSAGE
Dibucaine	NUPERCAINAL	Local Anesthetic Antihemorrhoidal	Cream: 0.5% Oint: 1%	Apply to affected areas prn and rub in gently. Apply to affected areas AM and PM and after each bowel movement.
Diclofenac Potassium	CATAFLAM	Antiinflammatory, Analgesic	Tab: 50 mg	**Osteoarthritis:** 100 - 150 mg/day po in divided doses (50 mg bid or tid). **Rheumatoid Arthritis:** 150 - 200 mg/day po in divided doses (50 mg tid or qid). **Ankylosing Spondylitis:** 100 - 125 mg/day po as: 25 mg qid with an extra 25 mg hs, prn. **Analgesia and Primary Dysmenorrhea:** 50 mg tid po or 100 mg initially, followed by 50 mg doses po. Except for the first day when the total dose may be 200 mg, do not exceed 150 mg daily.
Diclofenac Sodium	VOLTAREN	Antiinflammatory	Enteric-Coated Tab: 25, 50, 75 mg	**Osteoarthritis:** 100 - 150 mg/day po in divided doses (50 mg bid or tid, or 75 mg bid). **Rheumatoid Arthritis:** 150 - 200 mg/day po in div. doses (50 mg tid or qid, or 75 mg bid). **Ankylosing Spondylitis:** 100 - 125 mg/day po as: 25 mg qid with an extra 25 mg hs, prn.
			Ophth Solution: 0.1%	1 drop into affected eye(s) qid beginning 24 h after cataract surgery and continuing for the first 2 weeks of the postoperative period.
Dicloxacillin Sodium	DYNAPEN, PATHOCIL	Antibacterial	Powd for Susp: 62.5 mg/5 mL Cpsl: 250, 500 mg	**Mild to Moderate Infections:** 125 mg q 6 h po. **More Severe Infections:** 250 mg q 6 h po.
Dicyclomine Hydrochloride	BENTYL	Anticholinergic	Syrup: 10 mg/5 mL Cpsl: 10 mg Tab: 20 mg Inj: 10 mg/mL	Initially 80 mg/day po (in 4 equally divided doses). Dosage may be increased during the first week, if necessary, to 160 mg/day po. 80 mg daily IM (in 4 equally divided doses).

Didanosine	VIDEX	Antiviral	**Chewable/Dispersible Tab:** 25, 50, 100, 150 mg	**< 60 kg:** 125 mg bid q 12 h po. **≥ 60 kg:** 200 mg bid q 12 h po. Take 2 tablets at each dose for adequate buffering to prevent degradation by gastric acid. Chew or crush and disperse 2 tablets in at least 1 fl. oz. of water prior to consumption. Take on an empty stomach.
			Powd for Sol: 100, 167, 250, 375 mg packets	**< 60 kg:** 167 mg bid q 12 h po. **≥ 60 kg:** 250 mg bid q 12 h po. Dissolve contents of packet in 4 fl. oz. of water and drink on an empty stomach.
Dienestrol	ORTHO DIENESTROL	Estrogen	**Cream:** 0.01%	1 - 2 applicatorfuls intravaginally daily for 1 - 2 weeks, then gradually reduce to 1/2 initial dosage for a similar period. Maintenance dosage is 1 applicatorful 1 - 3 times a week.
Diethylpropion Hydrochloride (C-IV)	TENUATE TENUATE DOSPAN	Anorexiant	**Tab:** 25 mg **Controlled-Rel. Tab:** 75 mg	25 mg tid, 1 h ac po. 75 mg daily po in the midmorning.
Diethylstilbestrol		Antineoplastic	**Tab:** 1, 5 mg	**Prostatic Cancer:** 1 - 3 mg daily po; adjust dosage upward or downward as necessary. **Breast Cancer:** 15 mg daily po.
Diethylstilbestrol Diphosphate	STILPHOSTROL	Antineoplastic	**Tab:** 50 mg **Inj:** 250 mg/5 mL	**Prostatic Cancer:** Initially 50 mg tid po. Raise the dosage to 200 mg or more tid depending on the tolerance of the patient. **Prostatic Cancer:** 500 mg (in 250 mL of saline or 5% dextrose) slowly infused IV on the first day; then, 1000 mg (in 250 - 500 mL of fluid) for approx. 5 days. Thereafter, 250 - 500 mg (IV infusion) once or twice a week.
Diflorasone Diacetate	FLORONE, MAXIFLOR FLORONE E	Corticosteroid	**Cream & Oint:** 0.05% **Emollient Cream:** 0.05%	Apply to the affected area once daily to qid, depending on the severity of the condition. Apply to the affected area once daily to tid, depending on the severity of the condition.

GENERIC NAME	COMMON TRADE NAMES	THERAPEUTIC CATEGORY	PREPARATIONS	COMMON ADULT DOSAGE
Diflunisal	DOLOBID	Non-Opioid Analgesic, Antiinflammatory	Tab: 250, 500 mg	**Analgesic:** Initially 1000 mg po, followed by 500 mg q 12 h; or initially 500 mg po, followed by 250 mg q 8 - 12 h may also be appropriate. **Rheumatoid Arthritis & Osteoarthritis:** 250 to 500 mg bid po.
Digitoxin	CRYSTODIGIN	Heart Failure Drug, Inotropic Agent	Tab: 0.05, 0.1 mg	**Slow Digitalization:** 0.2 mg bid po for 4 days, followed by maintenance dosage. **Rapid Digitalization:** 0.6 mg po, followed by 0.4 mg and then 0.2 mg at intervals of 4 - 6 h. **Maintenance Dosage:** Ranges from 0.05 - 0.3 mg daily po; commonly 0.15 mg daily.
Digoxin	LANOXIN ELIXIR PEDIATRIC LANOXIN LANOXICAPS	Heart Failure Drug, Inotropic Agent	Elixir: 50 µg/mL (10% alcohol) Tab: 125, 250, 500 µg Inj: 250 µg/mL Cpsl: 50, 100, 200 µg	Variable; see Digoxin Dosage Tables, pp. 212 to 215. Variable; see Digoxin Dosage Tables, pp. 212 to 215.
Dihydrotachysterol	DHT HYTAKEROL	Vitamin D Analog	Tab: 0.125, 0.2, 0.4 mg Solution: 0.2 mg/mL Cpsl: 0.125 mg	**Initial:** 0.8 - 2.4 mg daily po for several days. **Maintenance:** 0.2 - 1.0 mg daily po. The average dose is 0.6 mg daily po.
Diltiazem Hydrochloride	CARDIZEM	Antianginal	Tab: 30, 60, 90, 120 mg	Initially, 30 mg qid po ac & hs. Dosage should be increased gradually at 1 - 2 day intervals. Usual optimum dosage: 180 - 360 mg/day.
	CARDIZEM SR	Antihypertensive	Sustained-Rel. Cpsl: 60, 90, 120 mg	Initially, 60 - 120 mg bid po; dosage may be adjusted after 14 days. Usual dosage: 240 to 360 mg/day.
	CARDIZEM CD	Antihypertensive, Antianginal	Extended-Rel. Cpsl: 120, 180, 240, 300 mg	**Hypertension:** Initially, 180 - 240 mg once daily po. Dosage may be increased up to 480 mg once daily po (over 14 days). Usual dosage: 240 - 360 mg once daily.

Generic	Brand	Category	Form/Strength	Dosage
	DILACOR XR	Antihypertensive	Extended-Rel. Cpsl: 180, 240 mg	**Angina:** Initially, 120 or 180 mg once daily po. Dosage may be increased up to 480 mg once daily po (over 7 - 14 days). 180 - 240 mg once daily po.
	CARDIZEM	Antiarrhythmic	Inj: 5 mg/mL	**IV Bolus (given over 2 min):** Initially, 0.25 mg/kg; if response is inadequate, in 15 min. give 0.35 mg/kg. Individualize subsequent IV bolus doses. **Continuous IV Infusion (following IV bolus):** Initially, 5 - 10 mg/hr; rate may be increased in 5 mg/hr increments up to 15 mg/hr prn for up to 24 h.
Dimenhydrinate	DRAMAMINE	Antivertigo Agent, Antiemetic	Liquid: 12.5 mg/4 mL (5% alcohol) Tab & Chewable Tab: 50 mg Inj: 50 mg/mL	50 - 100 mg q 4 - 6 h po. 50 mg q 4 - 6 h IM or slow IV.
Diphenhydramine Hydrochloride	BENADRYL DYE-FREE	Antihistamine	Elixir: 6.25 mg/5 mL Liqui-Gel Cpsl: 25 mg	25 - 50 mg (20 - 40 mL) q 4 - 6 h po. 25 - 50 mg q 4 - 6 h po.
	BENADRYL	Antihistamine, Antiemetic, Antiparkinsonian	Elixir: 12.5 mg/5 mL Cpsl: 25, 50 mg Tab: 25 mg Inj (per mL): 10, 50 mg	25 - 50 mg (10 - 20 mL) q 4 - 6 h po. 25 - 50 mg tid to qid po. 25 - 50 mg q 4 - 6 h po. 10 - 50 mg IV or deep IM.
		Antihistamine	Cream: 1, 2% Spray: 1, 2%	Apply to affected areas not more than tid or qid. Spray on affected areas not more than tid or qid.
Dipivefrin Hydrochloride	PROPINE	Anti-Glaucoma Agent	Ophth Solution: 0.1%	1 drop into the eye(s) q 12 h.
Dipyridamole	PERSANTINE	Platelet Aggregation Inhibitor	Tab: 25, 50, 75 mg	75 - 100 mg qid po.

GENERIC NAME	COMMON TRADE NAMES	THERAPEUTIC CATEGORY	PREPARATIONS	COMMON ADULT DOSAGE
Disopyramide Phosphate	NORPACE	Antiarrhythmic	Cpsl: 100, 150 mg	600 mg/day po given in divided doses, e.g., 150 mg q 6 h. For patients under 110 lbs, 400 mg/day po, e.g., 100 mg q 6 h.
	NORPACE CR		Extended-Rel. Cpsl: 100, 150 mg	600 mg/day po given in divided doses, e.g., 300 mg q 12 h. For patients under 110 lbs, 400 mg/day po, e.g., 200 mg q 12 h.
Disulfiram	ANTABUSE	Antialcoholic	Tab: 250, 500 mg	Initial: A maximum of 500 mg po, given as a single dose for 1 - 2 weeks. Maintenance: 250 mg daily po.
Divalproex Sodium	DEPAKOTE	Antiepileptic	Tab: 125, 250, 500 mg Cpsl: 125 mg	Initially, 15 mg/kg/day po; increase at 1 week intervals by 5 - 10 mg/kg/day (Maximum: 60 mg/kg/day). If total daily dosage exceeds 250 mg, it should be given in divided doses.
Dobutamine Hydrochloride	DOBUTREX	Sympathomimetic	Powd for Inj: 250 mg	2.5 - 10 µg/kg/min by IV infusion.
Docusate Calcium	SURFAK	Stool Softener	Cpsl: 240 mg	240 mg daily po.
Docusate Sodium	COLACE	Stool Softener	Syrup: 20 mg/5 mL Cpsl: 50, 100 mg	50 - 200 mg daily po.
	DIALOSE		Tab: 100 mg	100 mg once daily to tid po.
Dopamine Hydrochloride	INTROPIN	Sympathomimetic	Inj (per mL): 40, 80, 160 mg	2 - 10 µg/kg/min by IV infusion.
Doxacurium Chloride	NUROMAX	Neuromuscular Blocker	Inj: 1 mg/mL	Initially, 0.025 - 0.05 mg/kg IV (depending on duration of effect desired and other drugs given); then, 0.005 - 0.01 mg/kg IV prn.
Doxazosin Mesylate	CARDURA	Antihypertensive	Tab: 1, 2, 4, 8 mg	Initially, 1 mg once daily po. After 24 hours, dosage may be increased to 2 mg and there-after, if needed, to 4, 8, and 16 mg daily.

Doxepin Hydrochloride	SINEQUAN	Antianxiety Agent, Antidepressant	Cpsl: 10, 25, 50, 75, 100, 150 mg Oral Concentrate: 10 mg/mL	75 mg daily po in single or divided doses. The usual optimum dosage range is 75 - 150 mg daily.
	ZONALON	Antihistamine	Cream: 5%	Apply a thin film to affected areas qid, with at least 3 or 4 hours between applications.
Doxorubicin Hydrochloride	ADRIAMYCIN PFS ADRIAMYCIN RDF	Antineoplastic	Inj: 2 mg/mL Powd for Inj: 10, 20, 50 mg	60 - 75 mg/m² as a single IV injection given at 21-day intervals. Alternative: 20 mg/m² IV at weekly intervals.
Doxycycline Calcium	VIBRAMYCIN	Antibacterial, Antimalarial	Syrup: 50 mg/5 mL	**Usual Dosage**: 100 mg q 12 h po for the first day, followed by a maintenance dose of 100 mg/day given as 50 mg q 12 h or 100 mg once daily. **Urinary Tract Infections**: 100 mg q 12 h po. **Malaria Prophylaxis**: 100 mg once daily po.
Doxycycline Hyclate	VIBRAMYCIN VIBRA-TAB	Antibacterial, Antimalarial	Cpsl: 50, 100 mg Tab: 100 mg	Same dosages as for VIBRAMYCIN Syrup.
	DORYX	Antibacterial, Antimalarial	Cpsl (with coated pellets): 100 mg	Same dosages as for VIBRAMYCIN Syrup.
	VIBRAMYCIN INTRAVENOUS	Antibacterial	Powd for Inj: 100, 200 mg	**Usual Dosage**: 200 mg on the first day given in 1 or 2 IV infusions, then 100 - 200 mg a day, with 200 mg given in 1 or 2 infusions. **Syphilis**: 300 mg daily by IV infusion for at least 10 days.
Doxycycline Monohydrate	VIBRAMYCIN	Antibacterial, Antimalarial	Powd for Susp: 25 mg/5 mL	Same dosages as for VIBRAMYCIN Syrup.
Doxylamine Succinate	UNISOM	Sedative	Tab: 25 mg	25 mg po, 30 minutes before retiring.

73

GENERIC NAME	COMMON TRADE NAMES	THERAPEUTIC CATEGORY	PREPARATIONS	COMMON ADULT DOSAGE
Dronabinol (C-II)	MARINOL	Antiemetic, Appetite Stimulant	Cpsl: 2.5, 5, 10 mg	**Emesis:** 5 mg/m² po, 1 - 3 h prior to chemotherapy, then q 2 - 4 h after chemotherapy for a total of 4 - 6 doses/day. **Anorexia in AIDS patients:** Initially, 2.5 mg bid po, before lunch and supper. For patients who cannot tolerate this dosage, reduce to 2.5 mg once daily with supper or hs. When adverse reactions are absent or minimal or further therapeutic effect is desired, increase to 2.5 mg before lunch and 5 mg before supper (or 5 mg at lunch and 5 mg after supper). Approximately 50% of patients tolerate 10 mg bid po.
Droperidol	INAPSINE	Antianxiety Agent	Inj: 2.5 mg/mL	**Premedication:** 2.5 - 10 mg IM, 30 - 60 minutes preoperatively. **Adjunct to General Anesthesia: Induction:** 2.5 mg per 20 - 25 lb IV. **Maintenance:** 1.25 - 2.5 mg IV.
Dyphylline	LUFYLLIN	Bronchodilator	Tab: 200, 400 mg Elixir: 100 mg/15 mL (20% alcohol) Inj: 250 mg/mL	Variable: up to 15 mg/kg q 6 h po. 250 - 500 mg q 6 h IM (slowly). Do not exceed 15 mg/kg q 6 h.
Econazole Nitrate	SPECTAZOLE	Antifungal	Cream: 1%	**Tinea Infections:** Apply topically to affected areas once daily. **Cutaneous Candidiaisis:** Apply to affected areas bid.
Edrophonium Chloride	ENLON, TENSILON	Cholinomimetic	Inj: 10 mg/mL	**Diagnosis of Myasthenia:** 2 mg IV; if no reaction occurs after 45 seconds, give 8 mg IV. Test may be repeated in 30 minutes. May also administer 10 mg IM. Subject who shows hyperreactivity (cholinergic reaction), retest after 30 minutes with 2 mg IM.

74

Eflornithine Hydrochloride	ORNIDYL	Antiprotozoal	Inj: 200 mg/mL	**Evaluation of Treatment Requirements:** 1 - 2 mg IV, 1 hour after oral intake of the drug being used in treatment. **Curare Antagonism:** 10 mg IV, given slowly over 30 - 45 seconds. May be repeated prn, up to a maximum of 40 mg.
Enalapril Maleate	VASOTEC	Antihypertensive, Heart Failure Drug	Tab: 2.5, 5, 10, 20 mg	100 mg/kg/dose by IV infusion (over a minimum of 45 minutes) q 6 h for 14 days. **Hypertension:** 5 mg once daily po. Usual dosage range is 10 - 40 mg/day as a single dose or in 2 divided doses. **Heart Failure:** As adjunctive therapy with a diuretic or digoxin, use 2.5 mg once daily or bid po. Usual dosage range is 5 - 20 mg/day in 2 divided doses.
Enalaprilat	VASOTEC I.V.	Antihypertensive	Inj: 1.25 mg/mL	1.25 mg q 6 h IV (over 5 minutes).
Enoxacin	PENETREX	Antibacterial	Tab: 200, 400 mg	**Urinary Tract Infections (Uncomplicated):** 200 mg q 12 h po for 7 days. **Urinary Tract Infections (Complicated):** 400 mg q 12 h po for 14 days. **Gonorrhea (Uncomplicated):** 400 mg po as a single dose.
Enoxaparin Sodium	LOVENOX	Anticoagulant	Inj: 30 mg/0.3 mL	30 mg SC (as soon as possible after surgery, but not more than 24 h postoperatively); then 30 mg bid SC for 7 - 14 days.
Ephedrine Sulfate		Bronchodilator	Syrup: 20 mg/5 mL Cpsl: 25, 50 mg	25 - 50 mg q 3 - 4 h po.
			Inj: 25, 50 mg/mL	25 - 50 mg SC, IM or slowly IV.

GENERIC NAME	COMMON TRADE NAMES	THERAPEUTIC CATEGORY	PREPARATIONS	COMMON ADULT DOSAGE
Epinephrine	BRONKAID MIST, PRIMATENE MIST	Bronchodilator	**Aerosol:** 0.25 mg/spray **Aerosol:** 0.22 mg/spray	1 inhalation, then wait at least 1 minute. If not relieved, use once more. Do not use again for at least 3 h.
	EPIPEN		**Auto-injector:** 1:1000 soln (0.3 mg delivered per injection of 0.3 mL)	0.3 mg IM.
	SUS-PHRINE		**Inj:** 5 mg/mL (1:200)	0.1 - 0.3 mL SC. Do not use more often than q 6 h.
Epinephrine Bitartrate	MEDIHALER-EPI, BRONKAID MIST SUSPENSION, PRIMATENE MIST SUSPENSION	Bronchodilator	**Aerosol:** 0.3 mg/spray (equal to 0.16 mg of epinephrine)	1 inhalation, then wait at least 1 minute. If not relieved, use once more. Do not use again for at least 3 h.
Epinephrine Borate	EPINAL, EPPY/N	Anti-Glaucoma Agent	**Ophth Solution:** 0.5, 1% **Ophth Solution:** 0.5, 1, 2%	1 drop into affected eye(s) bid. 1 - 2 drops into affected eye(s) once daily hs.
Epinephrine Hydrochloride	ADRENALIN CHLORIDE	Sympathomimetic, Bronchodilator	**Solution:** 1:100 (10 mg/mL) **Inj:** 1:1000 (1 mg/mL)	Variable, by nebulizer. 0.2 - 1.0 mg SC or IM.
	EPIFRIN	Anti-Glaucoma Agent	**Ophth Solution:** 0.25, 0.5, 1, 2%	1 drop into affected eye(s) once or twice daily.
Ergonovine Maleate		Oxytocic	**Tab:** 0.2 mg	0.2 - 0.4 mg q 6 - 12 h po.
Ergotamine Tartrate	ERGOSTAT	Antimigraine Agent	**Sublingual Tab:** 2 mg	2 mg under tongue stat; repeat q 30 minutes, prn, for a maximum of 6 mg per 24 hours.
Erythrityl Tetranitrate	CARDILATE	Antianginal	**Tab:** 10 mg	5 - 10 mg sublingually prior to stress situation or 10 mg po ac, as well as mid-morning, mid-afternoon and hs.

Erythromycin	A/T/S ERYCETTE, ETS-2% T-STAT 2%	Anti-Acne Agent	Solution & Gel: 2% Solution: 2% Solution & Pads: 2%	Apply to affected areas bid.
	E-MYCIN ERY-TAB ERYC ERYTHROMYCIN BASE FILMTAB PCE	Antibacterial	Delayed-Rel. Tab: 250, 333 mg Delayed-Rel. Tab: 250, 333, 500 mg Delayed-Rel. Cpsl: 250 mg Tab: 250, 500 mg Dispersable Tab: 333, 500 mg	**Usual Dosage:** 250 mg qid po; 333 mg q 8 h po; or 500 mg bid (q 12 h) po. **Streptococcal Infections:** Administer the usual dosage for at least 10 days. **Primary Syphilis:** 30 - 40 g po in divided doses over a period of 10 - 15 days. **_Acute Pelvic Inflammatory Disease due to N. gonorrhoeae:_** After initial treatment with erythromycin lactobionate, give 250 mg q 6 h po for 7 days or 333 mg q 8 h for 7 days. **Urogenital Infections during pregnancy and Uncomplicated Urethral, Endocervical, or Rectal Infections due to _C. trachomatis:_** 500 mg qid po or 666 mg q 8 h po for at least 7 days. **Dysenteric Amebiasis:** 250 mg qid po or 333 mg q 8 h po for 10 - 14 days. **Legionnaires Disease:** 1 - 4 g daily po in divided doses.
	ILOTYCIN		Ophth Oint: 5 mg/g	Apply to affected eye(s) 1 or more times daily.
Erythromycin Estolate	ILOSONE	Antibacterial	Susp (per 5 mL): 125, 250 mg Cpsl: 250 mg Tab: 500 mg	**Usual Dosage:** 250 mg q 6 h po or 500 mg q 12 h po. **Streptococcal Infections:** Administer the usual dosage for at least 10 days. **Primary Syphilis:** 20 g po in divided doses over a period of 10 days. **Urogenital Infections during pregnancy and Uncomplicated Urethral, Endocervical, or Rectal Infections due to _C. trachomatis:_** 500 mg qid po for at least 7 days. **Dysenteric Amebiasis:** 250 mg qid po for 10 to 14 days. **Legionnaires Disease:** 1 - 4 g daily po in divided doses.

GENERIC NAME	COMMON TRADE NAMES	THERAPEUTIC CATEGORY	PREPARATIONS	COMMON ADULT DOSAGE
Erythromycin Ethylsuccinate	E.E.S.	Antibacterial	**Powd for Susp (per 5 mL):** 200 mg **Susp (per 5 mL):** 200, 400 mg **Tab:** 400 mg	**Usual Dosage:** 400 mg q 6 h po or 800 mg q 12 h po. **Streptococcal Infections:** Administer the usual dosage for at least 10 days. **Primary Syphilis:** 48 - 64 g po in divided doses over a period of 10 - 15 days.
	ERYPED		**Powd for Susp (per 5 mL):** 200, 400 mg **Chewable Tab:** 200 mg	**Urethritis due to C. trachomatis or U. urealyticum:** 800 mg tid po for 7 days. **Intestinal Amebiasis:** 400 mg qid po for 10 to 14 days. **Legionnaires Disease:** 1.6 - 4 g daily po in divided doses.
Erythromycin Gluceptate	ILOTYCIN GLUCEPTATE	Antibacterial	**Powd for Inj:** 1 g	**Usual Dosage:** 5 - 20 mg/kg/day by continuous IV infusion or in divided doses q 6 h IV. **Acute Pelvic Inflammatory Disease due to N. gonorrhoeae:** 500 mg q 6 h IV for at least 3 days, followed by 250 mg of oral erythromycin q 6 h for 7 days.
Erythromycin Lactobionate	ERYTHROCIN IV	Antibacterial	**Powd for Inj:** 500 mg; 1 g	**Severe Infections:** 15-20 mg/kg/day by contin. IV infusion or by intermittent IV infusion in 20 - 60 min periods at intervals of ≤ 6 h.
Erythromycin Stearate	ERYTHROCIN STEARATE	Antibacterial	**Tab:** 250, 500 mg	**Usual Dosage:** 250 mg q 6 h po or 500 mg q 12 h po on an empty stomach or ac. **Streptococcal Infections:** Administer the usual dosage for at least 10 days. **Acute Pelvic Inflammatory Disease due to N. gonorrhoeae:** After initial treatment with erythromycin lactobionate, give 250 mg q 6 h po for 7 days. **Urogenital Infections during pregnancy and Uncomplicated Urethral, Endocervical, or Rectal Infections due to C. trachomatis:** 500 mg qid po for at least 7 days. **Intestinal Amebiasis:** 250 mg qid po for 10 to 14 days.

Drug	Brand	Class	Form	Dosage
Esmolol Hydrochloride	BREVIBLOC	Antiarrhythmic	Inj (per mL): 10, 250 mg	500 μg/kg/min IV for 1 minute followed by a 4-minute infusion of 50 μg/kg/min. If an adequate effect is not seen within 5 min., repeat loading dose followed by a 4-minute infusion of 100 μg/kg/min. Continue process as above, increasing maintenance infusion by increments of 50 μg/kg/min. As the desired effect is reached, omit loading dose & lower incremental dose in maintenance infusion from 50 μg/kg/min to 25 μg/kg/min or lower. **Legionnaires Disease:** 1 - 4 g daily po in divided doses.
Estazolam (C-IV)	PROSOM	Hypnotic	Tab: 1, 2 mg	1 - 2 mg hs po.
Estradiol	ESTRACE	Estrogen	Tab: 0.5, 1, 2 mg	**Menopausal Symptoms:** 1 - 2 mg daily po. **Prostatic Cancer:** 1 - 2 mg tid po. **Breast Cancer:** 10 mg tid po for at least 3 mos. **Osteoporosis Prevention:** 0.5 mg daily po cyclically (3 weeks on, 1 week off) as soon as possible after menopause.
			Vaginal Cream: 0.01%	**Initial:** 2 - 4 g intravaginally daily for 1 - 2 weeks, then gradually reduce to 1/2 initial dose for a similar period. **Maintenance:** 1 g intravaginally 1 - 3 times a week.
	ESTRADERM		Transdermal: rate = 0.05, 0.1 mg/24 h	Apply 1 patch topically twice weekly.
Estradiol Cypionate	DEPO-ESTRADIOL	Estrogen	Inj (per mL): 1 - 5 mg (in oil)	**Menopausal Symptoms:** 1 - 5 mg IM q 3 - 4 weeks. **Female Hypogonadism:** 1.5 - 2 mg IM monthly.
Estradiol Valerate	DELESTROGEN	Estrogen, Antineoplastic	Inj (per mL): 10, 20, 40 mg (in oil)	**Menopausal Symptoms and Female Hypogonadism:** 10 - 20 mg IM q 4 weeks. **Prostatic Cancer:** 30 mg or more IM q 1 - 2 weeks.

GENERIC NAME	COMMON TRADE NAMES	THERAPEUTIC CATEGORY	PREPARATIONS	COMMON ADULT DOSAGE
Estramustine Phosphate	EMCYT	Antineoplastic	Cpsl: 140 mg	14 mg/kg/day (1 cpsl per 22 lb) in 3 or 4 divided doses po.
Estrogens, Conjugated	PREMARIN	Estrogen	Tab: 0.3, 0.625, 0.9, 1.25, 2.5 mg Vaginal Cream: 0.625 mg/g	0.3 - 1.25 mg daily po. 2 - 4 g (1/2 - 1 applicatorful) intravaginally daily. Administration should be cyclic (3 weeks on, 1 week off).
	PREMARIN INTRAVENOUS		Powd for Inj: 25 mg	25 mg IV or IM. Repeat in 6 - 12 h prn.
Estropipate	OGEN	Estrogen, Antiosteoporotic	Tab: 0.625, 1.25, 2.5, 5 mg Vaginal Cream: 1.5 mg/g	**Menopausal Symptoms:** 0.625 - 5 mg daily po. **Prevention of Osteoporosis:** 0.625 mg daily po for 25 days of a 31 day cycle per month. 2 - 4 g intravaginally daily. Administration should be cyclic (3 weeks on, 1 week off).
Ethacrynate Sodium	SODIUM EDECRIN	Diuretic	Powd for Inj: 50 mg	0.5 - 1.0 mg/kg IV (maximum 100 mg).
Ethacrynic Acid	EDECRIN	Diuretic	Tab: 25, 50 mg	50 - 100 mg daily po.
Ethambutol Hydrochloride	MYAMBUTOL	Tuberculostatic	Tab: 100, 400 mg	**Initial:** 15 mg/kg po as a single dose q 24 h. **Retreatment:** 25 mg/kg po as a single dose q 24 h. After 60 days, decrease dose to 15 mg/kg po as a single dose q 24 h.
Ethchlorvynol (C-IV)	PLACIDYL	Sedative - Hypnotic	Cpsl: 200, 500, 750 mg	500 mg hs po.
Ethinyl Estradiol	ESTINYL	Estrogen	Tab: 0.02, 0.05, 0.5 mg	**Menopausal Symptoms:** 0.02 - 0.05 mg daily po. Administration should be cyclic (3 weeks on, 1 week off). **Prostatic Cancer:** 0.15 - 2.0 mg daily po. **Breast Cancer:** 1.0 mg tid po.
Ethionamide	TRECATOR-SC	Tuberculostatic	Tab: 250 mg	0.5 - 1 g daily in divided doses po.

Drug	Brand	Class	Form	Dosage
Ethotoin	PEGANONE	Antiepileptic	Tab: 250, 500 mg	**Initial:** 1 g or less daily po in 4 - 6 divided doses, with gradual increases over a period of several days. - **Maintenance:** Usually 2 - 3 g daily po in 4 - 6 divided doses.
Etidronate Disodium	DIDRONEL	Bone Stabilizer	Tab: 200, 400 mg	**Paget's Disease:** Initially, 5 mg/kg daily po, not to exceed 6 months. May increase to 10 mg/kg daily po, not to exceed 6 months or to 11 - 20 mg/kg daily po, not to exceed 3 months.
	DIDRONEL I.V. INFUSION		Inj: 300 mg/6 mL	7.5 mg/kg daily by IV infusion (over at least 2 h) for 3 days. Daily dose must be diluted in at least 250 mL of sterile normal saline.
Etodolac	LODINE	Non-Opioid Analgesic, Antiinflammatory	Cpsl: 200, 300 mg Tab: 400 mg	**Analgesia:** 200 - 400 mg q 6 - 8 h po. **Osteoarthritis:** Initially, 800 - 1200 mg/day po in divided doses; adjust dosage within 600 to 1200 mg/day po, e.g., 400 mg bid - tid, 300 mg bid - qid, or 200 mg tid - qid.
Etoposide	VEPESID	Antineoplastic	Inj: 100 mg/5 mL	**Testicular Cancer:** Ranges from 50 - 100 mg/m²/day IV for days 1 - 5 to 100 mg/m²/day IV for day 1, 3 and 5. Repeat at 3 - 4 week intervals. **Small Cell Lung Cancer:** Ranges from 35 mg/m²/day IV for 4 days to 50 mg/m²/day IV for 5 days. Repeat at 3 - 4 week intervals.
			Cpsl: 50 mg	**Small Cell Lung Cancer:** Twice the IV dose po, rounded to the nearest 50 mg.
Etretinate	TEGISON	Anti-Psoriasis Agent	Cpsl: 10, 25 mg	**Initial:** 0.75 - 1 mg/kg/day po in divided doses. **Maintenance:** 0.5 - 0.75 mg/kg/day po (after 8 to 16 weeks).
Famciclovir	FAMVIR	Antiviral	Tab: 500 mg	500 mg q 8 h po for 7 days.

81

GENERIC NAME	COMMON TRADE NAMES	THERAPEUTIC CATEGORY	PREPARATIONS	COMMON ADULT DOSAGE
Famotidine	PEPCID	Histamine H₂-Blocker, Anti-Ulcer Agent	Powd for Susp: 40 mg/5 mL Tab: 20, 40 mg	**Duodenal Ulcer:** **Acute:** 40 mg hs po; or 20 mg bid po. **Maintenance:** 20 mg hs po. **Active Benign Gastric Ulcer:** 40 mg hs po. **Pathological Hypersecretory Conditions:** 20 mg q 6 h po. **Gastroesophageal Reflux Disease:** 20 mg bid po for up to 6 weeks.
	PEPCID INJECTION PEPCID INJECTION PREMIXED		Inj: 10 mg/mL Inj: 20 mg/50 mL	20 mg q 12 h IV. 20 mg q 12 h by IV infusion (over 15 - 30 minutes).
Felbamate	FELBATROL	Antiepileptic	Tab: 400, 600 mg Susp: 600 mg/5 mL	**Monotherapy:** Begin at 1200 mg/day po, in 3 to 4 divided doses. Titrate under close supervision, increasing the dosage in 600 mg increments q 2 weeks to 2400 mg/day, and thereafter to 3600 mg/day if indicated. **Adjunctive Therapy:** Add felbamate at 1200 mg/day po (in 3 to 4 divided doses) while decreasing the dose of present antiepileptic drug by 20%. Further reductions in these drug may be necessary to minimize adverse effects due to drug interactions. Increase the dosage of felbamate by 1200 mg/day increments at weekly intervals to 3600 mg/day if necessary.
Felodipine	PLENDIL	Antihypertensive	Extended-Rel. Tab: 2.5, 5, 10 mg	Initially, 5 mg once daily po. Dosage may be increased to 10 mg daily po after 2 weeks.
Fenfluramine Hydrochloride	PONDIMIN	Anorexiant	Tab: 20 mg	20 mg tid po ac. Dosage may be increased at weekly intervals by 20 mg daily until a maximum dosage of 40 mg tid is attained.
Fenoprofen Calcium	NALFON	Non-Opioid Analgesic, Antiinflammatory	Cps: 200, 300 mg Tab: 600 mg	**Analgesia:** 200 mg q 4 h po, prn. **Rheumatoid Arthritis and Osteoarthritis:** 300 to 600 mg tid to qid po.

Fentanyl (C-II)	DURAGESIC	Opioid Analgesic	**Transdermal:** rate = 25, 50, 75, 100 μg/hr	Individualize dosage. Each system may be worn for up to 72 h.
Fentanyl Citrate (C-II)	SUBLIMAZE	Opioid Analgesic	**Inj:** 50 μg/mL (as the base)	2 - 50 μg/kg IM or IV.
	FENTANYL ORALET	Opioid Analgesic	**Lozenge:** 200, 300, 400 μg	Administer only in a hospital setting. Individualize dosage. Fentanyl transmucosal doses of 5 μg/kg (400 μg) provide effects similar to usual doses of fentanyl citrate given IM, i.e., 0.75 - 1.25 μg/kg. Oral administration should begin 20 - 40 minutes prior to anticipated need of desired effect.
Ferrous Gluconate (11.6% iron)	FERGON	Hematinic	**Elixir:** 300 mg/5 mL (7% alcohol) **Tab:** 320 mg	5 mL (300 mg) daily po. 320 mg daily po.
Ferrous Sulfate (20% iron)	FEOSOL	Hematinic	**Elixir:** 220 mg/5 mL (5% alcohol)	5 - 10 mL tid po, preferably between meals.
	FER-IN-SOL		**Syrup:** 90 mg/5 mL (5% alcohol)	5 mL daily po.
	FERO-GRADUMET		**Controlled-Rel. Tab:** 525 mg	525 mg once daily or bid po.
	MOL-IRON		**Tab:** 195 mg	195 - 390 mg tid po.
Ferrous Sulfate, Exsiccated (30% iron)	FEOSOL	Hematinic	**Tab:** 200 mg **Cpsl:** 159 mg	200 mg tid - qid po pc & hs. 159 - 318 mg daily po.
	FER-IN-SOL		**Cpsl:** 190 mg	1 capsule daily po.
	SLOW FE		**Slow Release Tab:** 160 mg	160 - 320 mg daily po.
Finasteride	PROSCAR	Androgen Hormone Inhibitor	**Tab:** 5 mg	5 mg once daily po.
Flecainide Acetate	TAMBOCOR	Antiarrhythmic	**Tab:** 50, 100, 150 mg	Initially, 100 mg q 12 h po. May increase in increments of 50 mg bid q 4 days.

83

GENERIC NAME	COMMON TRADE NAMES	THERAPEUTIC CATEGORY	PREPARATIONS	COMMON ADULT DOSAGE
Floxuridine	STERILE FUDR	Antineoplastic	Powd for Inj: 500 mg	0.1 - 0.6 mg/kg/day by intra-arterial infusion.
Fluconazole	DIFLUCAN	Antifungal	Tab: 50, 100, 150, 200 mg Powd for Susp: 10, 40 mg/mL Inj: 200 mg/100 mL, 400 mg/200 mL	Oropharyngeal Candidiasis: 200 mg on the first day, followed by 100 mg once daily po or IV. Continue treatment for at least 2 weeks. Esophageal Candidiasis: 200 mg on the first day, followed by 100 mg once daily po or IV. Doses up to 400 mg may be used based on the patient response. Continue treatment for a minimum of 3 weeks and at least 2 weeks following resolution of symptoms. Systemic Candidiasis and Cryptococcal Meningitis: 400 mg on the first day, followed by 200 mg once daily po or IV. Vaginal Candidiasis: 150 mg po as a single dose.
Flucytosine	ANCOBON	Antifungal	Cpsl: 250, 500 mg	50 - 150 mg/kg/day po in divided doses at 6-hour intervals.
Fludrocortisone Acetate	FLORINEF ACETATE	Mineralocorticoid	Tab: 0.1 mg	0.1 mg daily po. If transient hypertension develops, reduce dosage to 0.05 mg daily.
Flumazenil	ROMAZICON	Benzodiazepine Antagonist	Inj: 0.1 mg/mL	Reversal of Conscious Sedation or in General Anesthesia: Initially 0.2 mg IV (over 15 seconds). After 45 seconds, a further dose of 0.2 mg can be injected and repeated at 60-second intervals where necessary (up to a maximum of 4 additional times) to a maximum total dose of 1 mg. Management of Suspected Benzodiazepine Overdose: Initially 0.2 mg IV (over 30 seconds). After 30 seconds, a further dose of 0.3 mg can be injected (over 30 seconds). Further doses of 0.5 mg can be given (over 30 seconds) at 60-second intervals up to a cumulative dose of 3 mg.

Flunisolide	AEROBID NASALIDE	Corticosteroid	**Aerosol:** 250 μg/spray **Spray:** 25 μg/spray	2 inhalations bid AM and PM. 2 sprays in each nostril bid.
Fluocinolone Acetonide	SYNALAR	Corticosteroid	**Cream:** 0.01, 0.025% **Oint:** 0.025% **Solution:** 0.01%	Apply as a thin film bid - qid.
	SYNALAR-HP		**Cream:** 0.2%	
Fluocinonide	LIDEX	Corticosteroid	**Cream, Oint, Gel & Solution:** 0.05%	Apply as a thin film bid - qid.
Fluorometholone	FML	Corticosteroid	**Ophth Susp:** 0.1%	1 drop into affected eye(s) bid - qid. During the initial 24 - 48 hours, the frequency of dosing may be increased if necessary.
	FML FORTE		**Ophth Susp:** 0.25%	
	FML S.O.P.		**Ophth Oint:** 0.1%	1 drop into affected eye(s) bid - qid.
Fluorouracil	FLUOROURACIL INJECTION	Antineoplastic	**Inj:** 500 mg/10 mL	Apply 1/2 inch ribbon to eye(s) q 4 h for the 1st 24 - 48 h. When a favorable response is observed, reduce dosage to 1 - 3 times daily. 12 mg/kg daily IV for 4 days. If no toxicity is observed, 6 mg/kg are given on days 6, 8, 10 and 12. May repeat course in 30 days.
	EFUDEX		**Cream:** 5% **Solution:** 2, 5%	**Actinic or Solar Keratosis:** Cover lesions bid; continue therapy for at least 2 - 4 weeks. **Superficial Basal Cell Carcinomas:** Use only 5% cream or solution. Cover lesions bid; continue therapy for at least 3 - 6 weeks.
	FLUOROPLEX		**Cream & Solution:** 1%	Cover all lesions bid. Continue therapy for 2 to 6 weeks.
Fluoxetine Hydrochloride	PROZAC	Antidepressant	**Cpsl:** 10, 20 mg **Liquid:** 20 mg/5 mL (0.23% alcohol)	20 mg daily po in the AM. May increase dose after several weeks to 20 mg bid po. Do not exceed maximum dose of 80 mg/day.

GENERIC NAME	COMMON TRADE NAMES	THERAPEUTIC CATEGORY	PREPARATIONS	COMMON ADULT DOSAGE
Fluoxymesterone (C-III)	HALOTESTIN	Androgen	Tab: 2, 5, 10 mg	**Male Hypogonadism:** 5 - 20 mg daily po as a single dose or in 3 - 4 divided doses. **Breast Cancer:** 10 - 40 mg daily po in 3 - 4 divided doses.
Fluphenazine Decanoate	PROLIXIN DECANOATE	Antipsychotic	Inj: 25 mg/mL	12.5 - 25 mg IM or SC.
Fluphenazine Enanthate	PROLIXIN ENANTHATE	Antipsychotic	Inj: 25 mg/mL	25 mg IM or SC q 2 weeks.
Fluphenazine Hydrochloride	PROLIXIN	Antipsychotic	Tab: 1, 2.5, 5, 10 mg Elixir: 2.5 mg/5 mL (14% alcohol) Conc Liquid: 5 mg/mL (14% alcohol)	2.5 - 10 mg daily po in divided doses at 6- to 8-hour intervals.
			Inj: 2.5 mg/mL	1.25 - 10 mg daily IM in divided doses at 6- to 8-hour intervals.
Flurandrenolide	CORDRAN	Corticosteroid	Cream & Oint: 0.025, 0.05% Lotion: 0.05% Tape: 4 mcg/cm^2	Apply as a thin film to affected areas bid - tid and rub in gently. Apply to affected areas; replace q 12 h.
Flurazepam (C-IV) Hydrochloride	DALMANE	Hypnotic	Cpsl: 15, 30 mg	15 - 30 mg hs po.
Flurbiprofen	ANSAID	Antiinflammatory	Tab: 50, 100 mg	200 - 300 mg daily, given bid, tid or qid po.
Flurbiprofen Sodium	OCUFEN	Antiinflammatory	Ophth Solution: 0.03%	1 drop in eye q 30 minutes, beginning 2 h before surgery (total of 4 drops).
Flutamide	EULEXIN	Antineoplastic	Cpsl: 125 mg	250 mg tid po at 8-hour intervals.

86

Fluticasone Propionate	CUTIVATE	Corticosteroid	Oint: 0.005% Cream: 0.05%	Apply a thin film to affected skin areas bid. Rub in gently.
	FLONASE	Corticosteroid	Nasal Spray: 50 µg/spray	Initially, 2 sprays in each nostril once daily or 1 spray in each nostril twice daily (morning and evening). May decrease to 1 spray in each nostril once daily based on response. **For Adolescents over 12 yrs:** Initially, 1 spray in each nostril once daily; may increase to 2 sprays in each nostril once daily, then may decrease to 1 spray in each nostril once daily based on response.
Fluvastatin Sodium	LESCOL	Hypolipidemic	Cpsl: 20, 40 mg	20 - 40 mg once daily po hs.
Fosinopril Sodium	MONOPRIL	Antihypertensive	Tab: 10, 20 mg	Initially, 10 mg once daily po. May increase dosage to usual range: 20 - 40 mg daily.
Furazolidone	FUROXONE	Antibacterial	Liquid: 50 mg/15 mL Tab: 100 mg	100 mg qid po.
Furosemide	LASIX	Diuretic, Antihypertensive	Solution: 10 mg/mL (11.5% alcohol) Tab: 20, 40, 80 mg	**Diuresis:** 20 - 80 mg daily po. May repeat in 6 to 8 h if needed. **Hypertension:** 40 mg bid po.
		Diuretic	Inj: 10 mg/mL	**Diuresis:** 20 - 40 mg IM or IV (over 1 - 2 min). **Acute Pulmonary Edema:** 40 mg IV (over 1 - 2 min). If response is not adequate after 1 h, dose may be doubled.
Gabapentin	NEURONTIN	Antiepileptic	Cpsl: 100, 300, 400 mg	Titrate with 300 mg po on day 1, 300 mg bid po on day 2, and 300 mg tid po on day 3. If necessary, the dosage may be increased by using 300 - 400 mg tid up to 1800 mg/day.
Gallium Nitrate	GANITE	Hypocalcemic	Inj: 25 mg/mL	200 mg/m² daily by IV infusion (over 24 h) for 5 consecutive days.

GENERIC NAME	COMMON TRADE NAMES	THERAPEUTIC CATEGORY	PREPARATIONS	COMMON ADULT DOSAGE
Ganciclovir Sodium	CYTOVENE	Antiviral	Powd for Inj: 500 mg	**CMV Retinitis:** **Induction:** 5 mg/kg IV (at a constant rate over 1 hour), q 12 h for 14 - 21 days. **Maintenance:** 5 mg/kg IV (at a constant rate over 1 hour), once daily 7 days each week, or 6 mg/kg IV once daily on 5 days each week. **Prevention of CMV in Transplant Recipients:** Initially, 5 mg/kg IV (at a constant rate over 1 hour), q 12 h for 7 - 14 days; then, 5 mg/kg IV once daily 7 days each week, or 6 mg/kg IV once daily on 5 days each week.
Gemfibrozil	LOPID	Hypolipidemic	Tab: 600 mg	600 mg bid po 30 minutes before the morning and evening meal.
Gentamicin Sulfate	GARAMYCIN	Antibacterial	Cream & Oint: 0.1% Ophth Solution: 3 mg/mL Ophth Oint: 3 mg/g Inj: 40 mg/mL	Apply to affected areas tid to qid. 1 - 2 drops into affected eye(s) q 4 h. In severe infections, dosage may be increased to as much as 2 drops once every hour. Apply to affected eye(s) bid or tid. **Usual Dosage:** 3 mg/kg/day IM or IV divided in 3 doses at 8-hour intervals. **Life-Threatening Infections:** Up to 5 mg/kg/day may be administered in 3 or 4 equal doses.
Glipizide	GLUCOTROL	Hypoglycemic	Tab: 5, 10 mg	**Initial:** 5 mg daily po before breakfast. **Titration:** As determined by blood glucose response, increase dosage in increments of 2.5 - 5 mg. At least several days should elapse between titration steps. **Maintenance:** Total daily doses above 15 mg should ordinarily be divided, e.g., bid.
	GLUCOTROL XL		Extended-Rel. Tab: 5, 10 mg	Initially, 5 mg daily po with breakfast. Usual dosage range: 5 - 10 mg daily po.

Generic	Brand	Class	Forms	Dosage
Glyburide	DIAβETA, MICRONASE	Hypoglycemic	**Tab:** 1.25, 2.5, 5 mg	**Initial:** 1.25 - 5 mg daily po with breakfast. **Maintenance:** 1.25 - 20 mg daily po as a single dose or in divided doses.
Glyburide Micronized	GLYNASE PRESTAB	Hypoglycemic	**Tab:** 1.5, 3, 6 mg	**Initial:** 0.75 - 3 mg daily po with breakfast. **Maintenance:** 0.75 - 12 mg daily po as a single dose or in divided doses.
Glycerin		Laxative	**Rectal Suppos:** (with sodium stearate)	Insert 1 suppository rectally prn.
Gold Sodium Thiomalate	MYOCHRYSINE	Antirheumatic	**Inj (per mL):** 25, 50 mg	Weekly IM injections as follows: 1st- 10 mg; 2nd- 25 mg; 3rd and subsequent- 25 - 50 mg until toxicity or major improvement. Maintenance doses: 25 - 50 mg every other week for 2 - 20 weeks. If condition remains stable, give 25 - 50 mg every 3rd week.
Granisetron Hydrochloride	KYTRIL	Antiemetic	**Inj:** 1.12 mg/mL (1 mg/mL as the base)	10 μg/kg, infused IV over 5 minutes, beginning within 30 minutes before initiation of chemotherapy, and only on the days that chemotherapy is given.
Griseofulvin Microsize	FULVICIN U/F	Antifungal	**Tab:** 250, 500 mg	500 mg daily po as a single dose or in divided doses.
	GRIFULVIN V, GRIVATE		**Susp:** 125 mg/5 mL **Tab:** 250, 500 mg	500 mg daily po.
	GRISACTIN		**Cpsl:** 250 mg **Tab:** 500 mg	500 mg daily po as a single dose or in divided doses, e.g., 125 mg qid or 250 mg bid.
Griseofulvin Ultramicrosize	FULVICIN P/G	Antifungal	**Tab:** 125, 165, 250, 330 mg	330 - 375 mg daily po as a single dose or in divided doses.
	GRISACTIN ULTRA		**Tab:** 250, 330 mg	330 mg daily po as a single dose or in divided doses.
	GRIS-PEG		**Tab:** 125, 250 mg	375 mg daily po (single dose or in div. doses).

89

GENERIC NAME	COMMON TRADE NAMES	THERAPEUTIC CATEGORY	PREPARATIONS	COMMON ADULT DOSAGE
Guaifenesin	ROBITUSSIN	Expectorant	Syrup: 100 mg/5 mL (3.5% alcohol) Liquid: 200 mg/5 mL	100 - 400 mg q 4 h po. 200 mg q 4 h po.
	NALDECON SENIOR EX			
	ORGANIDIN NR		Liquid: 100 mg/5 mL Tab: 200 mg	200 - 400 mg q 4 h po. 200 - 400 mg q 4 h po.
	HUMIBID SPRINKLE HUMIBID L.A.		Sustained-Rel. Cpsl: 300 mg Sustained-Rel. Tab: 600 mg	600 - 1200 mg q 12 h po.
Guanabenz Acetate	WYTENSIN	Antihypertensive	Tab: 4, 8 mg	Initially, 4 mg bid po. May increase dosage in increments of 4 - 8 mg/day q 1 - 2 weeks.
Guanadrel Sulfate	HYLOREL	Antihypertensive	Tab: 10, 25 mg	Initially, 5 mg bid po. Adjust dosage weekly; most require 20 - 75 mg/day (given bid).
Guanethidine Monosulfate	ISMELIN	Antihypertensive	Tab: 10, 25 mg	**Ambulatory Patients:** Initially, 10 mg daily po. Dosage should be increased gradually, no more often than every 5 - 7 days. Average daily dose is 25 - 50 mg po. **Hospitalized Patients:** Initially, 25 - 50 mg po. May increase by 25 or 50 mg daily or every other day.
Guanfacine Hydrochloride	TENEX	Antihypertensive	Tab: 1, 2 mg	1 mg daily po hs. Dose may be increased after 3 - 4 weeks to 2 mg if necessary.
Halazepam (C-IV)	PAXIPAM	Antianxiety Agent	Tab: 20, 40 mg	20 - 40 mg tid or qid po.
Halcinonide	HALOG	Corticosteroid	Cream, Oint & Solution: 0.1%	Apply to affected areas bid to tid.
Halobetasol Propionate	ULTRAVATE	Corticosteroid	Cream & Oint: 0.05%	Apply a thin layer to affected skin bid. Rub in gently and completely.
Haloperidol	HALDOL	Antipsychotic	Tab: 0.5, 1, 2, 5, 10, 20 mg	0.5 - 5 mg bid to tid po.

Haloperidol Decanoate	HALDOL DECANOATE 50 HALDOL DECANOATE 100	Antipsychotic	**Inj:** 70.5 mg/mL (50 mg/mL as the base) **Inj:** 141.0 mg/mL (100 mg/mL as the base)	Administer once q 4 wks by deep IM injection. For patients previously maintained on anti-psychotics, the recommended initial dose is 10 - 15 times the previous daily dose in oral haloperidol equivalents. The initial dose should not exceed 100 mg.
Haloperidol Lactate	HALDOL	Antipsychotic	**Liquid Conc:** 2 mg/mL **Inj:** 5 mg/mL	0.5 - 5 mg bid to tid po. 2 - 5 mg q 4 - 8 h IM.
Haloprogin	HALOTEX	Antifungal	**Cream & Solution:** 1%	Apply to affected areas bid for 2 - 3 weeks.
Heparin Calcium	CALCIPARINE	Anticoagulant	**Inj:** 5,000 units/0.2 mL	**Deep SC:** 5000 units IV, followed by 10,000 to 20,000 units SC. Then 8,000 - 10,000 units q 8 h or 15,000 - 20,000 units q 12 h. **Intermittent IV:** 10,000 units undiluted or in 50 - 100 mL of 0.9% sodium chloride injection. Then 5,000 - 10,000 units undiluted or in sodium chloride injection q 4 - 6 h. **IV Infusion:** 5,000 units IV; then 20,000 to 40,000 units/24 h in 1,000 mL of 0.9% NaCl injection by continuous IV infusion.
Heparin Sodium	LIQUAEMIN	Anticoagulant	**Inj:** 1,000 - 40,000 units/mL	Same dosages as for CALCIPARINE above.
Homatropine Hydrobromide	ISOPTO HOMATROPINE	Mydriatic - Cycloplegic	**Ophth Solution:** 2, 5%	**Refraction:** Instill 1 - 2 drops in the eye(s). May be repeated in 5 - 10 min, if necessary. **Uveitis:** Instill 1 - 2 drops in the eye(s) q 3 - 4 h.
Hydralazine Hydrochloride	APRESOLINE	Antihypertensive	**Inj:** 20 mg/mL	Initiate therapy in gradually increasing doses: 10 mg qid po for 2 - 4 days, increase to 25 mg qid for the rest of the week. For the 2nd and subsequent weeks, raise to 50 mg qid. 20 - 40 mg IM or IV, repeated as necessary.
Hydrochlorothiazide	ESIDRIX, HYDRODIURIL	Diuretic, Antihypertensive	**Tab:** 25, 50, 100 mg	**Diuresis:** 25 - 100 mg daily or bid po. **Hypertension:** 50 - 100 mg daily po in the AM.

GENERIC NAME	COMMON TRADE NAMES	THERAPEUTIC CATEGORY	PREPARATIONS	COMMON ADULT DOSAGE
Hydrocortisone	HYDROCORTONE	Corticosteroid	**Tab:** 10, 20 mg	Initial dosage varies from 20 - 240 mg daily po depending on the disease being treated and the patient's response.
	CORTEF		**Tab:** 5, 10, 20 mg	
	CORTENEMA		**Retention Enema:** 100 mg/60 mL	Use 1 enema rectally nightly for 21 days or until patient comes into remission.
	ANUSOL-HC 2.5%, PROCTOCREAM-HC 2.5%		**Cream:** 2.5%	Apply as a thin film to affected areas bid - qid.
	CORT-DOME		**Cream:** 0.5, 1%	Apply as a thin film to affected areas bid - qid.
	HYTONE		**Cream, Oint & Lotion:** 1, 2.5%	Apply as a thin film to affected areas bid - qid.
	NUTRACORT		**Cream:** 1% **Lotion:** 1, 2.5%	Apply as a thin film to affected areas tid - qid. Apply as a thin film to affected areas bid - qid.
Hydrocortisone Acetate	HYDROCORTONE ACETATE	Corticosteroid	**Inj (per mL):** 25, 50 mg [low solubility; provides a prolonged effect]	**Only for Intra-articular, Intralesional and Soft Tissue Injection:** Dose and frequency of injection are variable and must be individualized on the basis of the disease and the response of the patient. The initial dosage varies from 5 - 75 mg a day.
	ANUSOL HC-1 ANUSOL-HC		**Oint:** 1% **Rectal Suppos:** 25 mg	Apply as a thin film to affected areas bid - qid. Insert 1 rectally AM and PM for 2 weeks. In more severe cases, 1 rectally tid or 2 bid.
	CALDECORT CALDECORT LIGHT		**Cream & Spray:** 1% **Cream:** 0.5%	Apply to affected areas tid or qid. Apply to affected areas tid or qid.
	CARMOL-HC		**Cream:** 1%	Apply as a thin film to affected areas bid - qid.
	CORTICAINE		**Cream:** 0.5, 1%	Apply as a thin film to affected areas bid - qid.
	CORTAID		**Cream, Lotion, Oint and Spray:** 0.5%	Apply to affected areas up to qid.
				Apply to affected areas bid - qid.

92

Generic Name	Brand Name	Class	Formulation	Dosage
Hydrocortisone Sodium Phosphate	CORTIFOAM	Corticosteroid	Aerosol: 10% (with rectal applicator)	1 applicatorful rectally once or twice daily for 2 - 3 weeks, and every 2nd day thereafter.
	ORABASE HCA		Dental Paste: 0.5%	Apply to oral membranes bid - tid & hs.
	HYDROCORTONE PHOSPHATE		Inj: 50 mg/mL [water soluble; rapid onset, short duration]	For IV, IM & SC Injection: Dose requirements are variable and must be individualized on the basis of the disease and the response of the patient. The initial dosage varies from 15 - 240 mg a day.
Hydrocortisone Sodium Succinate	SOLU-CORTEF	Corticosteroid	Powd for Inj: 100, 250, 500, 1000 mg	100 - 500 mg IM, IV, or by IV infusion. Repeat at intervals of 2, 4, or 6 h.
Hydrocortisone Valerate	WESTCORT	Corticosteroid	Cream & Oint: 0.2%	Apply as a thin film to affected areas bid to tid.
Hydroflumethiazide	DIUCARDIN, SALURON	Diuretic, Antihypertensive	Tab: 50 mg	Diuresis: 50 mg once or twice daily po. Hypertension: 50 mg bid po.
Hydromorphone Hydrochloride (C-II)	DILAUDID	Opioid Analgesic	Tab: 2, 4, 8 mg	2 mg q 4 - 6 h po, prn. More severe pain may require 4 mg or more q 4 - 6 h po.
			Inj: 1, 2, 4 mg/mL	1 - 2 mg q 4 - 6 h SC or IM, prn. For IV use, give dose slowly over at least 2 - 3 minutes.
			Rectal Suppos: 3 mg	Insert 1 suppository rectally q 6 - 8 h.
	DILAUDID-5	Opioid Analgesic	Oral Liquid: 5 mg/5 mL	2.5 - 10 mg (2.5 - 10 mL) q 3 - 6 h po.
	DILAUDID-HP	Opioid Analgesic	Inj: 10 mg/mL	1 - 2 mg q 4 - 6 h SC or IM.
Hydroxyurea	HYDREA	Antineoplastic	Cpsl: 500 mg	Solid Tumors: Intermittent Therapy: 80 mg/kg po as a single dose every 3rd day. Continuous Therapy: 20 - 30 mg/kg po as a single dose daily. Resistant Chronic Myelocytic Leukemia: 20 to 30 mg/kg po as a single dose daily.

GENERIC NAME	COMMON TRADE NAMES	THERAPEUTIC CATEGORY	PREPARATIONS	COMMON ADULT DOSAGE
Hydroxyzine Hydrochloride	ATARAX	Sedative, Antipruritic, Antianxiety Agent	**Syrup:** 10 mg/5 mL (0.5% alcohol) **Tab:** 10, 25, 50, 100 mg	**Sedation:** 50 - 100 mg po. **Pruritus:** 25 mg tid or qid po. **Anxiety:** 50 - 100 mg qid po.
	VISTARIL	Antiemetic, Antianxiety Agent	**Inj (per mL):** 25, 50 mg	**Nausea & Vomiting:** 25 - 100 mg IM. **Anxiety:** 50 - 100 mg IM and q 4 - 6 h, prn.
Hydroxyzine Pamoate	VISTARIL	Sedative, Antipruritic, Antianxiety Agent	**Susp:** 25 mg/5 mL **Cpsl:** 25, 50, 100 mg	**Sedation:** 50 - 100 mg po. **Pruritus:** 25 mg tid or qid po. **Anxiety:** 50 - 100 mg qid po.
Hyoscyamine Sulfate	LEVSIN	Anticholinergic, Antispasmodic	**Solution:** 0.125 mg/mL (5% alcohol) **Elixir:** 0.125 mg/5 mL (20% alcohol) **Tab & Sublng Tab:** 0.125 mg **Inj:** 0.5 mg/mL	0.125 - 0.25 mg q 4 h po. 0.125 - 0.25 mg q 4 h po. 0.125 - 0.25 mg q 4 h po or sublingually. 0.25 - 0.5 mg SC, IM, or IV up to qid at 4-hour intervals.
	LEVSINEX TIMECAPS	Anticholinergic, Antispasmodic	**Timed-Rel. Cpsl:** 0.375 mg	0.375 - 0.750 mg q 12 h po.
Ibuprofen	ADVIL, MEDIPREN, MOTRIN IB	Non-Opioid Analgesic, Antipyretic	**Cplt & Tab:** 200 mg	200 mg q 4 - 6 h po.
	CHILDREN'S ADVIL, CHILDREN'S MOTRIN	Non-Opioid Analgesic, Antiinflammatory	**Susp:** 100 mg/5 mL	**Analgesia:** 400 mg q 4 - 6 h po prn pain. **Dysmenorrhea:** 400 mg q 4 h po prn pain. **Rheumatoid Arthritis and Osteoarthritis:** 1200 to 3200 mg daily po in divided doses (300 mg qid or 400, 600, or 800 mg tid or qid).
	MOTRIN	Non-Opioid Analgesic, Antiinflammatory	**Tab:** 300, 400, 600, 800 mg	Same dosages as for PEDIAPROFEN above.
	IBU		**Tab:** 400, 600, 800 mg	
Idarubicin Hydrochloride	IDAMYCIN	Antineoplastic	**Powd for Inj:** 5, 10 mg	12 mg/m^2 daily for 3 days by slow IV (10 - 15 minutes) in combination with cytarabine.

Idoxuridine	HERPLEX LIQUIFILM	Antiviral	**Ophth Solution:** 0.1%	1 drop into each infected eye q h during the day and q 2 h at night. Alternatively, 1 drop into each infected eye q 5 minutes; repeat q 4 h day and night.
Imipramine Hydrochloride	TOFRANIL	Antidepressant	**Tab:** 10, 25, 50 mg	**Outpatients:** Initially, 75 mg/day po in divided doses, increased to 150 mg/day. **Hospitalized Patients:** Initially, 100 mg/day po in divided doses, gradually increased to 200 mg/day po as required.
Imipramine Pamoate	TOFRANIL-PM	Antidepressant	**Inj:** 25 mg/2 mL **Cpsl:** 75, 100, 125, 150 mg	Up to 100 mg/day IM in divided doses. **Outpatients:** Initially, 75 mg/day po; may raise dosage to 150 mg/day (dosage at which the optimum response usually occurs). The usual maintenance dosage is 75 - 150 mg daily as a single dose hs or in divided doses. **Hospitalized Patients:** Initially, 100 - 150 mg daily po; may increase to 200 mg/day. If no response in 2 weeks, give 250 - 300 mg/day po.
Indapamide	LOZOL	Diuretic, Antihypertensive	**Tab:** 1.25, 2.5 mg	**Edema of CHF:** 2.5 mg daily po as a single dose in the AM. If response is not satisfactory, may double dose in 1 week. **Hypertension:** 1.25 mg daily po as a single dose in the AM. If response is not satisfactory, may double dose in 4 weeks.
Indomethacin	INDOCIN	Antiinflammatory	**Susp:** 25 mg/5 mL **Cpsl:** 25, 50 mg **Rectal Suppos:** 50 mg	**Rheumatoid Arthritis:** 25 mg bid or tid po pc; if well tolerated, increase the daily dosage by 25 or 50 mg. In persistent night pain or AM stiffness, giving a large portion of the daily dose (up to 100 mg) hs po or by suppository may be helpful. **Acute Painful Shoulder:** 75 - 150 mg daily po pc in 3 - 4 divided doses for 7 - 14 days. **Acute Gout:** 50 mg tid po pc until pain is tolerable.

GENERIC NAME	COMMON TRADE NAMES	THERAPEUTIC CATEGORY	PREPARATIONS	COMMON ADULT DOSAGE
Indomethacin [continued]	INDOCIN SR		Sustained-Rel. Cpsl: 75 mg	75 mg daily po.
Insulin	ILETIN, HUMULIN, etc.	Hypoglycemic	Inj: 100 units/mL	Variable: inject SC. See the Insulin Table, pp. 222 to 224 for preparations.
Interferon alfa-2a	ROFERON-A	Antineoplastic	Inj (per mL): 3, 18, 36 million IUnits Powd for Inj: 18 million Iunits	**Hairy Cell Leukemia:** For Induction- 3 million IUnits daily for 16 - 24 weeks SC or IM. For maintenance- 3 million IUnits 3 times a week SC or IM. **Kaposi's Sarcoma:** For Induction- 36 million IUnits daily for 10 - 12 weeks SC or IM. For maintenance- 36 million IUnits 3 times a week SC or IM.
Interferon alfa-2b	INTRON A	Antineoplastic	Powd for Inj: 3, 5, 10, 18, 25, 50 million IUnits/vial	**Hairy Cell Leukemia:** 2 million IUnits/m^2 IM or SC 3 times a week. **Kaposi's Sarcoma:** 30 million IUnits/m^2 IM or SC 3 times a week. **Chronic Hepatitis B:** 30 - 35 million IUnits per week SC or IM, either as 5 million IUnits daily or 10 million IUnits 3 times a week for 16 weeks. **Chronic Hepatitis Non-A, Non-B/C:** 3 million IUnits 3 times a week SC or IM. **Condylomata Acuminata (10 million IU vial):** 1 million IUnits into the base of each wart SC 3 times a week on alternate days, for 3 weeks. To reduce side effects, administer in the evening if possible.
Interferon alfa-n3	ALFERON N	Antineoplastic	Inj: 5 million IUnits/vial of 1 mL	**Condylomata Acuminata:** 250,000 IUnits per per wart. Maximum dose per treatment session is 2.5 million IUnits SC at base of each wart. Use twice weekly for up to 8 weeks.

Iodinated Glycerol		Expectorant	Elixir: 60 mg/5 mL (21.75% alcohol) Solution: 50 mg/mL Tab: 30 mg	5 mL (60 mg) qid po. 20 drops (= 60 mg) in fruit juice po. 60 mg qid po. with liquids.
Ipratropium Bromide	ATROVENT	Bronchodilator	Aerosol: 18 μg/spray Solution: 500 μg/2.5 mL	2 inhalations (36 μg) qid. 500 μg by nebulization tid - qid (q 6 - 8 h).
Isoetharine	BRONKOSOL	Bronchodilator	Solution: 1%	**Hand Nebulizer:** 4 inhalations, up to q 4 h. **Oxygen Aerosolization:** 0.5 mL, diluted 1:3 with saline or other diluent, administered with O$_2$ flow adjusted to 4 - 6 L/min, over 15 - 20 minutes. **IPPB:** 0.5 mL, diluted 1:3 with saline or other diluent (with an inspiratory flow rate of 15 L/min at a cycling pressure of 15 cm H$_2$O).
	BRONKOMETER		Aerosol: 340 μg/spray	1 - 2 inhalations, up to q 4 h.
Isoflurophate	FLOROPRYL	Anti-Glaucoma Agent	Ophth Oint: 0.025%	Initially, place a 1/4 inch strip into the glaucomatous eye q 8 - 72 h.
Isoniazid	INH	Tuberculostatic	Tab: 300 mg	300 mg daily po.
Isoproterenol Hydrochloride	ISUPREL	Bronchodilator	Solution: 1:200 (0.5%), 1:100 (1.0%)	**Acute Bronchial Asthma (Hand-Bulb Nebulizer):** 5 - 15 inhalations (of 1:200) or 3 - 7 inhalations (of 1:100) up to 5 times daily. **Bronchospasm in COPD:** **Hand-Bulb Nebulizer:** Same dosage as for Acute Bronchial Asthma above. **Nebulization by Compressed Air or Oxygen:** 0.5 mL (of 1:200) diluted to 2 - 2.5 mL with water or isotonic saline. Flow rate is regulated to deliver over 10 - 20 minutes. Breath in mist up to 5 times daily. **IPPB:** 0.5 mL (of 1:200) diluted to 2 - 2.5 mL with water or isotonic saline. The IPPB treatments are usually given for 15 - 20 minutes, up to 5 times daily.

GENERIC NAME	COMMON TRADE NAMES	THERAPEUTIC CATEGORY	PREPARATIONS	COMMON ADULT DOSAGE
Isoproterenol Hydrochloride [continued]	ISUPREL MISTOMETER		Aerosol: 131 µg/spray	1 - 2 inhalations up to 5 times daily.
Isosorbide	ISMOTIC	Osmotic Diuretic	Solution: 100 g/220 mL (45%)	Initially 1.5 g/kg po, followed by 1 - 3 g/kg bid - qid po as indicated.
Isosorbide Dinitrate	ISORDIL	Antianginal	Sublingual Tab: 2.5, 5, 10 mg	2.5 - 10 mg q 2 - 3 h sublingually.
			Oral Tab: 5, 10, 20, 30, 40 mg	Initially, 5 - 20 mg po. For maintenance, 10 - 40 mg q 6 h po.
			Controlled-Rel. Cpsl & Tab: 40 mg	Initially, 40 mg po. For maintenance, 40 - 80 mg q 8 - 12 h po.
	SORBITRATE		Sublingual Tab: 2.5, 5, 10 mg	2.5 - 10 mg q 2 - 3 h sublingually.
			Chewable Tab: 5, 10 mg	5 - 10 mg q 2 - 3 h po.
			Oral Tab: 5, 10, 20, 30, 40 mg	Initially, 5 - 20 mg po. For maintenance, 10 - 40 mg q 6 h po.
			Sustained-Action Tab: 40 mg	Initially, 40 mg po. For maintenance, 40 - 80 mg q 8 - 12 h po.
	DILATRATE-SR		Sustained-Rel. Cpsl: 40 mg	Initially, 40 mg po. For maintenance, 40 - 80 mg q 8 - 12 h po.
Isosorbide Mononitrate	ISMO	Antianginal	Tab: 20 mg	20 mg bid po, with the two doses given 7 h apart.
	MONOKET		Tab: 10, 20 mg	20 mg bid po, with the doses given 7 h apart.
	IMDUR		Extended-Rel. Tab: 60 mg	Initially, 30 - 60 mg once daily po. May increase to 120 mg once daily po.
Isotretinoin	ACCUTANE	Anti-Cystic Acne Agent	Cpsl: 10, 20, 40 mg	0.5 - 2 mg/kg/day divided in 2 doses po for 15 - 20 weeks.
Isoxsuprine Hydrochloride	VASODILAN	Vasodilator	Tab: 10, 20 mg	10 - 20 mg tid or qid po.

Isradipine	DYNACIRC	Antihypertensive	**Cpsl:** 2.5, 5 mg	Initially, 2.5 mg bid po. May increase in increments of 5 mg/day at 2 - 4 week intervals to a maximum of 20 mg/day.
Itraconazole	SPORANOX	Antifungal	**Cpsl:** 100 mg	**Blastomycosis and Histoplasmosis:** 200 mg once daily po with food. May increase the dosage in 100 mg increments to a maximum of 400 mg daily. Doses over 200 mg/day should be given in 2 divided doses. **Aspergillosis:** 200 - 400 mg daily po.
Kanamycin Sulfate	KANTREX	Antibacterial	**Cpsl:** 500 mg **Powd for Inj:** 500, 1000 mg	**Suppression of Intestinal Bacteria:** 1000 mg q h po for 4 hours, followed by 1000 mg q 6 h po for 36 - 72 h. 7.5 mg/kg q 12 h deep IM.
Ketoconazole	NIZORAL	Antifungal	**Tab:** 200 mg **Cream:** 2% **Shampoo:** 2%	200 mg once daily po. In very severe infections, 400 mg once daily po. Apply topically once daily. Shampoo twice a week for 4 weeks with at least 3 days between shampooing; then shampoo intermittently prn.
Ketoprofen	ORUDIS	Non-Opioid Analgesic, Antiinflammatory	**Cpsl:** 25, 50, 75 mg	**Analgesia & Dysmenorrhea:** 25 - 50 mg q 6 - 8 h po. **Rheumatoid Arthritis & Osteoarthritis:** 75 mg tid po or 50 mg qid po.
	ORUVAIL	Antiinflammatory	**Extended-Rel. Cpsl:** 200 mg	**Rheumatoid Arthritis & Osteoarthritis:** 200 mg once daily po.
Ketorolac Tromethamine	ACULAR	Antiinflammatory	**Ophth Solution:** 0.5%	1 drop into affected eye(s) qid.

GENERIC NAME	COMMON TRADE NAMES	THERAPEUTIC CATEGORY	PREPARATIONS	COMMON ADULT DOSAGE
Ketorolac Tromethamine [continued]	TORADOL [IV/IM]	Non-Opioid Analgesic	Inj (per mL): 15, 30 mg	**Single-Dose Treatment (IM or IV[*]):** < 65 yrs: 1 dose of 60 mg IM or 30 mg IV. ≥ 65 yrs, renally impaired, or under 50 kg (110 lbs): 1 dose of 30 mg IM or 15 mg IV. **Multiple-Dose Treatment (IM or IV[*]):** < 65 yrs: 30 mg q 6 h IM or IV, not to exceed 120 mg per day. ≥ 65 yrs, renally impaired, or under 50 kg (110 lbs): 15 mg q 6 h IM or IV, not to exceed 60 mg per day. * The IV bolus dose must be given over no less than 15 seconds.
	TORADOL [ORAL]		Tab: 10 mg	Indicated only as continuation therapy to TORADOL [IV/IM]. The maximum combined duration of use (parenteral and oral) is 5 days. < 65 yrs: 20 mg po as a first dose for those who received 60 mg IM (single dose), 30 mg IV (single dose), or 30 mg (multiple dose) of TORADOL [IV/IM], followed by 10 mg q 4 - 6 h po, not to exceed 40 mg/day. ≥ 65 yrs, renally impaired, or under 50 kg (110 lbs): 10 mg po as a first dose for those who received 30 mg IM or 15 mg IV (single dose), or 15 mg (multiple dose) of TORADOL [IV/IM], followed by 10 mg q 4 - 6 h po, not to exceed 40 mg/day.
Labetalol Hydrochloride	NORMODYNE, TRANDATE	Antihypertensive	Tab: 100, 200, 300 mg	**Initial:** 100 mg bid po. Titrate dosage upward in increments of 100 mg bid q 2 - 3 days. **Maintenance:** Usually, 200 - 400 mg bid po.
			Inj: 5 mg/mL	**Repeated IV:** 20 mg IV (over 2 minutes). May give additional injections of 40 - 80 mg at 10-minute intervals (maximum: 300 mg). **IV Infusion:** 200 mL of a diluted solution (1 mg/mL) given at a rate of 2 mL/min.

Lactulose	CHRONULAC	Laxative	**Syrup:** 10 g/15 mL	15 - 30 mL (10 - 20 g) daily po. Dose may be increased to 60 mL daily if necessary.
Levobunolol Hydrochloride	BETAGAN LIQUIFILM	Anti-Glaucoma Agent	**Ophth Solution:** 0.25, 0.5%	1 drop into affected eye(s) once daily or bid.
Levocabastine Hydrochloride	LIVOSTIN	Antiallergic	**Ophth Solution:** 0.05%	1 drop into affected eye(s) qid for up to 2 weeks.
Levodopa	LARODOPA	Antiparkinsonian	**Tab:** 100, 250, 500 mg	Initially, 500 mg to 1 g daily po divided in 2 or more doses with food. May increase dosage gradually in increments not more than 750 mg q 3 - 7 days. Maximum 8 g daily.
Levonorgestrel	NORPLANT SYSTEM	Implant Contraceptive	**Kit:** 6 cpsles (each with 36 mg levonorgestrel) plus trocar, scalpel, forceps, syringe, 2 syringe needles, package of skin closures, gauze sponges, stretch bandages, surgical drapes	Total implanted dose is 216 mg. Perform implantation of all 6 capsules during the first 7 days of the onset of menses. Insertion is subdermal in the mid-portion of the upper arm; distribute capsules in a fan-like pattern, about 15 degrees apart, for a total of 75 degrees.
Levorphanol Tartrate (C-II)	LEVO-DROMORAN	Opioid Analgesic	**Tab:** 2 mg **Inj:** 2 mg/mL	2 mg po. May be increased to 3 mg if needed. 2 mg SC. May be increased to 3 mg if needed.
Levothyroxine Sodium	LEVOTHROID	Thyroid Hormone	**Tab:** 25, 50, 75, 88, 100, 112, 125, 137, 150, 175, 200, 300 µg	**Usual Dosage:** 50 µg daily po with increases of 25 - 50 µg at 2 - 4 week intervals until the patient is euthyroid or symptoms preclude further dose increases. The usual maintenance dosage is 100 - 200 µg daily po.
	SYNTHROID		**Tab:** 25, 50, 75, 88, 100, 112, 125, 150, 175, 200, 300 µg	**Myxedema Coma or Hypothyroid Patients with Angina:** Starting dose should be 25 µg daily po with increases of 25 - 50 µg at 2 - 4 week intervals as determined by response.
			Powd for Inj: 200, 500 µg	**Myxedema Coma:** Initially, 200 - 500 µg (100 µg/mL) IV. Then, 100 - 200 µg daily IV. After evaluation of thyroid state, 50 - 100 µg daily IV is usually sufficient.

101

GENERIC NAME	COMMON TRADE NAMES	THERAPEUTIC CATEGORY	PREPARATIONS	COMMON ADULT DOSAGE
Lidocaine	XYLOCAINE	Local Anesthetic	Oint: 2.5% Oint: 5% Oral Spray: 10%	Apply topically prn. Apply topically. Maximum single application-5 g (= 6 inches of ointment). Maximum daily application- 1/2 tube (= 17 - 20 g). 2 metered doses per quadrant are recommended as the upper limit.
Lidocaine Hydrochloride	XYLOCAINE	Antiarrhythmic	Inj (per mL): 10 mg (1%), 20 mg (2%)	IV Injection: 50 - 100 mg IV bolus (at a rate of 25 - 50 mg/min). May repeat dose in 5 min. IV Infusion: Following bolus administration, give at a rate of 1 - 4 mg/min.
	4% XYLOCAINE-MPF	Local Anesthetic	Inj: 40 mg/mL (4%)	Retrobulbar Injection: 3 - 5 mL/70 kg (1.7 - 3 mg/kg. Transtracheal Injection: 2 - 3 mL injected rapidly through a large needle. Topical: Spray pharynx with 1 - 5 mL.
	XYLOCAINE 2% VISCOUS	Local Anesthetic	Solution: 2%	Mouth: 15 mL swished around mouth and spit out. Readminister q 3 - 8 h prn. Pharynx: 15 mL gargled & may be swallowed. Readminister q 3 - 8 h prn.
Lincomycin Hydrochloride	LINCOCIN	Antibacterial	Cpsl: 500 mg	Serious Infections: 500 mg tid (q 8 h) po. More Severe Infections: 500 mg or more qid (q 6 h) po.
			Inj: 300 mg/mL	Serious Infections: 600 mg q 24 h IM or 600 to 1000 mg (diluted in 100 mL of fluid) q 8 to 12 h by IV infusion (over 1 hour). More Severe Infections: 600 mg q 12 h IM or up to 8 g daily by IV infusion (at a rate of 1 g/100 mL/hour).
Lindane	KWELL	Antiparasitic, Scabicide	Cream & Lotion: 1%	Scabies: Apply to dry skin as a thin layer and rub in thoroughly. Leave on for 8 - 12 h, then remove by thorough washing.

Drug	Category	Form	Dosage
		Shampoo: 1%	**Head & Crab Lice:** Apply 30 - 60 mL to dry hair. Work thoroughly into hair and allow to remain in place for 4 minutes. Add small amounts of water to form a good lather. Rinse thoroughly and towel dry.
Liothyronine Sodium / CYTOMEL	Thyroid Hormone	Tab: 5, 25, 50 μg	**Usual Dosage:** 25 μg daily po. Daily dosage may be increased by 12.5 - 25 μg q 1 - 2 weeks. Usual maintenance dose is 25 - 75 μg daily po. **Myxedema:** Starting dose is 5 μg daily po. May increase by 5 - 10 μg daily q 1 - 2 weeks. When 25 μg daily is reached, dosage may be increased by 12.5 - 25 μg q 1 - 2 weeks. Usual maintenance dose is 50 - 100 μg daily.
Lisinopril / PRINIVIL ZESTRIL	Antihypertensive, Heart Failure Drug	Tab: 2.5, 5, 10, 20, 40 mg Tab: 5, 10, 20, 40 mg	**Hypertension:** Initially, 10 mg once daily po. Usual dosage range is 20 - 40 mg as a single daily dose. **Heart Failure:** Initially, 5 mg once daily po with diuretics and digitalis. Usual dosage range is 5 - 20 mg once daily.
Lithium Carbonate / ESKALITH	Antimaniacal	Cpsl & Tab: 300 mg	**Usual Dosage:** 300 mg tid or qid po. **Acute Mania:** 900 mg bid po or 600 mg tid po. **Long-Term Control:** 900 - 1200 mg daily po in 2 or 3 divided doses.
ESKALITH CR		Controlled-Rel. Tab: 450 mg	**Usual Dosage:** 450 mg bid po.
LITHOBID		Slow-Rel. Tab: 300 mg	**Acute Mania:** 900 mg bid po or 600 mg tid po. **Long-Term Control:** 900 - 1200 mg daily po in 2 or 3 divided doses.
Lithium Citrate	Antimaniacal	Syrup: 8 mEq (= 300 mg of lithium carbonate)/5 mL	**Acute Mania:** 10 mL (16 mEq) tid po. **Long-Term Control:** 5 mL (8 mEq) tid or qid po.
Lobeline Sulfate / BANTRON	Smoking Deterrent	Tab: 2 mg	2 mg po after each meal with half a glass of water.

103

GENERIC NAME	COMMON TRADE NAMES	THERAPEUTIC CATEGORY	PREPARATIONS	COMMON ADULT DOSAGE
Lodoxamide Tromethamine	ALOMIDE	Antiallergic	Ophth Sol: 0.1%	1 - 2 drops in each affected eye qid for up to 3 months.
Lomefloxacin Hydrochloride	MAXAQUIN	Antibacterial	Tab: 400 mg	**Lower Respiratory Tract and Urinary Tract Infections (Uncomplicated):** 400 mg once daily po for 10 days. **Urinary Tract Infections, Complicated:** 400 mg once daily po for 14 days.
Lomustine	CeeNU	Antineoplastic	Cpsl: 10, 40, 100 mg	130 mg/m^2 po as a single dose q 6 weeks. Dosage adjustments are made in 6 weeks based on platelet and leukocyte counts.
Loperamide Hydrochloride	IMODIUM	Antidiarrheal	Cpsl: 2 mg	4 mg po followed by 2 mg after each unformed stool. Maximum daily dosage- 16 mg.
	IMODIUM A-D		Liquid: 1 mg/5 mL (5.25% alcohol) Cplt: 2 mg	4 mg po followed by 2 mg after each unformed stool. Maximum daily dosage- 8 mg.
	PEPTO DIARRHEA CONTROL		Solution: 1 mg/5 mL (5.25% alcohol)	4 mg po followed by 2 mg after each loose bowel movement. Maximum: 8 mg daily.
Loracarbef	LORABID	Antibacterial	Powd for Susp (per 5 mL): 100, 200 mg Cpsl: 200, 400 mg	**Lower Respiratory Tract Infections (Except Pneumonia:** 200 - 400 mg q 12 h po for 7 days. **Pneumonia:** 400 mg q 12 h po for 14 days. **Upper Respiratory Tract Infections:** 200 - 400 mg q 12 h po for 10 days. **Skin and Skin Structure Infections:** 200 mg q 12 h po for 7 days. **Urinary Tract Infections (Uncomplicated Cystitis):** 200mg q 24 h po for 7 days. **Urinary Tract Infections (Uncomplicated Pyelonephritis):** 400 mg q 12 h po for 14 days.
Loratadine	CLARITIN	Antihistamine	Tab: 10 mg	10 mg once daily po on an empty stomach.

Lorazepam (C-IV)	ATIVAN	Antianxiety Agent	Tab: 0.5, 1, 2 mg	**Anxiety:** 2 - 3 mg daily po given bid or tid. **Insomnia due to Anxiety:** 2 - 4 mg hs po.
			Inj (per mL): 2, 4 mg	**Premedicant:** 0.05 mg/kg (maximum 4 mg) IM. **Anxiety:** 0.044 mg/kg (maximum 2 mg) IV.
Lovastatin	MEVACOR	Hypolipidemic	Tab: 10, 20, 40 mg	Initially, 20 mg once daily po with the evening meal. Dosage adjustments may be made at 4 week intervals. Usual dosage range is 20 to 80 mg/day po in single or divided doses.
Loxapine Hydrochloride	LOXITANE C	Antipsychotic	Conc Liquid: 25 mg/mL	Initially, 10 mg bid po. Dosage should be increased rapidly over 7 - 10 days; usual maintenance range is 60 - 100 mg daily, but many patients do well at 20 - 60 mg daily.
	LOXITANE IM		Inj: 50 mg/mL	12.5 - 50 mg q 4 - 6 h IM.
Loxapine Succinate	LOXITANE	Antipsychotic	Cpsl: 5, 10, 25, 50 mg	Same dosage as for LOXITANE C above.
Lypressin	DIAPID	Posterior Pituitary Hormone	Nasal Spray: 0.185 mg/mL	1 - 2 sprays in one or both nostrils qid. An additional dose hs often eliminates nocturia.
Mafenide Acetate	SULFAMYLON	Burn Preparation	Cream: 85 mg/g	Apply to the clean and debrided wound with a sterile gloved hand, once or twice daily, to a thickness of about 1/16 in.
Magaldrate	RIOPAN	Antacid	Susp: 540 mg/5 mL	5 - 10 mL po, between meals & hs.
Magnesium Hydroxide	MILK OF MAGNESIA	Antacid, Saline Laxative	Susp: 400 mg/5 mL	**Antacid:** 5 - 15 mL with a little water, up to qid po. **Laxative:** 30-60 mL followed by 8 oz. of fluid.
Magnesium Sulfate		Anticonvulsant	Inj: 12.5, 50%	**IM:** 4 - 5 g of a 50% solution q 4 h prn. **IV:** 4 g of a 10 - 20% solution (not exceeding 1.5 mL/min of a 10% solution) **IV Infusion:** 4 - 5 g in 250 mL of 5% Dextrose or Sodium Chloride Solution (not exceeding 3 mL/min).

GENERIC NAME	COMMON TRADE NAMES	THERAPEUTIC CATEGORY	PREPARATIONS	COMMON ADULT DOSAGE
Malathion	OVIDE	Antiparasitic	**Lotion:** 0.5%	Sprinkle on dry hair, rub gently until scalp is thoroughly wet. Allow to dry. After 8 - 12 h, wash & rinse hair; remove nits with fine toothed comb. Repeat in 7 - 9 days if necessary.
Malt Soup Extract	MALTSUPEX	Bulk Laxative	**Liquid:** 16 grams/15 mL **Powder:** 16 grams/heaping tablespoonful **Tab:** 750 mg	2 tablespoonfuls bid po for 3 or 4 days, or until relief is noted; then 1 - 2 tablespoonfuls daily po hs for maintenance, prn. Initially 4 tablets qid po with meals and hs. Adjust dosage according to response. Drink a full glass of liquid (8 fl. oz.) with each dose.
Maprotiline Hydrochloride	LUDIOMIL	Antidepressant	**Tab:** 25, 50, 75 mg	**Outpatients:** Initially, 75 mg daily po as a single dose or in divided doses. May increase dosage gradually after 2 weeks in increments of 25 mg. Usual maintenance dosage is 75 to 150 mg daily po. **Hospitalized Patients:** Initially, 100 - 150 mg daily po as a single dose or in divided doses. May increase dosage gradually, if needed, up to a maximum dose of 225 mg daily.
Mazindol (C-IV)	SANOREX	Anorexiant	**Tab:** 1, 2 mg	1 mg tid po 1 hour ac or 2 mg once daily po 1 hour before lunch.
Mebendazole	VERMOX	Anthelmintic	**Chew Tab:** 100 mg	Pinworm: 100 mg daily po (1 dose). Common Roundworm, Whipworm, Hookworm: 100 mg bid AM & PM for 3 days po.
Mechlorethamine Hydrochloride	MUSTARGEN	Antineoplastic	**Powd for Inj:** 10 mg	0.4 mg/kg IV either as a single dose or in divided doses of 0.1 - 0.2 mg/kg/day.
Meclizine Hydrochloride	ANTIVERT	Antivertigo Agent	**Tab:** 12.5, 25, 50 mg **Chewable Tab:** 25 mg	Vertigo: 25 - 100 mg daily po in divided doses. Motion Sickness: 25 - 50 mg po, 1 hour prior to embarkation; repeat dose q 24 h prn.

Meclocycline Sulfosalicylate	MECLAN	Anti-Acne Agent	Cream: 1%	Apply to affected area bid, AM and PM.
Meclofenamate Sodium	MECLOMEN	Non-Opioid Analgesic, Antiinflammatory	Cpsl: 50, 100 mg	**Analgesia:** 50 - 100 mg q 4 - 6 h po. **Dysmenorrhea:** 100 mg tid po, for up to 6 days, starting at the onset of menses. **Rheumatoid Arthritis & Osteoarthritis:** 200 to 400 mg daily po in 3 or 4 equal doses.
Medroxyprogesterone Acetate	PROVERA	Progestin	Tab: 2.5, 5, 10 mg	5 - 10 mg daily po for 5 - 10 days.
	DEPO-PROVERA	Antineoplastic	Inj (per mL): 100, 400 mg	Initially, 400 - 1000 mg weekly IM. If improvement is noted within a few weeks, patient may be maintained with as little as 400 mg per month.
		Injectable Contraceptive	Inj: 150 mg/mL	150 mg q 3 months by deep IM injection in the gluteal or deltoid muscle.
Medrysone	HMS	Corticosteroid	Ophth Susp: 1%	1 drop into affected eye(s) up to q 4 h.
Mefenamic Acid	PONSTEL	Non-Opioid Analgesic	Cpsl: 250 mg	500 mg po, then 250 mg q 6 h po with food.
Mefloquine Hydrochloride	LARIAM	Antimalarial	Tab: 250 mg	**Treatment:** 1250 mg po as a single dose with food and with at least 8 oz. of water. **Prophylaxis:** 250 mg once weekly po for 4 weeks, then 250 mg every other week. Take with food and at least 8 oz of water. Start 1 week prior to departure to endemic area.
Megestrol Acetate	MEGACE	Progestin	Susp: 40 mg/mL	**Appetite Stimulant in Patients with AIDS:** 800 mg/day (20 mL/day) po.
		Antineoplastic	Tab: 20, 40 mg Susp: 40 mg/mL	**Breast Cancer:** 40 mg qid po. **Endometrial Cancer:** 40 - 320 mg daily po in divided doses for at least 2 months.

GENERIC NAME	COMMON TRADE NAMES	THERAPEUTIC CATEGORY	PREPARATIONS	COMMON ADULT DOSAGE
Melphalan	ALKERAN	Antineoplastic	Tab: 2 mg	**Multiple Myeloma:** 6 mg daily po as a single dose. After 2 - 3 weeks, discontinue drug for up to 4 weeks; when WBC and platelet counts begin rising, maintenance dose of 2 mg daily po may be initiated. **Epithelial Ovarian Cancer:** 0.2 mg/kg daily for 5 days. Repeat q 4 - 5 weeks.
Meperidine Hydrochloride (C-II)	DEMEROL	Opioid Analgesic	**Powd for Inj:** 50 mg **Tab:** 50, 100 mg **Syrup:** 50 mg/5 mL **Inj (per mL):** 25, 50, 75, 100 mg	Usual dose is 16 mg/m² given as a single IV infusion over 15 - 20 min. Administer at 2 week intervals for 4 doses, then, after recovery from toxicity, at 4 week intervals. **Analgesia:** 50 - 150 mg q 3 - 4 h po, IM or SC. **Preoperatively:** 50 - 100 mg IM or SC, 30 - 90 minutes prior to anesthesia. **Obstetrical Analgesia:** 50 - 100 mg IM or SC when pain becomes regular; may repeat at 1 - 3 hour intervals.
Mephenytoin	MESANTOIN	Antiepileptic	**Tab:** 100 mg	Initially 50 - 100 mg daily po, increasing the daily dose by 50 - 100 mg at weekly intervals to a maintenance dose of 200 to 600 mg daily.
Mephobarbital (C-IV)	MEBARAL	Antiepileptic, Sedative	**Tab:** 32, 50, 100 mg	**Epilepsy:** 400 - 600 mg daily po. **Sedation:** 32 - 100 mg tid or qid po. Optimum dosage is 50 mg tid or qid po.
Meprobamate (C-IV)	EQUANIL, MILTOWN MILTOWN MEPROSPAN	Antianxiety Agent	**Tab:** 200, 400 mg **Tab:** 600 mg **Sust.-Rel. Cpsl:** 200, 400 mg	1200 - 1600 mg/day po in 3 - 4 divided doses. 600 mg bid po. 400 mg tid or qid po.
Mercaptopurine	PURINETHOL	Antineoplastic	**Tab:** 50 mg	**Induction:** 2.5 mg/kg daily po. May increase after 4 weeks to 5 mg/kg daily po. **Maintenance:** 1.5 - 2.5 mg/kg po as a single dose.

Mesalamine	ASACOL PENTASA	Bowel Antiinflammatory Agent	Delayed-Rel. Tab: 400 mg Controlled-Rel. Cpsl: 250 mg	800 mg tid po for 6 weeks. 1000 mg qid po for up to 8 weeks.
	ROWASA		Rectal Susp: 4 g/60 mL Rectal Suppos: 500 mg	One rectal instillation (4 g) once a day, preferably hs, and retained for approx. 8 h. Insert 1 rectally bid, and retained for 1 - 3 h.
Mesoridazine Besylate	SERENTIL	Antipsychotic	Tab: 10, 25, 50, 100 mg Conc Liquid: 25 mg/mL (0.61% alcohol) Inj: 25 mg/mL	**Schizophrenia:** 50 mg tid po. **Behavioral Problems in Mental Deficiency and Chronic Brain Syndrome:** 25 mg tid po. **Alcoholism:** 25 mg bid po. **Psychoneurotic Manifestations:** 10 mg tid po. 25 mg IM. May repeat in 30 - 60 minutes.
Metaproterenol Sulfate	ALUPENT, METAPREL	Bronchodilator	Syrup: 10 mg/5 mL Tab: 10, 20 mg Aerosol: 650 μg/spray	20 mg tid or qid po. 20 mg tid or qid po. 2 - 3 inhalations q 3 - 4 h.
Methadone Hydrochloride (C-II)	DOLOPHINE HYDROCHLORIDE	Opioid Analgesic	Tab: 5, 10 mg Inj: 10 mg/mL	2.5 - 10 mg q 3 - 4 h po, IM or SC prn pain.
Methamphetamine Hydrochloride (C-II)	DESOXYN	Anorexiant	Sustained-Rel. Tab: 5, 10, 15 mg	10 - 15 mg once daily po in the AM.
Methdilazine Hydrochloride	TACARYL	Antihistamine	Syrup: 4 mg/5 mL Chew Tab: 4 mg Tab: 8 mg	8 mg bid to qid po.
Methenamine Hippurate	HIPREX, UREX	Urinary Anti-infective	Tab: 1 g	1 g bid (morning and night) po.
Methenamine Mandelate	MANDELAMINE	Urinary Anti-infective	Tab: 0.5, 1 g Susp: 0.5 g/5 mL	1 g qid po, pc and hs. 1 g qid po, pc and hs.
Methicillin Sodium	STAPHCILLIN	Antibacterial	Powd for Inj: 1, 4, 6 g	4 - 12 g/day IM or IV (diluted in Sodium Chloride Injection) in divided doses q 4 - 6 h.

GENERIC NAME	COMMON TRADE NAMES	THERAPEUTIC CATEGORY	PREPARATIONS	COMMON ADULT DOSAGE
Methimazole	TAPAZOLE	Antithyroid Drug	**Tab:** 5, 10 mg	**Initial:** 15 mg daily po (mild disease), 30 - 40 mg daily po (moderately severe), and 60 mg daily po (severe), divided into 3 doses q 8 h. **Maintenance:** 5 - 15 mg daily po.
Methocarbamol	ROBAXIN	Skeletal Muscle Relaxant	**Tab:** 500 mg	**Initial:** 1500 mg qid po. **Maintenance:** 1000 mg qid po.
	ROBAXIN-750		**Tab:** 750 mg	**Initial:** 1500 mg qid po. **Maintenance:** 750 mg q 4 h po or 1500 mg tid po.
Methotrexate		Anti-Psoriasis Agent	**Tab:** 2.5 mg **Powd for Injection:** 20 mg (as the sodium salt) **Inj:** 25 mg/mL (as the sodium salt)	Individualize dosage. A test dose may be given prior to therapy to detect extreme sensitivity. 10 - 25 mg once a week po, IM, or IV until response is achieved. For po use, may given 2.5 mg q 12 h for 3 doses, once a week. Do not exceed 30 mg per week.
Methsuximide	CELONTIN	Antiepileptic	**Cpsl:** 150, 300 mg	300 mg daily po for the 1st week. May raise dosage at weekly intervals by 300 mg/day for 3 weeks to a daily dosage of 1200 mg.
Methyclothiazide	ENDURON	Diuretic, Antihypertensive	**Tab:** 2.5, 5 mg	**Diuresis:** 2.5 - 10 mg once daily po. **Hypertension:** 2.5 - 5 mg once daily po.
Methylcellulose	CITRUCEL CITRUCEL (Sugar-Free)	Bulk Laxative	**Powder:** 2 g/heaping tablespoonful (19 g) **Powder:** 2 g/heaping tablespoonful (10.2 g)	1 heaping tablespoonful stirred into 8 fl. oz. of cold water 1 - 3 times daily po at the first sign of constipation.
Methyldopa	ALDOMET	Antihypertensive	**Susp:** 250 mg/5 mL (1 % alcohol) **Tab:** 125, 250, 500 mg	**Initial:** 250 mg bid or tid po for the first 48 h. Adjust dosage at intervals of not less than 2 days. **Maintenance:** 500 mg - 2 g daily po in 2 - 4 divided doses.

Generic Name	Brand Name	Class	Form	Dosage
Methyldopate Hydrochloride	ALDOMET	Antihypertensive	Inj: 250 mg/5 mL	250 - 500 mg q 6 h IV.
Methylergonovine	METHERGINE	Oxytocic	Tab: 0.2 mg Inj: 0.2 mg/mL	0.2 mg tid or qid po for a maximum of 1 week. 0.2 mg q 2 - 4 h IM.
Methylphenidate Hydrochloride (C-II)	RITALIN RITALIN SR	CNS Stimulant	Tab: 5, 10, 20 mg Sustained-Rel. Tab: 20 mg	10 - 30 mg daily po in divided dose 2 or 3 times daily, preferably 30 - 45 minutes ac. 20 mg q 8 h po, preferably 30 - 45 minutes ac.
Methylprednisolone	MEDROL	Corticosteroid	Tab: 2, 4, 8, 16, 24, 32 mg	Initial dosage varies from 4 - 48 mg daily po, depending on the disease being treated. This dosage should be maintained or adjusted until the patient's response is satisfactory.
Methylprednisolone Acetate	DEPO-MEDROL	Corticosteroid	Inj (per mL): 20, 40, 80 mg	Initial dosage varies from 20 - 80 mg weekly to monthly, depending on the disease being treated; the dosage may be given intra-articularly or IM. The dosage should be maintained or adjusted until the patient's response is satisfactory.
Methylprednisolone Sodium Succinate	SOLU-MEDROL	Corticosteroid	Powd for Inj: 40, 125, 500 mg; 1, 2 g	30 mg/kg IV (administered over at least 30 minutes) q 4 - 6 h for 48 hours.
Methyltestosterone (C-III)	ANDROID	Androgen, Antineoplastic	Tab: 10, 25 mg	Replacement Therapy in Males: 10 - 50 mg daily po. Breast Carcinoma in Females: 50 - 200 mg daily po.
	ORETON METHYL TESTRED		Tab: 10 mg Cpsl: 10 mg	Same dosages as for ANDROID above. Same dosages as for ANDROID above.
Methysergide Maleate	SANSERT	Antimigraine Agent	Tab: 2 mg	4 - 8 mg daily with meals po.
Metipranolol Hydrochloride	OPTIPRANOLOL	Anti-Glaucoma Agent	Ophth Solution: 0.3%	1 drop into affected eye(s) bid.

111

GENERIC NAME	COMMON TRADE NAMES	THERAPEUTIC CATEGORY	PREPARATIONS	COMMON ADULT DOSAGE
Metoclopramide Hydrochloride	REGLAN	GI Stimulant, Antiemetic	**Syrup:** 5 mg/5 mL **Tab:** 5, 10 mg	**Gastroesophageal Reflux:** 10 - 15 mg po up to qid 30 minutes ac & hs. If symptoms are intermittent, single doses of up to 20 mg may be used prior to the provoking stimulus. **Diabetic Gastroparesis (early symptoms):** 10 mg po 30 minutes ac & hs for 2 - 8 weeks.
			Inj: 5 mg/mL	**Diabetic Gastroparesis (severe symptoms):** 10 mg slow IV (over 1 - 2 minutes) for up to 10 days; then switch to oral therapy. **Nausea and Vomiting associated with Cancer Chemotherapy:** 1 - 2 mg/kg slow IV (over 15 minutes), 30 min before beginning cancer therapy; repeat q 2 h for 2 doses, then q 3 h for 3 doses. **Postoperative Nausea and Vomiting:** 10 mg IM. **Facilitate Small Bowel Intubation:** 10 mg slow IV (over 1 - 2 minutes).
Metocurine Iodide	METUBINE IODIDE	Neuromuscular Blocker	**Inj:** 2 mg/mL	0.2 - 0.4 mg/kg IV (over 30 - 60 seconds). Supplemental doses (average, 0.5 - 1 mg) may be made as required.
Metolazone	MYKROX	Antihypertensive	**Tab:** 0.5 mg	0.5 mg once daily po, usually in the morning. If necessary, the dosage may be increased to 1 mg daily po.
	ZAROXOLYN	Diuretic, Antihypertensive	**Tab:** 2.5, 5, 10 mg	**Diuresis:** 5 - 20 mg once daily po. **Hypertension:** 2.5 - 5 mg once daily po.
Metoprolol Succinate	TOPROL XL	Antihypertensive, Antianginal	**Extended-Rel. Tab:** 47.5, 95, 190 (equivalent to 50, 100, 200 mg of metoprolol tartrate, respectively)	**Hypertension:** Initially, 50 - 100 mg daily po in a single dose. May increase dosage at weekly (or longer) intervals up to a maximum of 400 mg daily. **Angina:** Initially 100 mg daily po in a single dose. May increase dosage at weekly intervals up to a maximum of 400 mg daily.

112

Metoprolol Tartrate	LOPRESSOR	Antihypertensive, Antianginal, Post-MI Drug	Tab: 50, 100 mg	**Hypertension and Angina:** Initially, 100 mg daily po in a single or divided doses. May increase at weekly intervals. The effective dosage range is 100 - 400 mg/day. **Post-Myocardial Infarction:** **Early Treatment:** In patients who tolerate the full IV dose (15 mg; see below), 50 mg po q 6 h, initiated 15 minutes after the last IV dose and continue for 48 h. Then give a maintenance dose of 100 mg bid po. In patients who do <u>not</u> tolerate the full IV dose, 25 - 50 mg po q 6 h, initiated 15 minutes after the last IV dose or as soon as their condition allows. **Late Treatment:** Patients who appear not to tolerate full Early Treatment or those with contraindications to treatment, 100 mg po bid, as soon as their condition allows.
		Post-MI Drug	Inj: 1 mg/mL	**Post-Myocardial Infarction:** Start with 3 bolus IV injections of 5 mg each, at approximately 2-minute intervals. Then, switch to oral dosing as described above.
Metronidazole	FLAGYL	Antitrichomonal, Amebicide, Antibacterial	Tab: 250, 500 mg	**Trichomoniasis:** 250 mg tid po for 7 days or 2 g as a single dose po. **Acute Intestinal Amebiasis:** 750 mg tid po for 5 - 10 days. **Amebic Liver Abscess:** 500 - 750 mg tid po for 5 - 10 days. **Anaerobic Bacterial Infections:** Following IV dosing (as described below) 7.5 mg/kg q 6 h for 7 - 10 days.

113

GENERIC NAME	COMMON TRADE NAMES	THERAPEUTIC CATEGORY	PREPARATIONS	COMMON ADULT DOSAGE
Metronidazole [continued]	FLAGYL I.V. FLAGYL I.V. RTU	Antibacterial	Powd for Inj: 500 mg Inj: 500 mg/100 mL	**Treatment of Anaerobic Infections:** 15 mg/kg infused IV (over 1 h) as a loading dose; then, 7.5 mg/kg infused IV (over 1 h) q 6 h. **Surgical Prophylaxis:** 15 mg/kg infused IV (over 30 - 60 minutes) and completed 1 hour before surgery; then 7.5 mg/kg infused IV (over 30 - 60 minutes) at 6 and 12 h after the initial dose.
	METROGEL	Anti-Acne Agent	Gel: 0.75%	Apply and rub in a thin film to affected areas bid, morning and evening.
	METROGEL VAGINAL	Antibacterial	Vaginal Gel: 0.75%	Insert 1 applicatorful intravaginally bid, morning and evening, for 5 days.
Mexiletine Hydrochloride	MEXITIL	Antiarrhythmic	Cpsl: 150, 200, 250 mg	Initially, 200 mg q 8 h po with food or antacid. After 2 - 3 days, dosage may be adjusted in in 50 or 100 mg increments. For rapid control of arrhythmias, 400 mg po may be used as an initial loading dose.
Mezlocillin Sodium	MEZLIN	Antibacterial	Powd for Inj: 1, 2, 3, 4 g	**Urinary Tract Infections (Uncomplicated):** 100 to 125 mg/kg as 1.5 - 2.0 g q 6 h IV or IM. **Urinary Tract (Complicated) and Lower Respiratory Tract Infections:** 150 - 200 mg/kg as 3.0 g q 6 h IV. **Intra-Abdominal, Gynecological, Skin & Skin Structure Infections and Septicemia:** 225 to 300 mg/kg as 3.0 g q 4 h IV or 4.0 g q 6 h IV.
Miconazole	MONISTAT I.V.	Antifungal	Inj: 10 mg/mL	200 - 1200 mg per IV infusion. The following daily doses may be divided over 3 infusions: **Candidiasis:** 600 - 1800 mg/day. **Cryptococcosis:** 1200 - 2400 mg/day. **Coccidioidomycosis:** 1800 - 3600 mg/day. **Pseudoallescheriosis:** 600 - 3000 mg/day. **Paracoccidioidomycosis:** 200 - 1200 mg/day.

Miconazole Nitrate	MICATIN	Antifungal	Cream, Liquid, Powder & Spray Powder: 2%	Apply to affected areas bid, AM and PM.
	MONISTAT-DERM		Cream: 2%	Apply to affected areas bid, AM and PM.
	MONISTAT 3		Vaginal Suppos: 200 mg	200 mg intravaginally once daily hs for 3 days.
	MONISTAT 7		Vaginal Cream: 2%	Insert 1 applicatorful intravaginally once daily hs for 7 days.
			Vaginal Suppos: 100 mg	100 mg intravaginally once daily hs for 7 days.
Midazolam Hydrochloride (C-IV)	VERSED	Sedative - Hypnotic	Inj (per mL): 1, 5 mg	**Preoperative Sedation:** 0.07 - 0.08 mg/kg deep IM (approx. 5 mg) 1 h before surgery. **Conscious Sedation:** Titrate IV dose slowly to the desired effect. Give no more than 2.5 mg (over at least 2 minutes). Wait another 2 minutes to fully evaluate effect. If further titration is needed, use small increments.
Milrinone Lactate	PRIMACOR	Inotropic Agent	Inj: 1 mg/mL	**Loading Dose:** 50 µg/kg IV (over 10 minutes). **Maintenance:** 0.375 - 0.75 µg/kg/min by IV infusion. Total daily dosage: 0.59 - 1.13 mg/kg per 24 hours.
Mineral Oil	FLEET MINERAL OIL ENEMA	Emollient Laxative	Rectal Liquid: (pure)	Administer 1 bottle (118 mL) rectally as a single dose.
Minocycline Hydrochloride	MINOCIN	Antibacterial	Susp: 50 mg/5 mL (5% alcohol) Cpsl: 50, 100 mg Powd for Inj: 100 mg	200 mg initially po, followed by 100 mg q 12 h po. 200 mg initially po, followed by 100 mg q 12 h po; or, 100 - 200 mg initially po, followed by 50 mg qid po. 200 mg initially IV, followed by 100 mg q 12 h IV.
Minoxidil	LONITEN	Antihypertensive	Tab: 2.5, 5, 10 mg	Initially, 5 mg once daily po. May increase to 10, 20 and then to 40 mg daily po as a single dose or in divided doses. Intervals between dosage adjustments should be at least 3 days.

115

GENERIC NAME	COMMON TRADE NAMES	THERAPEUTIC CATEGORY	PREPARATIONS	COMMON ADULT DOSAGE
Minoxidil [continued]	ROGAINE	Hair Growth Stimulator	**Solution:** 20 mg/mL (2%)	Apply 1 mL to the total affected areas of the scalp bid.
Misoprostol	CYTOTEC	Anti-Ulcer Agent	**Tab:** 100, 200 μg	200 μg qid with food po.
Mivacurium Chloride	MIVACRON	Neuromuscular Blocker	**Inj (per mL):** 0.5, 2 mg	**Initial:** 0.15 mg/kg IV (over 5-15 sec), or 0.20 mg/kg IV (over 30 sec), or 0.25 mg/kg IV (0.15 mg/kg followed in 30 sec by 0.10 mg/kg) for tracheal intubation. **Maintenance:** 0.1 mg/kg IV.
Molindone Hydrochloride	MOBAN	Antipsychotic	**Conc Liquid:** 20 mg/mL (alcohol) **Tab:** 5, 10, 25, 50, 100 mg	**Initial:** 50 - 75 mg/day po; increase to 100 mg/day in 3 - 4 days. **Maintenance:** 5 - 15 mg tid or qid po (mild); 10 - 25 mg tid or qid po (moderate); 225 mg/day may be needed (severe psychosis).
Mometasone Furoate	ELOCON	Corticosteroid	**Cream, Oint & Lotion:** 0.1 %	Apply a thin film to affected areas once daily.
Moricizine Hydrochloride	ETHMOZINE	Antiarrhythmic	**Tab:** 200, 250, 300 mg	600 - 900 mg/day po, given q 8 h in 3 equally divided doses. Within this range, the dosage can be adjusted in increments of 150 mg/day at 3-day intervals.
Morphine Sulfate (C-II)	ASTRAMORPH/PF, DURAMORPH	Opioid Analgesic	**Inj (per mL):** 0.5, 1 mg	**IV:** 2 - 10 mg/70 kg. **Epidural:** Initially, 5 mg in the lumbar region; after 1 hour, incremental doses of 1 - 2 mg at interval sufficient to assess effectiveness may be given carefully. Max: 10 mg/24 h. **Intrathecal:** 0.2 - 1 mg in the lumbar area.
	INFUMORPH		**Inj (per mL):** 10, 25 mg	**Intrathecal Infusion:** Initially, 0.2 - 1 mg/day (patients with no opioid tolerance) and 1 - 10 mg/day (opioid tolerance) in the lumbar area. **Epidural Infusion:** 3.5 - 7.5 mg/day (patients with no opioid tolerance) and 4.5 - 10 mg/day (opioid tolerance).

	Brand	Category	Dosage Forms	Dosing
	MS CONTIN ORAMORPH SR		Controlled-Rel. Tab: 15, 30, 60, 100, 200 mg Sustained-Rel. Tab: 30, 60, 100 mg	Variable po dosages based on patient tolerance to opioids and type of conversion, e.g., from oral morphine, parenteral morphine, or other opioid analgesics.
	MSIR		Solution (per 5 mL): 10, 20 mg Conc Solution: 20 mg/mL Cpsl & Tab: 15, 30 mg	5 - 30 mg q 4 h po prn pain.
	ROXANOL		Rectal Suppos: 5, 10, 20, 30 mg Oral Solution: 20 mg/5 mL Oral Solution: 20 mg/5 mL Oral Solution: 100 mg/5 mL	10 - 30 mg q 4 h rectally. 10 - 30 mg q 4 h po prn pain. 10 - 30 mg q 4 h po prn pain. 10 - 30 mg q 4 h po prn pain.
	ROXANOL RESCUDOSE ROXANOL 100			
	ROXANOL SR		Sustained-Rel. Tab: 30 mg	30 mg q 8 h po.
Mupirocin	BACTROBAN	Antibacterial	Oint: 2%	Apply a small amount to affected area tid.
Nabumetone	RELAFEN	Antiinflammatory	Tab: 500, 750 mg	Initially 1000 mg po as a single dose with or without food. Dosage may be increased to 1500 - 2000 mg/day as a single dose or in 2 divided doses.
Nadolol	CORGARD	Antihypertensive, Antianginal	Tab: 20, 40, 80, 120, 160 mg	**Hypertension:** Initially, 40 mg once daily po. May increase dosage in increments of 40 to 80 mg until optimal response occurs. Usual maintenance dose is 40 - 80 mg once daily. **Angina:** Initially, 40 mg once daily po. May increase dosage in increments of 40 - 80 mg at 3 - 7 day intervals until optimal response occurs. Usual maintenance dosage is 40 to 80 mg once daily.

GENERIC NAME	COMMON TRADE NAMES	THERAPEUTIC CATEGORY	PREPARATIONS	COMMON ADULT DOSAGE
Nafcillin Sodium	UNIPEN	Antibacterial	Cpsl: 250 mg Tab: 500 mg Powd for Solution: 250 mg/5 mL Powd for Inj: 0.5, 1, 2 g	**Mild to Moderate Infections:** 250 - 500 mg q 4 to 6 h po. **Severe Infections:** 1000 mg q 4 - 6 h po. **IV:** 500 mg q 4 h; double the dose in very severe infections. **IM:** 500 mg q 6 h, decrease the interval to 4 h in severe infections.
Naftifine Hydrochloride	NAFTIN	Antifungal	Cream: 1% Gel: 1%	Gently massage into affected areas once daily. Gently massage into affected areas bid, morning and evening.
Nalbuphine Hydrochloride	NUBAIN	Opioid Analgesic	Inj (per mL): 10, 20 mg	10 mg/70 kg SC, IM, or IV; dose may be repeated q 3 - 6 h prn.
Nalidixic Acid	NEG-GRAM	Urinary Anti-Infective	Susp: 250 mg/5 mL Cplt: 250, 500 mg: 1 g	Initially, 1 g qid po for 1 - 2 weeks. For prolonged therapy, may reduce dosage to 500 mg qid after the initial treatment period.
Naloxone Hydrochloride	NARCAN	Opioid Antagonist	Inj (per mL): 0.4, 1 mg	**Opioid Overdose (Known or Suspected):** Initially, 0.4 - 2 mg IV. Dose may be repeated at 2 - 3 minute intervals. Maximum: 10 mg. **Postoperative Opioid Respiratory Depression:** 0.1 - 0.2 mg IV at 2 - 3 minute intervals. Doses may be repeated in 1 - 2 hours.
Nandrolone Decanoate (C-III)	DECA-DURABOLIN	Anabolic Steroid	Inj (per mL): 50, 100, 200 mg (in oil)	**Women:** 50 - 100 mg per week by deep IM. **Men:** 100 - 200 mg per week by deep IM.
Nandrolone Phenpropionate (C-III)	DURABOLIN	Anabolic Steroid	Inj (per mL): 25, 50 mg (in oil)	50 - 100 mg weekly by deep IM.

Naphazoline Hydrochloride	PRIVINE	Nasal Decongestant	**Nasal Solution:** 0.05% **Nasal Spray:** 0.05%	2 drops in each nostril no more than q 3 h. 2 sprays in each nostril q 4 - 6 h.
	NAPHCON NAPHCON FORTE	Ocular Decongestant	**Ophth Solution:** 0.012% **Ophth Solution:** 0.1%	1 - 2 drops into the affected eye(s) up to qid. 1 - 2 drops into the affected eye(s) q 3 - 4 h.
Naproxen	NAPROSYN	Non-Opioid Analgesic, Antiinflammatory	**Susp:** 125 mg/5 mL **Tab:** 250, 375, 500 mg	**Analgesia, Dysmenorrhea, Acute Tendonitis and Bursitis:** 500 mg po, followed by 250 mg po q 6 - 8 h prn. **Acute Gout:** 750 mg po, followed by 250 mg po q 8 h until the attack has subsided. **Rheumatoid Arthritis, Osteoarthritis and Ankylosing Spondylitis:** 250 - 500 mg bid po, morning and evening. **Juvenile Arthritis:** 5 mg/kg bid po.
Naproxen Sodium	ALEVE	Non-Opioid Analgesic	**Tab:** 220 mg	**Analgesia:** 220 mg q 8 - 12 h po with a full glass of liquid, while symptoms persist or 440 mg initially, followed by 220 mg 12 h later.
	ANAPROX ANAPROX DS	Non-Opioid Analgesic, Antiinflammatory	**Tab:** 275 mg **Tab:** 550 mg	**Analgesia, Dysmenorrhea, Acute Tendonitis and Bursitis:** 550 mg po, followed by 275 mg po q 6 - 8 h prn. **Acute Gout:** 825 mg po, followed by 275 mg po q 8 h until the attack has subsided. **Rheumatoid Arthritis, Osteoarthritis and Ankylosing Spondylitis:** 275 or 550 mg bid po, morning and evening.
Natamycin	NATACYN	Antifungal	**Ophth Susp:** 5%	**Fungal Keratitis:** 1 drop into the affected eye(s) at 1 or 2 hour intervals. The frequency of application can usually be reduced to 1 drop 6 - 8 times daily after the first 3 or 4 days. **Fungal Blepharitis & Conjunctivitis:** 4 to 6 daily applications may be sufficient.
Nedocromil Sodium	TILADE	Antiasthmatic	**Aerosol:** 1.75 mg/spray	2 inhalations qid at regular intervals.
Neomycin Sulfate	MYCIFRADIN	Antibacterial	**Cream & Oint:** 0.5%	Apply to affected areas up to qid.

GENERIC NAME	COMMON TRADE NAMES	THERAPEUTIC CATEGORY	PREPARATIONS	COMMON ADULT DOSAGE
Neostigmine Bromide	PROSTIGMIN	Cholinomimetic	**Tab:** 15 mg	15 - 375 mg/day po. Average dose is 150 mg po administered over a 24-hour period.
Neostigmine Methylsulfate	PROSTIGMIN	Cholinomimetic	**Inj (per mL):** 0.25, 0.5, 1 mg	**Myasthenia Gravis:** 0.5 mg SC or IM. Adjust subsequent doses based on response. **Postoperative Distension & Urinary Retention: Prevention:** 0.25 mg SC or IM as soon as possible after operation; repeat q 4 - 6 h for 2 - 3 days. **Treatment:** 0.5 mg SC or IM. **Reversal of Neuromuscular Blockade:** 0.5 - 2 mg by slow IV, repeated as required. Also administer IV atropine sulfate, 0.6 - 1.2 mg.
Netilmicin Sulfate	NETROMYCIN	Antibacterial	**Inj:** 100 mg/mL	**Urinary Tract Infections (Complicated):** 1.5 - 2.0 mg/kg q 12 h IM or IV. **Serious Systemic Infections:** 1.3 - 2.2 mg/kg q 8 h IM or IV; or, 2.0 - 3.25 mg/kg q 12 h IM or IV.
Nicardipine Hydrochloride	CARDENE	Antianginal, Antihypertensive	**Cpsl:** 20, 30 mg	**Angina:** Initially, 20 mg tid po; may increase dosage after 3 days. Doses in the range of 20 - 40 mg tid are effective. **Hypertension:** Initially, 20 mg tid po. Doses in the range of 20 - 40 mg tid are effective.
	CARDENE SR	Antihypertensive	**Sustained-Rel. Cpsl:** 30, 45, 60 mg	Initially, 30 mg bid po. Effective doses range from 30 - 60 mg bid po.

| Nicardipine Hydrochloride [continued] | CARDENE I.V. | Antihypertensive | Inj: 2.5 mg/mL | **Initiation in a Drug-free Patient:** Administer by continuous IV infusion at a concentration of 0.1 mg/mL.
Titration: For <u>gradual reduction</u> in blood pressure, start at 5 mg/h (50 mL/h); may increase rate by 2.5 mg/h (25 mL/h) q 15 min up to a max. of 15 mg/h (150 mL/h). For <u>rapid reduction</u> in blood pressure, begin at 5 mg/h (50 mL/h); may increase rate by 2.5 mg/h (25 mL/h) q 5 min up to a maximum of 15 mg/h (150 mL/h). In either case, after desired effect is achieved reduce infusion rate to 30 mL/h.
Maintenance: Adjust infusion rate as needed.
Substitution for Oral Nicardipine: Use the infusion rate as indicated in the table below: |

Oral Dose	Equivalent IV Infusion Rate
20 mg q 8 h	0.5 mg/h
30 mg q 8 h	1.2 mg/h
40 mg q 8 h	2.2 mg/h

| Niclosamide | NICLOCIDE | Anthelmintic | Chewable Tab: 500 mg | **Beef & Fish Tapeworm:** Chew and swallow 4 tablets in a single dose po.
Dwarf Tapeworm: Chew and swallow 4 tablets once daily for 7 days. |

| Nicotine | HABITROL, NICODERM | Smoking Deterrent | Transdermal: rate = 7, 14, 21 mg/24 hr | Apply to clean, dry, non-hairy site on upper body or upper outer arm. Initially, one 21 mg/24 h patch daily for 6 weeks; then, one 14 mg/24 h patch daily for 2 - 4 weeks; then, one 7 mg/24 h patch daily for 2 - 4 weeks. |

121

GENERIC NAME	COMMON TRADE NAMES	THERAPEUTIC CATEGORY	PREPARATIONS	COMMON ADULT DOSAGE
Nicotine	NICOTROL		Transdermal: rate = 5, 10, 15 mg/16 hr	Apply to clean, dry, non-hairy site on upper body or upper outer arm. Initially, one 15 mg/16 h patch daily for 4 - 12 weeks; then, one 10 mg/16 h patch daily for 2 - 4 weeks; then, one 5 mg/16 h patch daily for 2 - 4 weeks.
	PROSTEP		Transdermal: rate = 11, 22 mg/24 hr	Apply to clean, dry, non-hairy site on upper body or upper outer arm. Initially, one 22 mg/24 h patch daily for 4 - 8 weeks; then, one 11 mg/24 h patch daily for 2 - 4 weeks.
Nicotine Polacrilex	NICORETTE	Smoking Deterrent	Chewing Gum: 2 mg/piece	**Less Dependent Smokers:** Chew 1 piece slowly and intermittently for 30 minutes. Most patients require 9 - 12 pieces of gum per day. Maximum: 30 pieces per day.
	NICORETTE DS		Chewing Gum: 4 mg/piece	**Highly Dependent Smokers:** Chew 1 piece slowly and intermittently for 30 minutes. Most patients require 9 - 12 pieces of gum per day. Maximum: 20 pieces per day.
Nifedipine	ADALAT, PROCARDIA	Antianginal	Cpsl: 10, 20 mg	Initially, 10 mg tid po; may increase dosage over a 7 - 14 day period. Usual effective dosage range is 10 - 20 mg tid po.
	ADALAT CC, PROCARDIA XL	Antianginal, Antihypertensive	Extended-Rel. Tab: 30, 60, 90 mg	Initially, 30 or 60 mg once daily po; adjust the dosage over a 7 - 14 day period.
Nitrofurantoin	FURADANTIN	Urinary Anti-infective, Antibacterial	Oral Susp: 25 mg/5 mL	50 - 100 mg qid po with food. For long-term suppressive therapy, reduce dosage to 50 - 100 mg po hs.
Nitrofurantoin Macrocrystals	MACRODANTIN	Urinary Anti-infective, Antibacterial	Cpsl: 25, 50, 100 mg	**Usual Dosage:** 50 - 100 mg qid po with food. **Urinary Tract Infections (Uncomplicated):** 50 mg qid po with food.
Nitrofurantoin Monohydrate	MACROBID	Urinary Anti-infective	Cpsl: 100 mg	100 mg q 12 h po with food for 7 days.

Nitrofurazone	FURACIN	Burn Preparation	Cream, Oint & Sol: 0.2%	Apply directly to the lesion or place on gauze. Reapply daily or every few days.
Nitroglycerin	DEPONIT	Antianginal	Transdermal: rate = 0.2, 0.4 mg/h	Apply a 0.2 mg/h or 0.4 mg/h patch for 12 to 14 h daily as a starting dose.
	MINITRAN, TRANSDERM-NITRO		Transdermal: rate = 0.1, 0.2, 0.4, 0.6 mg/h	Same dosage as for DEPONIT above.
	NITRODISC		Transdermal: rate = 0.2, 0.3, 0.4 mg/h	Same dosage as for DEPONIT above.
	NITRO-DUR		Transdermal: rate = 0.1, 0.2, 0.3, 0.4, 0.6, 0.8 mg/h	Same dosage as for DEPONIT above.
	NITRO-BID		Oint: 2%	Apply 0.5 inch of ointment to a 1 x 3-inch area of skin q 8 h. Titrate upward (1 inch on a 2 x 3-in area q 8 h) until angina is controlled.
	NITROSTAT		Sublingual Tab: 0.15, 0.3, 0.4, 0.6 mg	Dissolve 1 tablet under tongue or in the buccal pouch at first sign of attack. May repeat q 5 minutes until relief is obtained.
	NITROGARD		Extended-Rel. Buccal Tab: 1, 2, 3 mg	Place tablet under the upper lip or in the buccal pouch; allow tablet to dissolve slowly over a 3 - 5 hour period. Initial dose is 1 mg, with subsequent increases guided by symptoms and side effects.
	NITROLINGUAL SPRAY		Aerosol: 0.4 mg/dose	1 - 2 sprays onto or under tongue at onset of attack. No more than 3 sprays within a 15 minute period.
	NITRO-BID IV, TRIDIL		Inj (per mL): 5 mg; Inj (per mL): 0.5, 5 mg	Initially, 5 μg/min by IV infusion. Titrate dosage based upon clinical situation; increases of 5 μg/min can be made at 3 - 5 min intervals. If no response occurs at 20 μg/min, increments of 10 and later 20 μg/min can be used.

GENERIC NAME	COMMON TRADE NAMES	THERAPEUTIC CATEGORY	PREPARATIONS	COMMON ADULT DOSAGE
Nizatidine	AXID	Histamine H$_2$-Blocker, Anti-Ulcer Agent	Cpsl: 150, 300 mg	**Active Duodenal Ulcer or Benign Gastric Ulcer:** 300 mg once daily po hs or 150 mg bid po. **Maintenance of Healed Duodenal Ulcer:** 150 mg once daily po hs. **Gastroesophageal Reflux Disease:** 150 mg bid po.
Norethindrone	NORLUTIN	Progestin	Tab: 5 mg	**Amenorrhea:** 5 - 20 mg once daily po, from the 5th to the 25th days of the menstrual cycle. **Endometriosis:** 10 mg once daily po for 2 weeks, with increments of 5 mg/day q 2 weeks until 30 mg/day is reached.
	MICRONOR, NOR-Q.D.	Oral Contraceptive	Tab: 0.35 mg	1 tablet daily po, every day of the year starting on the first day of menstruation.
Norethindrone Acetate	AYGESTIN	Progestin	Tab: 5 mg	**Amenorrhea:** 2.5 - 10 mg once daily po, for 5 to 10 days during the second half of the menstrual cycle. **Endometriosis:** 5 mg once daily po for 2 weeks, with increments of 2.5 mg/day q 2 weeks until 15 mg/day is reached.
	NORLUTATE		Tab: 5 mg	**Amenorrhea:** 2.5 - 10 mg once daily po, from the 5th - 25th days of the menstrual cycle. **Endometriosis:** 5 mg once daily po for 2 weeks, with increments of 2.5 mg/day q 2 weeks until 15 mg/day is reached.
Norfloxacin	NOROXIN	Urinary Anti-Infective	Tab: 400 mg	**Urinary Tract Infections (Uncomplicated):** 400 mg bid po for 7 - 10 days. **Urinary Tract Infections (Complicated):** 400 mg bid po for 10 - 21 days.
	CHIBROXIN	Antibacterial	Ophth Solution: 0.3%	1 - 2 drops into the eye(s) qid for up to 7 days.
Norgestrel	OVRETTE	Oral Contraceptive	Tab: 0.075 mg	1 tablet daily po, every day of the year starting on the first day of menstruation.

Nortriptyline Hydrochloride	PAMELOR	Antidepressant	**Solution:** 10 mg/5 mL (4% alcohol) **Cpsl:** 10, 25, 50, 75 mg	25 mg tid or qid po; or, total daily dosage may be given once daily po.
Nystatin	MYCOSTATIN, NILSTAT	Antifungal	**Susp:** 100,000 Units/mL	400,000 - 600,000 Units qid po (1/2 dose in each side of the mouth).
	MYCOSTATIN		**Tab:** 500,000 Units **Pastilles:** 200,000 Units	500,000 - 1,000,000 Units tid po. 200,000 - 400,000 Units 4 or 5 times daily po. Allow to dissolve slowly in the mouth.
			Vaginal Tab: 100,000 Units **Cream & Oint:** 100,000 Units/g **Powder:** 100,000 Units/g	1 tablet daily intravaginally for 2 weeks. Apply liberally to affected areas bid. Apply to candidal lesions bid or tid.
Ofloxacin	FLOXIN FLOXIN I.V.	Antibacterial	**Tab:** 200, 300, 400 mg **Inj (per mL):** 4, 10, 20 mg	**Lower Respiratory Tract, Skin & Skin Structure Infections:** 400 mg q 12 h po or by IV infusion (over 60 min.) for 10 days. **Gonorrhea (Uncomplicated):** 400 mg po or by IV infusion (over 60 min.) as a single dose. **Cervicitis or Urethritis due to *N. gonorrhoeae* and/or *C. trachomatis*:** 300 mg q 12 h po or by IV infusion (over 60 min.) for 7 days. **Cystitis due to *E. coli* or *K. pneumoniae*:** 200 mg q 12 h po or by IV infusion (over 60 min.) for 3 days. **Cystitis due to other Organisms:** 200 mg q 12 h po or by IV infusion (over 60 min.) for 7 days. **Urinary Tract Infections (Complicated):** 200 mg q 12 h po or by IV infusion (over 60 min.) for 10 days. **Prostatitis:** 300 mg q 12 h po for 6 weeks or by IV infusion (over 60 min.) for up to 10 days, then switch to oral therapy.
	OCUFLOX	Antibacterial	**Ophth Solution:** 0.3%	1 - 2 drops in affected eye(s) q 2 - 4 h for 2 days, then qid for up to 5 more days.

GENERIC NAME	COMMON TRADE NAMES	THERAPEUTIC CATEGORY	PREPARATIONS	COMMON ADULT DOSAGE
Olsalazine Sodium	DIPENTUM	Bowel Antiinflammatory Agent	**Cpsl:** 250 mg	1000 mg daily po in 2 divided doses.
Omeprazole	PRILOSEC	Gastric Acid Pump Inhibitor	**Delayed-Rel. Cpsl:** 20 mg	**Acute Duodenal Ulcer, Severe Erosive Esophagitis or Poorly Responsive Gastro-esophageal Reflux Disease:** 20 mg once daily po for up to 4 - 8 weeks. **Pathological Hypersecretory Conditions:** 60 mg once daily po, initially; adjust dosage as indicated. Daily dosages over 80 mg po should be given in divided doses.
Ondansetron Hydrochloride	ZOFRAN	Antiemetic	**Tab:** 4, 8 mg	**Nausea & Vomiting Associated With Cancer Chemotherapy:** Administer first dose (8 mg po) 30 minutes before the start of emetogenic chemotherapy, with subsequent doses 4 and 8 hours after the first dose. Then, 8 mg tid po for 1 to 2 days after completion of chemotherapy.
			Inj: 2 mg/mL	**Nausea & Vomiting Associated With Cancer Chemotherapy:** Three 0.15 mg/kg doses IV: The first dose is infused over 15 minutes beginning 30 minutes before the start of emetogenic chemotherapy. Alternatively, 32 mg IV (infused over 15 min) beginning 30 minutes before the start of emetogenic chemotherapy. Subsequent doses are given 4 and 8 h after the first dose. **Prevention of postoperative nausea & vomiting:** Immediately before induction of anesthesia or postoperatively, 4 mg IV (over 2 to 5 min).
Orphenadrine Citrate	NORFLEX	Skeletal Muscle Relaxant	**Tab:** 100 mg **Inj:** 60 mg/2 mL	100 mg bid po, AM and PM. 60 mg q 12 h IM or IV.

Generic	Brand	Class	Forms/Strengths	Dosage
Oxacillin Sodium	BACTOCILL, PROSTAPHLIN	Antibacterial	**Cpsl:** 250, 500 mg **Cpsl:** 250, 500 mg **Powd for Susp:** 250 mg/5 mL	**Mild to Moderate Infections of the Skin, Soft Tissue or Upper Respiratory Tract:** 500 mg q 4 - 6 h po for a minimum of 5 days. **Serious or Life-Threatening Infections:** After initial parenteral treatment, 1 g q 4 - 6 h po.
	BACTOCILL, PROSTAPHLIN		**Powd for Inj:** 250, 500 mg; 1, 2, 4 g	**Mild to Moderate Upper Respiratory and Local Skin and Soft Tissue Infections:** 250 - 500 mg q 4 - 6 h IM or IV. **Severe Lower Respiratory or Disseminated Infections:** 1 g q 4 - 6 h IM or IV.
Oxamniquine	VANSIL	Anthelmintic	**Cpsl:** 250 mg	12 - 15 mg/kg as a single dose po with food.
Oxandrolone (C-III)	OXANDRIN	Anabolic Steroid	**Tab:** 2.5 mg	2.5 mg bid - qid po. Usually a course of therapy of 2 - 4 weeks is adequate.
Oxaprozin	DAYPRO	Antiinflammatory	**Tab:** 600 mg	1200 mg once daily po. For patients of low body weight or mild disease, an initial dose of 600 mg once a day may be appropriate.
Oxazepam (C-IV)	SERAX	Antianxiety Agent	**Cpsl:** 10, 15, 30 mg **Tab:** 15 mg	10 - 30 mg tid or qid po. 15 - 30 mg tid or qid po.
Oxiconazole Nitrate	OXISTAT	Antifungal	**Cream & Lotion:** 1%	Apply to affected areas once daily.
Oxtriphylline	CHOLEDYL	Bronchodilator	**Syrup:** 50 mg/5 mL **Elixir:** 100 mg/5 mL (20% alcohol) **Delayed-Rel. Tab:** 100, 200 mg	7.8 mg/kg po, followed by 4.7 mg/kg q 8 h po (in nonsmokers) and 4.7 mg/kg q 6 h po (in smokers).
	CHOLEDYL SA		**Sustained-Action Tab:** 400, 600 mg	Therapy should be initiated and daily dosage requirements established using a non-sustained-action form of oxtriphylline. If the total daily dosage of the nonsustained prep. is 1200 mg, then 600 mg of CHOLEDYL SA may be used q 12 h. Similarly, if the total daily dosage is 800 mg, then 400 mg of CHOLEDYL SA may be used q 12 h.

GENERIC NAME	COMMON TRADE NAMES	THERAPEUTIC CATEGORY	PREPARATIONS	COMMON ADULT DOSAGE
Oxybutynin Chloride	DITROPAN	Urinary Antispasmodic	**Syrup:** 5 mg/5 mL **Tab:** 5 mg	5 mg bid - tid po.
Oxycodone Hydrochloride (C-II)	ROXICODONE	Opioid Analgesic	**Solution:** 5 mg/5 mL **Conc Solution:** 20 mg/mL **Tab:** 5 mg	5 mg q 6 h po prn pain.
Oxymetazoline Hydrochloride	AFRIN, NTZ	Nasal Decongestant	**Nasal Solution:** 0.05% **Nasal Spray:** 0.05%	2 - 3 drops into each nostril bid, AM and PM. Spray 2 - 3 times into each nostril bid, AM and PM.
	CHERACOL NASAL, DRISTAN 12-HOUR, 4-WAY LONG LASTING, NEO-SYNEPHRINE MAXIMUM STRENGTH, NOSTRILLA LONG ACTING, VICKS SINEX LONG-ACTING		**Nasal Spray:** 0.05%	Same dosage as AFRIN Spray above.
Oxymetholone (C-III)	ANADROL-50	Anabolic Steroid	**Tab:** 50 mg	1 - 2 mg/kg daily po.
	VISINE L.R.	Ocular Decongestant	**Ophth Solution:** 0.025%	1 - 2 drops in the affected eye(s) q 6 h.
Oxymorphone Hydrochloride (C-II)	NUMORPHAN	Opioid Analgesic	**Inj (per mL):** 1, 1.5 mg **Rectal Suppos:** 5 mg	**IM or SC:** 1 - 1.5 mg q 4 - 6 h, prn pain. **IV:** 0.5 mg q 4 - 6 h, prn pain. Insert 1 rectally q 4 - 6 h.
Oxytetracycline	TERRAMYCIN	Antibacterial	**Inj (per mL):** 50, 125 mg	250 mg q 24 h IM or 300 mg daily in divided doses IM at 8- to 12-hour intervals.
Oxytetracycline Hydrochloride	TERRAMYCIN	Antibacterial	**Cpsl:** 250 mg	**Usual Dosage:** 250 - 500 mg q 6 h po. **Brucellosis:** 500 mg qid po with streptomycin for 3 weeks. **Gonorrhea:** Initially 1.5 g po, followed by 500 mg qid po, for a total of 9.0 g. **Syphilis:** 30 - 40 g po in equally divided doses over a period of 10 - 15 days.

Oxytocin	SYNTOCINON	Posterior Pituitary Hormone	Nasal Spray: 40 Units/mL	1 spray into one or both nostrils 2 - 3 minutes before nursing or pumping breasts.
Pamidronate Disodium	AREDIA	Bone Stabilizer	Powd for Inj: 30, 60, 90 mg	**Hypercalcemia of Malignancy:** **Moderate:** 60 mg - 90 mg by IV infusion. The 60 mg dose is given over at least 4 hours; the 90 mg dose is given over 24 hours. **Severe:** 90 mg by IV infusion, given over 24 hours. **Paget's Disease:** 30 mg daily by IV infusion over 4 hours, on 3 consecutive days, for a total dose of 90 mg.
Pancuronium Bromide	PAVULON	Neuromuscular Blocker	Inj (per mL): 1, 2 mg	Initially 0.04 - 0.1 mg/kg IV. Later, use incremental doses starting at 0.01 mg/kg.
Papaverine Hydrochloride	PAVABID	Vasodilator	Timed-Rel. Cpsl: 150 mg	150 mg q 12 h po.
Paramethadione	PARADIONE	Antiepileptic	Cpsl: 150, 300 mg	0.9 - 2.4 g daily po in 3 or 4 equally divided doses, i.e., 300 - 600 mg tid or qid po.
Paromomycin Sulfate	HUMATIN	Amebicide	Cpsl: 250 mg (of paromomycin base)	**Intestinal Amebiasis: 25 - 35 mg/kg/day po in 3 divided doses with meals for 5 - 10 days.**
Paroxetine Hydrochloride	PAXIL	Antidepressant	Tab: 20, 30 mg	Initially, 20 mg once daily in the AM. May increase in 10 mg/day increments, up to a maximum of 50 mg/day.
Pegaspargase	ONCASPAR	Antineoplastic	Inj: 750 IUnits/mL	2500 IU/m² q 14 days by IM (preferred) or IV.
Pemoline (C-IV)	CYLERT	CNS Stimulant	Chewable Tab: 37.5 mg Tab: 18.75, 37.5, 75 mg	Starting dose is 37.5 mg/day po. Gradually increase daily dose by 18.75 mg at 1 week intervals until the desired response is obtained (Maximum: 112.5 mg).
Penbutolol Sulfate	LEVATOL	Antihypertensive	Tab: 20 mg	20 mg once daily po.

GENERIC NAME	COMMON TRADE NAMES	THERAPEUTIC CATEGORY	PREPARATIONS	COMMON ADULT DOSAGE
Penicillin G Benzathine	BICILLIN L-A	Antibacterial	**Inj (per mL):** 300,000; 600,000 Units	**Streptococcal Upper Respiratory Infections (e.g., Pharyngitis):** 1,200,000 Units IM. **Syphilis (Primary, Secondary & Latent):** 2,400,000 Units IM. **Syphilis (Late):** 2,400,000 Units IM at 7-day intervals for 3 doses. **Rheumatic Fever and Glomerulonephritis (Prophylaxis):** 1,200,000 Units IM once a month or 600,000 Units IM q 2 weeks.
Penicillin G Potassium	PFIZERPEN	Antibacterial	**Powd for Inj:** 5,000,000; 20,000,000 Units	5,000,000 to 80,000,000 Units daily IM or by IV drip, depending on the severity of the infection and the susceptibility of the infecting organism.
Penicillin G Procaine	PFIZERPEN-AS, WYCILLIN	Antibacterial	**Inj:** 300,000 Units/mL; **Inj:** 600,000 Units/mL	**Usual Dosage:** 600,000 - 1,000,000 Units daily IM. **Syphilis:** 600,000 Units daily IM for 8 - 15 days. **Gonorrhea:** 4,800,000 Units IM divided into at least 2 doses and inj. at diff. sites at the same visit, with probenecid (1 g po).
Penicillin V Potassium	BETAPEN-VK, PEN-VEE K, VEETIDS	Antibacterial	**Tab:** 250, 500 mg; **Powd for Solution (per 5 mL):** 125, 250 mg	**Streptococcal Upper Respiratory Infections:** 125 - 250 mg q 6 - 8 h po for 10 days. **Pneumococcal Infections:** 250 - 500 mg q 6 h po until afebrile for at least 48 hours. **Staphylococcal Infections:** 250 - 500 mg q 6 to 8 h po. **Vincent's Gingivitis and Pharyngitis:** 250 - 500 mg q 6 - 8 h po.
Pentaerythritol Tetranitrate	PERITRATE	Antianginal	**Tab:** 10, 20, 40 mg	Initially, 10 - 20 mg qid po; titrate upward to 40 mg qid po, 30 minutes ac or 60 minutes pc and hs.
	PERITRATE SA		**Sustained-Action Tab:** 80 mg	80 mg q 12 h po (on an empty stomach).

Pentamidine Isethionate	NEBUPENT PENTAM 300	Antiprotozoal	**Powd for Solution:** 300 mg **Powd for Inj:** 300 mg	300 mg once q 4 weeks, administered via a Respigard II nebulizer. 4 mg/kg once daily IV (over 60 minutes) or IM for 14 days.
Pentazocine Lactate (C-IV)	TALWIN	Opioid Analgesic	**Inj:** 30 mg/mL	**Usual Dosage:** 30 mg q 3 - 4 h IM, SC or IV. **Patients in Labor:** 30 mg IM or 20 mg q 2 - 3 h IV.
Pentobarbital Sodium (C-II)	NEMBUTAL SODIUM	Sedative - Hypnotic	**Cpsl:** 50, 100 mg **Elixir:** 20 mg/5 mL (18% alcohol) **Rectal Suppos:** 30, 60, 120, 200 mg	**Sedation:** Reduce hypnotic dose appropriately. **Hypnosis:** 100 mg hs.
		Hypnotic	**Inj:** 50 mg/mL	**Sedation:** Reduce hypnotic dose appropriately. **Hypnosis:** 120 - 200 mg rectally. **IM:** 150 - 200 mg as a single dose. **IV:** Initially, 100 mg/70 kg. May increase in small increment to 200 - 500 mg if needed.
Pentoxifylline	TRENTAL	Hemorheologic Agent	**Tab:** 400 mg	400 mg tid po with meals.
Pergolide Mesylate	PERMAX	Antiparkinsonian	**Tab:** 0.05, 0.25, 1 mg	0.05 mg po for first 2 days; then increase the dosage by 0.1 or 0.15 mg/day every third day for the next 12 days. The dosage may then be increased by 0.25 mg/day every 3rd day until optimal response is reached. Daily dose is usually given in 3 divided doses.
Permethrin	ELIMITE	Scabacide	**Cream:** 5%	Throughly massage into skin from the head to the soles of the feet. Wash off (bath or shower) after 8 - 14 h.
	NIX		**Liquid:** 1%	Shampoo hair, rinse with water and towel dry. Saturate the hair and scalp; allow solution to remain for 10 minutes before rinsing off with water. If live lice are observed 7 days or more after the first application, a second treatment should be given.

GENERIC NAME	COMMON TRADE NAMES	THERAPEUTIC CATEGORY	PREPARATIONS	COMMON ADULT DOSAGE
Perphenazine	TRILAFON	Antipsychotic, Antiemetic	Tab: 2, 4, 8, 16 mg Liquid Conc: 16 mg/5 mL Inj: 5 mg/mL	**Psychoses:** **Outpatients:** 4 - 8 mg tid po. **Hospitalized Patients:** 8 - 16 mg bid - qid po; or 5 mg q 6 h IM. **Nausea & Vomiting:** 8 - 16 mg daily in divided doses po; or 5 mg IM.
Phenacemide	PHENURONE	Antiepileptic	Tab: 500 mg	Initially, 500 mg tid po. After 1 week, another 500 mg may be taken on arising; in the third week, another 500 mg may be taken hs.
Phenazopyridine Hydrochloride	PYRIDIUM	Urinary Analgesic	Tab: 100, 200 mg	200 mg tid po after meals.
Phendimetrazine Tartrate (C-III)	BONTRIL PRELU-2	Anorexiant	Slow-Rel. Cpsl: 105 mg Timed-Rel. Cpsl: 105 mg	105 mg po, 30 - 60 minutes before the morning meal.
Phenelzine Sulfate	NARDIL	Antidepressant	Tab: 15 mg	Initially, 15 mg tid po. Increase dosage to at least 60 mg/day at a rapid pace as patient tolerates drug. After several weeks, dosage may be reduced (over several weeks) to as low as 15 mg daily or every other day.
Phenindamine Tartrate	NOLAHIST	Antihistamine	Tab: 25 mg	25 mg q 4 - 6 h po.
Phenobarbital (C-IV)		Sedative - Hypnotic, Anticonvulsant	Tab: 15, 30, 60, 100 mg Elixir: 20 mg/5 mL (alcohol)	**Sedation:** 30 - 120 mg daily po in 2 - 3 divided doses. **Hypnosis:** 100 - 200 mg hs po. **Convulsions:** 60 - 200 mg daily po.
Phenobarbital Sodium (C-IV)		Sedative - Hypnotic, Anticonvulsant	Inj (per mL): 30, 60, 65, 130 mg	**Sedation:** 30 - 120 mg daily IM or IV in 2 - 3 divided doses. **Preoperative Sedation:** 100 - 200 mg IM, 60 to 90 minutes before surgery. **Hypnosis:** 100 - 320 mg IM or IV. **Acute Convulsions:** 200 - 320 mg IM or IV, repeated in 6 h prn.

Phenol	CHILDREN'S CHLORASEPTIC	Local Anesthetic	**Spray:** 0.5%	Spray 5 times daily directly on throat or affected area and swallow. Repeat q 2 h prn.
Phenolphthalein, Yellow	EVAC-U-GEN	Irritant Laxative	**Tab:** 97.2 mg	1 - 2 tab once daily po.
	EX-LAX		**Chewable Tab:** 90 mg **Pill:** 90 mg	90 - 180 mg po, preferably hs.
	EX-LAX MAXIMUM RELIEF		**Pill:** 135 mg	135 - 270 mg po, preferably hs.
Phenoxybenzamine Hydrochloride	DIBENZYLINE	Antihypertensive	**Cpsl:** 10 mg	Initially, 10 bid po; increase dosage every other day, usually to 20 - 40 mg, bid - tid po.
Phentermine Hydrochloride (C-IV)	ADIPEX-P	Anorexiant	**Cpsl & Tab:** 37.5 mg	37.5 mg daily po, before breakfast or 1 - 2 h after breakfast.
	FASTIN		**Cpsl:** 30 mg	30 mg daily po, approx. 2 h after breakfast.
Phentermine Resin (C-IV)	IONAMIN	Anorexiant	**Cpsl:** 15, 30 mg	15 - 30 mg daily po, before breakfast or 10 to 14 hours before retiring.
Phentolamine Mesylate	REGITINE	Antihypertensive	**Powd for Inj:** 5 mg	**Preoperative:** 5 mg IM or IV, 1 - 2 h before surgery, and repeated if necessary. **During Surgery:** 5 mg IV as required.
Phenylephrine Hydrochloride	NEO-SYNEPHRINE	Sympathomimetic	**Inj:** 10 mg/mL (1%)	**Mild or Moderate Hypotension:** 2 - 5 mg SC; or 0.2 mg by slow IV. Repeat injections no more often than every 10 - 15 minutes. **Severe Hypotension & Shock:** Infuse a dilute solution IV (10 mg in 500 mL of Dextrose Injection) at 100 - 180 μg/min (approx. 100 to 180 drops/min). When blood pressure stabilizes, use maintenance rate of 40 - 60 μg/min (approx. 40 - 60 drops/min).

GENERIC NAME	COMMON TRADE NAMES	THERAPEUTIC CATEGORY	PREPARATIONS	COMMON ADULT DOSAGE
	NEO-SYNEPHRINE	Nasal Decongestant	Nasal Solution & Spray: 0.25, 0.5, 1%	1 - 2 drops or sprays (of 0.25%) in each nostril q 3 - 4 h. The 0.5 or 1% solutions may be used in resistant cases.
	NŌSTRIL		Nasal Spray: 0.25, 0.5%	2 - 3 sprays (of 0.25%) in each nostril q 3 - 4 h. The 0.5% spray may be used in resistant cases.
Phenytoin	DILANTIN	Antiepileptic	Susp: 125 mg/5 mL Chewable Tab: 50 mg	Initially, 125 mg tid po; adjust dosage prn. Initially, 100 mg tid po; adjust dosage prn.
Phentoin Sodium	DILANTIN	Antiepileptic	Inj: 50 mg/mL	**Status Epilepticus:** A loading dose of 10 - 15 mg/kg slow IV (at a rate not exceeding 50 mg/min). Follow with maintenance doses of 100 mg po or IV q 6 - 8 h.
			Cpsl: 100 mg	Initially, 100 mg tid po; adjust dosage prn. For patients controlled at 100 mg tid, a single daily dose of 300 mg po may be given.
Phytonadione	AQUA-MEPHYTON	Vitamin K_1	Inj (per mL): 2, 10 mg	2.5 - 25 mg SC or IM. Repeat in 6 - 8 h if necessary.
Pilocarpine	OCUSERT PILO-20	Anti-Glaucoma Agent	Ocular Therapeutic System: releases 20 µg/h for 1 week	Place in conjunctival cul-de-sac hs; replace every 7 days.
	OCUSERT PILO-40	Anti-Glaucoma Agent	Ocular Therapeutic System: releases 40 µg/h for 1 week	Place in conjunctival cul-de-sac hs; replace every 7 days.
Pilocarpine Hydrochloride	ISOPTO CARPINE	Anti-Glaucoma Agent	Ophth Solution: 0.25, 0.5, 1, 2, 3, 4, 5, 6, 8, 10%	1 or 2 drops in eye(s) up to 6 times daily. The usual range is 0.5 to 4%.
	PILOCAR, PILOSTAT		Ophth Solution: 0.5, 1, 2, 3, 4, 6%	1 or 2 drops in eye(s) up to 6 times daily. The usual range is 0.5 to 4%.
	PILOPINE HS GEL		Ophth Gel: 4%	Apply a 0.5 in. ribbon in the lower conjunctival sac of the affected eye(s) once daily hs.

	SALAGEN	Cholinomimetic	**Tab:** 5 mg	Initially, 5 mg tid po. Dosage may be increased to 10 mg tid, if necessary and tolerated.
Pilocarpine Nitrate	PILAGAN	Anti-Glaucoma Agent	**Ophth Solution:** 1, 2, 4%	1 or 2 drops in the affected eye(s) bid to qid.
Pimozide	ORAP	Antipsychotic	**Tab:** 2 mg	Initially, 1 - 2 mg daily in divided doses po; may increase thereafter every other day. Most are maintained at less than 0.2 mg/kg daily or 10 mg daily, whichever is less.
Pindolol	VISKEN	Antihypertensive	**Tab:** 5, 10 mg	Initially, 5 mg bid po. After 3 - 4 weeks dosage may be increased in increments of 10 mg/day q 2 - 4 weeks, to a maximum of 60 mg/day.
Pipecuronium Bromide	ARDUAN	Neuromuscular Blocker	**Powd for Inj:** 10 mg	**Endotracheal Intubation:** 70 - 85 μg/kg IV. **Maintenance:** 10 - 15 μg/kg IV.
Piperacillin Sodium	PIPRACIL	Antibacterial	**Powd for Inj:** 2, 3, 4 g	**Urinary Tract Infections (Uncomplicated) and Most Community-Acquired Pneumonia:** 100 to 125 mg/kg/day IM or IV in divided doses q 6 - 12 h. **Urinary Tract Infections (Complicated):** 125 to 200 mg/kg/day IV in divided doses q 6 - 8 h. **Serious Infections:** 200 - 300 mg/kg/day IV in divided doses q 4 - 6 h. **Gonorrhea (Uncomplicated):** 2 g IM as a single dose with probenecid (1 g po).
Pirbuterol Acetate	MAXAIR	Bronchodilator	**Aerosol:** 200 μg/spray	2 inhalations q 4 - 6 h.
Piroxicam	FELDENE	Antiinflammatory	**Cpsl:** 10, 20 mg	20 mg daily po.
Plicamycin	MITHRACIN	Antineoplastic	**Powd for Inj:** 2.5 mg	**Testicular Tumors:** 25 - 30 μg/kg daily by IV infusion (over 4 - 6 h) for 8 - 10 days. Repeat monthly if necessary. **Hypercalcemia & Hypercalciuria:** 25 μg/kg daily by IV infusion (over 4 - 6 h) for 3 or 4 days.

GENERIC NAME	COMMON TRADE NAMES	THERAPEUTIC CATEGORY	PREPARATIONS	COMMON ADULT DOSAGE
Polymyxin B Sulfate	AEROSPORIN	Antibacterial	Powd for Inj: 500,000 Units	IV: 15,000 - 25,000 Units/kg/day by IV infusion. Infusions may be given q 12 h but not more than 25,000 Units/kg/day. IM: 25,000 - 30,000 Units/kg/day. Dosage may be divided and given at 4 or 6 hour intervals.
Polythiazide	RENESE	Diuretic, Antihypertensive	Tab: 1, 2, 4 mg	Diuresis: 1 - 4 mg daily po. Hypertension: 2 - 4 mg daily po.
Potassium Chloride	K-DUR	Potassium Supplement	Extended-Rel. Tab: 10, 20 mEq	Dosage must be adjusted to the individual needs of each patient. Typical dosages are given below.
	K-TAB KLOTRIX K-NORM KLOR-CON MICRO-K EXTENCAPS SLOW-K TEN-K		Extended-Rel. Tab: 10 mEq Slow-Rel. Tab: 10 mEq Extended-Rel. Cpsl: 10 mEq Extended-Rel. Tab: 8, 10 mEq Extended-Rel. Cpsl: 8, 10 mEq Extended-Rel. Tab: 8 mEq Extended-Rel. Tab: 10 mEq	Prevention of Hypokalemia: 20 - 30 mEq daily po as a single dose or in divided doses with meals and with water or other liquids. Treatment of Potassium Depletion: 40 - 100 mEq daily po in divided doses with meals and with water or other liquids.
	KLORVESS 10% LIQUID		Liquid: 20 mEq/15 mL (0.75% alcohol)	15 mL (20 mEq) diluted in 3 - 4 oz. of cold water bid - qid po.
	K-LOR		Powd for Solution: 15, 20 mEq	Same dosages as shown above. Dissolve each packet in at least 3 oz. of fluid.
	KLOR-CON POWDER		Powd for Solution: 20, 25 mEq	Same dosages as shown above. Dissolve each packet in at least 3 oz. of fluid.
	KATO		Powd for Solution: 20 mEq	Dissolve each packet in 2 oz. of cold water. Drink solution bid with meals.
	MICRO-K LS		Extended-Rel. Formulation (Powd for Suspl): 20 mEq	Dissolve each packet in 2 - 6 oz. of cold water. Drink solution 1 - 5 times daily with meals.
	KLORVESS		Effervescent Powd for Solution: 20 mEq	Dissolve each packet in 3 - 4 oz. of cold water, fruit juice or other liquid. Drink solution bid to qid.

136

Potassium Gluconate	K-LYTE/CL	**Effervescent Tab:** 25, 50 mEq	Dissolve 1 tablet completely in cold water (3 to 4 oz. for the 25 mEq tab and 6 to 8 oz. for the 50 mEq tab); drink solution bid - qid.
	KLORVESS	**Effervescent Tab:** 20 mEq	Dissolve 1 tablet completely in 3 - 4 oz. of cold water or fruit juice. Drink solution bid to qid.
	KAON	**Elixir:** 20 mEq/15 mL (5% alcohol)	15 mL (20 mEq) diluted in 3 - 4 oz. of cold water bid - qid po.
Pramoxine Hydrochloride	TRONOTHANE	**Cream:** 1%	**Topical:** Apply to affected areas tid or qid. **Anorectal:** Apply up to 5 times daily, especially morning, night, and after bowel movements. **Intrarectal:** Insert 1 applicatorful into rectum.
Pravastatin Sodium	PRAVACHOL	**Tab:** 10, 20, 40 mg	10 - 20 mg once daily po, hs.
Prazepam (C-IV)	CENTRAX	**Cpsl:** 5, 10, 20 mg **Tab:** 10 mg	30 mg daily po in divided doses; or, 20 mg po as a single daily dose hs.
Praziquantel	BILTRICIDE	**Tab:** 600 mg	Three 20 mg/kg doses po for 1 day only.
Prazosin Hydrochloride	MINIPRESS	**Cpsl:** 1, 2, 5 mg	Initially, 1 mg bid - tid po. Dosage may be slowly increased to 20 mg daily, given in divided doses.
Prednicarbate	DERMATOP	**Cream:** 0.1%	Apply a thin film to skin bid.
Prednisolone Acetate	PRED-MILD PRED FORTE	**Ophth Susp:** 0.12% **Ophth Susp:** 1%	1 - 2 drops into affected eye(s) bid - qid. During the initial 24 - 48 h, the dosing frequency may be increased if necessary.

137

GENERIC NAME	COMMON TRADE NAMES	THERAPEUTIC CATEGORY	PREPARATIONS	COMMON ADULT DOSAGE
Prednisolone Sodium Phosphate	HYDELTRASOL	Corticosteroid	Inj: 20 mg/mL	**For IV and IM Injection:** Dose requirements are variable and must be individualized on the basis of the disease and the response of the patient. The initial dosage varies from 4 to 60 mg a day. Usually the daily parenteral dose of HYDELTRASOL is the same as the oral dose of prednisolone and the dosage interval is q 4 to 8 h. **For Intra-articular, Intralesional and Soft Tissue Injection:** Dose requirements are variable and must be individualized on the basis of the disease, the response of the patient, and the site of injection. The usual dose is from 2 to 30 mg. The frequency usually ranges from once every 3 to 5 days to once every 2 to 3 weeks.
	INFLAMASE MILD 1/8% INFLAMASE FORTE 1%	Corticosteroid	**Ophth Solution:** 0.125% **Ophth Solution:** 1%	1 - 2 drops into affected eye(s) up to q h during the day & q 2 h at night. When a favorable response occurs, reduce dosage to 1 drop q 4 h.
Prednisolone Tebutate	HYDELTRA-T.B.A.	Corticosteroid	Inj: 20 mg/mL	**For Intra-articular, Intralesional & Soft Tissue Injection:** Dose requirements are variable and must be individualized on the basis of the disease and the response of the patient. The initial dosage varies from 4 to 40 mg a day and frequency is usually once every 2 to 3 weeks. Severe conditions may require injection once a week.
Prednisone	DELTASONE	Corticosteroid	**Tab:** 2.5, 5, 10, 20, 50 mg	Initial dosage may vary from 5 - 60 mg daily po, depending on the disease being treated.
Primaquine Phosphate	PRIMAQUINE PHOSPHATE	Antimalarial	**Tab:** 26.3 mg (equal to 15 mg of primaquine base)	15 mg (of base) daily po for 14 days.

Drug	Brand	Class	Forms	Dosage
Primidone	MYSOLINE	Antiepileptic	Susp: 250 mg/5 mL Tab: 50, 250 mg	100 - 125 mg hs po (for 3 days); 100 - 125 mg bid po (for 3 days); 100 - 125 mg tid po (for 3 days); then 250 mg tid po
Probenecid	BENEMID	Anti-Gout Agent, Penicillin/Cephalosporin Adjunct	Tab: 500 mg	Gout: 250 mg bid po for 1 week, followed by 500 mg bid thereafter. Penicillin/Cephalosporin Therapy: The recommended dosage is 2 g po daily in divided doses. Usually 1 g po with or just before each administration of antibacterial therapy.
Probucol	LORELCO	Hypolipidemic	Tab: 250, 500 mg	500 mg bid po, AM and PM with meals.
Procainamide Hydrochloride	PRONESTYL	Antiarrhythmic	Cpsl & Tab: 250, 375, 500 mg Inj (per mL): 100, 500 mg	Up to 50 mg/kg daily in divided doses q 3 h po. IM: 50 mg/kg daily in divided doses given q 3 to 6 h until oral therapy is possible. IV: 100 mg q 5 minutes (at a rate not to exceed 50 mg/min) until the arrhythmia is suppressed or until 500 mg has been given. IV Infusion: Loading dose of 20 mg/mL (1 g diluted in 50 mL of 5% Dextrose Injection) at a rate of 1 mL/min for 25 - 30 min; then a maintenance dose of 2 or 4 mg/mL (1 g diluted in 500 or 250 mL of 5% Dextrose Injection) at a rate of 0.5 - 1.5 mL/min.
	PROCAN SR PRONESTYL-SR		Extended-Rel. Tab: 250, 500, 750, 1000 mg Extended-Rel. Tab: 500 mg	Up to 50 mg/kg daily in divided doses q 6 h po.
Procarbazine Hydrochloride	MATULANE	Antineoplastic	Cpsl: 50 mg	2 - 4 mg/kg/day po as a single dose or in divided doses for 1 week; then maintain the dosage at 4 - 6 mg/kg/day until maximum response occurs. Then give 1 - 2 mg/kg/day.
Prochlorperazine	COMPAZINE	Antiemetic	Rectal Suppos: 25 mg	Nausea & Vomiting: 25 mg bid rectally.

139

GENERIC NAME	COMMON TRADE NAMES	THERAPEUTIC CATEGORY	PREPARATIONS	COMMON ADULT DOSAGE
Prochlorperazine Edisylate	COMPAZINE	Antiemetic, Antipsychotic	Syrup: 5 mg/5 mL Inj: 5 mg/mL	**Nausea & Vomiting:** 5 - 10 mg tid or qid po. **Nausea & Vomiting:** 5 - 10 mg q 3 - 4 h deep IM; or 2.5 - 10 mg by slow IV injection or IV infusion (maximum rate of 5 mg/min). **Psychosis:** Initially, 10 - 20 mg deep IM. May repeat q 2 - 4 h, if necessary, for a few doses; then switch to oral medication.
Prochlorperazine Maleate	COMPAZINE	Antiemetic, Antipsychotic	Tab: 5, 10, 25 mg Sustained-Rel. Cpsl: 10, 15, 30 mg	**Nausea & Vomiting:** 5 - 10 mg tid or qid po. **Non-Psychotic Anxiety:** 5 mg tid or qid po. **Psychosis:** **Mild or in Outpatients:** 5 - 10 mg tid - qid po. **Moderate-to-Severe or in Hospitalized Patients:** Initially, 10 mg tid - qid po; raise the dosage slowly until symptoms are controlled. **More Severe Cases:** Optimum dosage is 100 to 150 mg daily po. **Nausea & Vomiting or Non-Psychotic Anxiety:** 15 mg po on arising or 10 mg q 12 h po.
Procyclidine Hydrochloride	KEMADRIN	Antiparkinsonian	Tab: 5 mg	Initially, 2.5 mg tid po pc. If well tolerated, gradually increase to 5 mg tid po.
Progesterone	PROGESTASERT	Intrauterine Contraceptive	Intrauterine System: unit containing a reservoir of 38 mg of progesterone	Insert a single unit into the uterine cavity. Replace 1 year after insertion.
Promazine Hydrochloride	SPARINE	Antipsychotic	Tab: 25, 50, 100 mg Inj: 50 mg	10 - 200 mg q 4 - 6 h po. 10 - 200 mg q 4 - 6 h IM.

Promethazine Hydrochloride	PHENERGAN	Antihistamine, Antiemetic, Sedative	**Tab:** 12.5, 25, 50 mg **Syrup (PLAIN):** 6.25 mg/5 mL (7% alcohol) **Syrup (FORTIS):** 25 mg/5 mL (1.5% alcohol) **Inj (per mL):** 25, 50 mg **Rectal Suppos:** 12.5, 25, 50 mg	**Allergy:** 25 mg po hs, or 12.5 mg po ac & hs. By deep IM injection, 25 mg; may repeat once in 2 h, then switch to oral medication. **Motion Sickness:** 25 mg po, taken 30 - 60 min before travel; repeat once in 8 - 12 h. On succeeding days, 25 mg bid, on arising & hs. **Nausea & Vomiting:** 25 mg po, followed by 12.5 - 25 mg q 4 - 6 h po. When oral medication is not tolerated, dose by injection (deep IM) or by rectal suppositories. **Sedation:** 25 - 50 mg hs po or by deep IM.
Propafenone Hydrochloride	RYTHMOL	Antiarrhythmic	**Tab:** 150, 225, 300 mg	Initiate with 150 mg q 8 h po. Dosage may be increased at a minimum of 3 - 4 day intervals to 225 mg q 8 h po, and if needed to 300 mg q 8 h po.
Propantheline Bromide	PRO-BANTHINE	Anticholinergic	**Tab:** 7.5, 15 mg	15 mg po 30 minutes ac and 30 mg hs. For mild symptoms, 7.5 mg tid po may be used.
Propoxyphene Hydrochloride (C-IV)	DARVON	Opioid Analgesic	**Cpsl:** 65 mg	65 mg q 4 h po, prn pain.
Propoxyphene Napsylate (C-IV)	DARVON-N	Opioid Analgesic	**Tab:** 100 mg	100 mg q 4 h po, prn pain.
Propranolol Hydrochloride	INDERAL	Antihypertensive, Antianginal, Antiarrhythmic, Antimigraine Agent, Post-MI Drug	**Tab:** 10, 20, 40, 60, 80 mg	**Hypertension:** Initially, 40 mg bid po; increase dosage gradually. The usual maintenance dosage is 120 - 240 mg daily. **Angina:** 80 - 320 mg daily po in divided doses (bid to qid). **Hypertrophic Subaortic Stenosis:** 20 - 40 mg tid - qid po. ac & hs. **Arrhythmias:** 10 - 30 mg tid - qid po, ac & hs. **Migraine Headaches:** Initially, 80 mg daily po in divided doses; increase dosage gradually. The usual maintenance dosage is 160 - 240 mg daily. **Post-Myocardial Infarction:** 180 - 240 mg daily po in divided doses (bid to tid).

141

GENERIC NAME	COMMON TRADE NAMES	THERAPEUTIC CATEGORY	PREPARATIONS	COMMON ADULT DOSAGE
Propranolol Hydrochloride [continued]		Antiarrhythmic	Inj: 1 mg/mL	**Life-Threatening Arrhythmias:** 1 - 3 mg IV (at a rate not exceeding 1 mg/min). May repeat dose after 2 minutes, if necessary. Then no additional drug should be given for 4 h.
	INDERAL LA	Antihypertensive, Antianginal, Antimigraine Agent	Long-Acting Cpsl: 60, 80, 120, 160 mg	**Hypertension:** Initially, 80 mg once daily po; may increase to usual maintenance dosage of 120 - 160 mg daily. **Angina:** Initially, 80 mg once daily po; increase at 3 - 7 day intervals. The average optimal dosage is 160 mg once daily. **Hypertrophic Subaortic Stenosis:** 80 - 160 mg once daily po. **Migraine Headaches:** Initially, 80 mg once daily po; increase gradually. The usual effective dosage range is 160 - 240 mg once daily.
Propylthiouracil		Antithyroid Agent	Tab: 50 mg	Initial: 300 mg/day po, usually administered in 3 equal doses at 8 hour intervals. **Maintenance:** Usually, 100 - 150 mg daily po in 3 equal doses at 8 hour intervals.
Protamine Sulfate		Heparin Antagonist	Inj: 10 mg/mL	1 mg per 90 - 115 Units of heparin activity by slow IV (over 10 minutes). Maximum dose: 50 mg.
Protriptyline Hydrochloride	VIVACTIL	Antidepressant	Tab: 5, 10 mg	15 - 40 mg daily po in 3 - 4 divided doses.
Pseudoephedrine Hydrochloride	SUDAFED SUDAFED 12 HOUR	Decongestant	**Liquid:** 30 mg/5 mL **Tab:** 30, 60 mg **Extended-Rel. Cplt:** 120 mg	10 mL (60 mg) q 4 - 6 h po. 60 mg q 4 - 6 h po. 120 mg q 12 h po.
	EFIDAC/24		**Extended-Rel. Tab:** 240 mg	240 mg once daily po.

Pseudoephedrine Sulfate	DRIXORAL NON-DROWSY, AFRIN; CHLOR-TRIMETON NON-DROWSY DECONGESTANT	Decongestant	**Extended-Rel. Tab:** 120 mg **Tab:** 60 mg	120 mg q 12 h po. 60 mg q 4 - 6 h po.
Psyllium	PERDIEM FIBER	Bulk Laxative	**Granules:** 4.03 g/rounded teaspoonful (6.0 g)	In the evening and/or before breakfast, 1 - 2 rounded teaspoonfuls should be swallowed with at least 8 oz. of a cool beverage.
Psyllium Hydrophilic Mucilloid	EFFER-SYLLIUM	Bulk Laxative	**Powder:** 3 g/rounded teaspoonful **Packet:** 3 g	1 rounded teaspoonful, or 1 packet, in a glass of water 1 - 3 times daily po.
	FIBERALL		**Powder:** 3.4 g/rounded teaspoonful (5.0 - 5.9 g) **Wafer:** 3.4 g	1 rounded teaspoonful in 8 oz. of liquid 1 - 3 times daily po. 1 - 2 wafers with 8 oz. of liquid 1 - 3 times daily po.
	METAMUCIL		**Powder (Regular):** 3.4 g per rounded teaspoonful **Powder (Flavored):** 3.4 g per tablespoonful **Wafer:** 3.4 g	1 rounded teaspoonful (Regular) or tablespoonful (Flavored) in 8 oz. of liquid 1 - 3 times daily po. 2 wafers with 8 oz. of liquid 1 - 3 times daily po.
	SERUTAN		**Granules:** 2.5 g/heaping teaspoonful **Powder:** 3.4 g/heaping teaspoonful	1 - 3 heaping teaspoonfuls on cereal or other food 1 - 3 times daily po. Drink at least 8 oz. of liquid with the food. 1 heaping teaspoonful in 8 oz. of water 1 - 3 times daily po, preferably with meals.
	SYLLACT		**Powder:** 3.3 g/rounded teaspoonful	1 rounded teaspoonful in 8 oz. of liquid 1 - 3 times daily po.

GENERIC NAME	COMMON TRADE NAMES	THERAPEUTIC CATEGORY	PREPARATIONS	COMMON ADULT DOSAGE
Pyrantel Pamoate	ANTIMINTH	Anthelmintic	**Susp:** 144 mg/mL (equivalent to 50 mg/mL of pyrantel)	5 mg/lb (to a maximum of 1 g) as a single dose po.
	REESE'S PINWORM MEDICINE		**Susp:** 144 mg/mL (equivalent to 50 mg/mL of pyrantel) **Cpt:** 180 mg (equivalent to 62.5 mg of pyrantel)	5 mg/lb (to a maximum of 1 g) as a single dose po.
Pyrazinamide		Tuberculostatic	**Tab:** 500 mg	15 - 30 mg/kg once daily po (Maximum: 3 g/day).
Pyridostigmine Bromide	MESTINON	Cholinomimetic	**Syrup:** 60 mg/5 mL (5% alcohol) **Tab:** 60 mg	600 mg (10 tsp. or 10 tab) daily po in divided doses, spaced to provide maximum relief when maximum strength is needed.
	MESTINON TIMESPAN		**Slow-Rel. Tab:** 180 mg	1 - 3 tablets once or twice daily po.
Pyrimethamine	DARAPRIM	Antimalarial	**Tab:** 25 mg	**Chemoprophylaxis:** 25 mg once weekly po.
Quazepam (C-IV)	DORAL	Hypnotic	**Tab:** 7.5, 15 mg	7.5 - 15 mg hs po.
Quinapril Hydrochloride	ACCUPRIL	Antihypertensive, Heart Failure Drug	**Tab:** 5, 10, 20, 40 mg	**Hypertension:** **Initial:** 10 mg once daily po. Adjust dosage at intervals of at least 2 weeks. **Maintenance:** Most patients require 20 - 80 mg daily po as a single dose or in 2 equally divided doses. **Heart Failure:** Used in conjunction with other conventional therapies including diuretics or digoxin. Initially, give 5 mg bid po. Titrate patients at weekly intervals until an effective dose is attained, usually 10 - 20 mg bid.
Quinestrol	ESTROVIS	Estrogen	**Tab:** 100 μg	100 μg daily po for 7 days, followed by 100 μg weekly as a maintenance schedule, commencing 2 wks after starting treatment.

144

Quinidine Gluconate	QUINAGLUTE	Antiarrhythmic	Sustained-Rel. Tab: 324 mg	324 - 648 mg q 8 - 12 h po.
Quinidine Polygalacturonate	CARDIOQUIN	Antiarrhythmic	Tab: 275 mg	Initial: 275 - 825 mg q 3 - 4 h po. If normal sinus rhythm is not restored after 3 - 4 equal doses, the dose may be increased by 137.5 to 275 mg and given 3 - 4 times before any further dosage increase. Maintenance: 275 mg bid - tid po.
Quinidine Sulfate	QUINIDEX EXTENTABS	Antiarrhythmic	Extended-Rel. Tab: 300 mg	300 - 600 mg q 8 - 12 h po.
Quinine Sulfate		Antimalarial	Cpsl: 200, 300, 325 mg Tab: 260 mg	Chloroquine-sensitive Malaria: 600 mg q 8 h po for 5 - 7 days. Chloroquine-resistant Malaria: 650 mg q 8 h po for 5 - 7 days.
Ramipril	ALTACE	Antihypertensive	Cpsl: 1.25, 2.5, 5, 10 mg	Initially, 2.5 mg once daily po. The usual maintenance dosage range is 2.5 - 20 mg daily administered as a single dose or in two equally divided doses.
Ranitidine Hydrochloride	ZANTAC	Histamine H_2-Blocker, Anti-ulcer Agent	Syrup: 15 mg/mL (7.5% alcohol) Cpsl & Tab: 150, 300 mg Effervescent Tab: 150 mg Effervescent Granules: 150 mg/packet	Active Duodenal Ulcer: 150 mg bid po; or 300 mg once daily po hs. Maintenance Therapy: 150 mg daily po hs. Pathological Hypersecretory Conditions: 150 mg bid po, or more frequently if needed. Gastroesophageal Reflux and Benign Gastric Ulcer: 150 mg bid po. Erosive Esophagitis: 150 mg qid po.
			Inj: 25 mg/mL	IM: 50 mg q 6 - 8 h. Intermittent IV: 50 mg q 6 - 8 h as a bolus (diluted solution) or as an infusion (at a rate not greater than 5 - 7 mL/min). Continuous IV Infusion: 6.25 mg/h.
Reserpine		Antihypertensive	Tab: 0.1, 0.25 mg	Initially, 0.5 mg daily po for 1 - 2 weeks; for maintenance, reduce to 0.1 - 0.25 mg daily.

GENERIC NAME	COMMON TRADE NAMES	THERAPEUTIC CATEGORY	PREPARATIONS	COMMON ADULT DOSAGE
Rifabutin	MYCOBUTIN	Tuberculostatic	**Cpsl:** 150 mg	300 mg once daily po.
Rifampin	RIFADIN RIFADIN I.V.	Tuberculostatic	**Cpsl:** 150, 300 mg **Powd for Inj:** 600 mg	600 mg daily in a single administration, po (1 hour before or 2 hours a after meal) or IV.
Rimantadine Hydrochloride	FLUMADINE	Antiviral	**Syrup:** 50 mg/5 mL **Tab:** 100 mg	**Prophylaxis:** 100 mg bid po. **Treatment:** 100 mg bid po. Start therapy within 48 h of symptoms; continue for 7 days from initial onset of symptoms.
Risperidone	RISPERDAL	Antipsychotic	**Tab:** 1, 2, 3, 4 mg	Initially, 1 mg bid po. Increase in increments of 1 mg bid on 2nd & 3rd day, as tolerated, to a target dose of 3 mg bid. Further dosage adjustments should be made at intervals of ≥ 1 week.
Salmeterol	SEREVENT	Bronchodilator	**Aerosol:** 25 μg base/spray (as the xinafoate salt)	**Asthma & Bronchospasm:** 2 inhalations bid, approximately q 12 h. **Prevention of Exercise-Induced Bronchospasm:** 2 inhalations at least 30 - 60 min. before exercise.
Salsalate	DISALCID	Antiinflammatory	**Cpsl:** 500 mg **Tab:** 500, 750 mg	3000 mg daily po, given in divided doses as 1500 mg bid or 1000 mg tid.
	SALFLEX		**Tab:** 500, 750 mg	Same dosage as for DISALCID above.
Scopolamine	TRANSDERM SCŌP	Anticholinergic, Antiemetic	**Transdermal:** 1.5 mg/patch	Apply 1 patch to the area behind one ear at least 4 hours before the antiemetic effect is required. Effective for 3 days.
Scopolamine Hydrobromide	ISOPTO HYOSCINE	Mydriatic - Cycloplegic	**Ophth Solution:** 0.25%	**Refraction:** Instill 1 - 2 drops in the eye(s) 1 hour before refracting. **Uveitis:** Instill 1 - 2 drops in the eye(s) up to qid.

146

Secobarbital Sodium (C-II)	Sedative - Hypnotic	Inj: 50 mg/mL	**Hypnotic:** 100 - 200 mg IM or 50 - 250 mg IV. **Preoperative Sedation:** 1 mg/kg IM, 10 - 15 minutes before the procedure.
Selegiline Hydrochloride	Antiparkinsonian	Tab: 5 mg	5 mg bid po, at breakfast and lunch.
Selenium Sulfide	Antiseborrheic, Antifungal	Lotion: 2.5%	**Seborrheic Dermatitis & Dandruff:** Massage 5 to 10 mL into wet scalp; let stand for 2 - 3 minutes. Rinse & repeat. Apply twice a week for 2 weeks; then may be used once weekly or once every 2 - 4 weeks. **Tinea Versicolor:** Apply to affected areas and lather with water; leave on skin for 10 minutes, then rinse. Repeat once daily for 7 days.
EXSEL, SELSUN			
Senna Concentrate	Irritant Laxative	**Syrup:** 218 mg/5 mL (7% alcohol) **Tab:** 187 mg	10 - 15 mL daily po, preferably hs. (Maximum: 15 mL bid po). 2 tablets daily po, preferably hs. (Maximum: 2 bid po).
		Granules: 326 mg/tsp.	1 teaspoonful daily po, preferably hs. (Maximum: 2 teaspoonfuls bid po).
		Rectal Suppos: 652 mg	Insert 1 rectally hs.
SENOKOT			
SENOKOTXTRA		**Tab:** 374 mg	1 tablet daily po, preferably hs. (Maximum: 2 tablets bid po).
Sertraline Hydrochloride	Antidepressant	**Tab:** 50, 100 mg	Initially, 50 mg once daily po, either in the morning or evening. The dosage may be increased, at intervals of not less than 1 week, up to a maximum of 200 mg daily.
ZOLOFT			
Silver Sulfadiazine	Burn Preparation	**Cream:** 1%	Apply to a thickness of 1/16 inch once or twice daily.
SSD			

147

GENERIC NAME	COMMON TRADE NAMES	THERAPEUTIC CATEGORY	PREPARATIONS	COMMON ADULT DOSAGE
Simethicone	MYLICON	Antiflatulant	**Solution (Drops):** 40 mg/0.6 mL	0.6 mL (40 mg) qid po pc and hs.
	MYLANTA GAS		**Chewable Tab:** 40, 80, 125 mg	Chew 40 - 125 mg qid, pc and hs.
	GAS-X		**Chewable Tab:** 80, 125 mg	Chew 80 - 125 mg qid, pc and hs.
	PHAZYME		**Solution (Drops):** 40 mg/0.6 mL	1.2 mL (80 mg) qid po pc and hs.
	PHAZYME-95 PHAZYME-125		**Tab:** 60 mg **Tab:** 95 mg **Cpsl:** 125 mg	60 mg qid po, pc and hs. 95 mg qid po, pc and hs. 125 mg qid po, pc and hs.
Simvastatin	ZOCOR	Hypolipidemic	**Tab:** 5, 10, 20, 40 mg	Initially 5 - 10 mg once daily po, in the evening. Dosage range: 5 - 40 mg once daily po, in the evening. Adjust dose at intervals of at least 4 weeks.
Sodium Nitroprusside		Antihypertensive	**Inj:** 50 mg (in 1 L D$_5$W)	The average effective IV infusion rate is about 3 μg/kg/min. At this rate, some patients will become dangerously hypotensive. Begin IV infusion at a very low rate (0.3 μg/kg/min), with gradual upward titration every few minutes until the desired effect is achieved or the maximum rate (10 μg/kg/min) has been reached.
Sodium Polystyrene Sulfonate	KAYEXALATE	Potassium-Removing Resin	**Powder:** 10 - 12 g/heaping teaspoonful	Average daily dose is 15 - 60g po. Usually, 15 g mixed in liquid 1 - 4 times daily po.
	SODIUM POLYSTYRENE SULFONATE SUSP.		**Susp:** 15 g/60 mL (0.1% alcohol)	Same dosage as for KAYEXALATE above.
Sotalol Hydrochloride	BETAPACE	Antiarrhythmic	**Tab:** 80, 160, 240 mg	Initially, 80 mg bid po. Dosage may be increased at 2 - 3 day intervals up to 320 mg/day po given in 2 or 3 divided doses.

148

Spectinomycin Hydrochloride	TROBICIN	Antibacterial	Powd for Inj: 2, 4 g	2 g as a single deep IM injection.
Spironolactone	ALDACTONE	Antihypertensive, Diuretic	Tab: 25, 50, 100 mg	**Diuresis:** Initially, 100 mg po, as a single dose or in divided doses, for at least 5 days. **Hypertension:** Initially 50 - 100 mg po as a single dose or in divided doses.
Stanozolol (C-III)	WINSTROL	Anabolic Steroid	Tab: 2 mg	Initially, 2 mg tid po. After a favorable response, decrease dosage at intervals of 1 to 3 months to a maintenance dosage of 2 mg once daily.
Stavudine	ZERIT	Antiviral	Cpsl: 15, 20, 30, 40 mg	**Initial Dosage:** **Under 60 kg:** 30 mg twice daily (q 12 h) po. **Equal to or Over 60 kg:** 40 mg twice daily (q 12 h) po. **Dosage Adjustment:** Monitor patients for the development of peripheral neuropathy. If symptoms develop, stop the drug. If the symptoms resolve completely, consider resumption of therapy with half of the above mg dosages.
Streptokinase	STREPTASE	Thrombolytic	Powd for Inj: 250,000 IUnits, 750,000 IUnits, and 1,500,000 IUnits	250,000 IU IV (over 30 minutes), followed by 100,000 IU/h by IV infusion. Length of therapy determined by condition (see below). **Pulmonary Embolism:** 24 h (72 h if concurrent deep vein thrombosis is suspected). **Deep Vein Thrombosis:** 72 h. **Arterial Thrombosis or Embolism:** 24 - 72 h.
Streptozocin	ZANOSAR	Antineoplastic	Powd for Inj: 1 g	**Daily Schedule:** 500 mg/m² IV for 5 consecutive days q 6 weeks. **Weekly Schedule:** 1000 mg/m² IV weekly for the first 2 weeks. Dosage may be increased in selected patients to a maximum of 1500 mg/m² IV once a week.

GENERIC NAME	COMMON TRADE NAMES	THERAPEUTIC CATEGORY	PREPARATIONS	COMMON ADULT DOSAGE
Succinylcholine Chloride	ANECTINE	Neuromuscular Blocker	Inj: 20 mg/mL Powd for IV Infusion: 500, 1000 mg	**Short Surgical Procedures:** 0.6 mg/kg IV. **Long Surgical Procedures:** 2.5 - 4.3 mg/min by IV infusion; or 0.3 - 1.1 mg/kg initially by IV injection followed, at appropriate intervals, by 0.04 - 0.07 mg/kg.
Sucralfate	CARAFATE	Anti-ulcer Agent	**Tab:** 1 g **Susp:** 1 g/10 mL	**Active Duodenal Ulcer:** 1 g qid po on an empty stomach. **Maintenance:** 1 g bid po.
Sulconazole Nitrate	EXELDERM	Antifungal	Cream & Solution: 1%	Gently massage a small amount into the skin once or twice daily.
Sulfacetamide Sodium	BLEPH-10	Antibacterial	Ophth Solution: 10%	**Conjunctivitis and other Superficial Ocular Infections:** 1 - 2 drops into the affected eye(s) q 2 - 3 h initially. Dosage may be reduced as the condition responds. The usual duration of therapy is 7 to 10 days. **Trachoma:** 2 drops into eye(s) q 2 h.
			Ophth Oint: 10%	**Conjunctivitis and other Superficial Ocular Infections:** Apply a small amount (approx. 1/2 inch) into the affected eye(s) q 3 - 4 h and hs. Dosage may be reduced as the condition responds. The usual duration of therapy is 7 to 10 days.
	SODIUM SULAMYD		Ophth Solution: 10%	1 - 2 drops into the affected eye(s) q 2 - 3 h during the day, less often at night. Apply a small amount to affected eye(s) q 3 - 4 h and hs.
	SODIUM SULAMYD		Ophth Oint: 10% Ophth Solution: 30%	**Conjunctivitis or Corneal Ulcer:** 1 drop into the affected eye(s) q 2 h or less frequently. **Trachoma:** 2 drops into eye(s) q 2 h.
Sulfamethizole	THIOSULFIL FORTE	Antibacterial	Tab: 500 mg	500 - 1000 mg tid or qid po.

Drug	Brand	Class	Forms	Dosage
Sulfamethoxazole	GANTANOL	Antibacterial	Tab: 500 mg	**Mild to Moderate Infections:** Initially, 2 g po; then 1 g bid po thereafter. **Severe Infections:** Initially 2 g po; then 1 g tid po thereafter.
Sulfanilamide	AVC	Antibacterial	**Vaginal Cream:** 15% **Vaginal Suppos:** 1.05 g	1 applicatorful intravaginally once daily or bid. Insert 1 vaginally once daily or bid.
Sulfasalazine	AZULFIDINE	Bowel Antiinflammatory Agent	**Susp:** 250 mg/5 mL **Tab:** 500 mg **Enteric-Coated Tab:** 500 mg	**Initial:** 3 - 4 g daily po in evenly divided doses. **Maintenance:** 2 g daily po.
Sulfinpyrazone	ANTURANE	Anti-Gout Agent	**Tab:** 100 mg **Cpsl:** 200 mg	**Initial:** 200 - 400 mg daily po in 2 divided doses with meals or milk. **Maintenance:** 400 mg daily po in 2 divided doses with meals or milk.
Sulfisoxazole	GANTRISIN	Antibacterial	**Cpsl:** 200 mg	
			Tab: 500 mg	Initially 2 - 4 g po, then 4 - 8 g/day divided in 4 - 6 doses.
Sulfisoxazole Acetyl	GANTRISIN	Antibacterial	**Pediatric Susp:** 500 mg/5 mL (0.3% alcohol) **Syrup:** 500 mg/5 mL (0.9% alcohol)	Initially 2 - 4 g po, then 4 - 8 g/day divided in 4 - 6 doses.
Sulfisoxazole Diolamine	GANTRISIN	Antibacterial	**Ophth Solution:** 4%	2 - 3 drops in eye(s) 3 or more times daily.
Sulindac	CLINORIL	Antiinflammatory	**Tab:** 150, 200 mg	**Osteoarthritis, Rheumatoid Arthritis and Ankylosing Spondylitis:** 150 mg bid po with food. **Acute Painful Shoulder:** 200 mg bid po with food for 7 - 14 days. **Acute Gouty Arthritis:** 200 mg bid po with food for 7 days.
Sumatriptan Succinate	IMITREX	Antimigraine Agent	**Inj:** 12 mg/mL	6 mg SC. A second 6 mg dose may be given in patients who failed to respond to the first dose. Maximum: two 6 mg doses in 24 h.

151

GENERIC NAME	COMMON TRADE NAMES	THERAPEUTIC CATEGORY	PREPARATIONS	COMMON ADULT DOSAGE
Suprofen	PROFENAL	Antiinflammatory	Ophth Solution: 1%	On the day of surgery, instill 2 drops into the conjunctival sac at 3, 2, and 1 hour prior to surgery. Two drops may be instilled into the conjunctival sac q 4 h, while awake, the day preceding surgery.
Tacrolimus	PROGRAF	Immunosuppressant	Cpsl: 1, 5 mg	0.15 - 0.3 mg/kg/day po in 2 divided doses (q 12 h). Administer initial dose no sooner than 6 h after transplantation. If IV therapy was initiated, begin 8 - 12 h after discontinuing IV therapy.
			Inj: 5 mg/mL	0.05 - 0.1 mg/kg/day as a continuous IV infusion. Administer initial dose no sooner than 6 h after transplantation. Convert to oral therapy as soon as the patient can tolerate oral dosing.
Tamoxifen Citrate	NOLVADEX	Antineoplastic	Tab: 10 mg	10 - 20 mg q 12 h po, morning and evening.
Temazepam (C-IV)	RESTORIL	Hypnotic	Cpsl: 7.5, 15, 30 mg	7.5 - 30 mg po hs.
Terazosin Hydrochloride	HYTRIN	Antihypertensive	Tab: 1, 2, 5, 10 mg	Initially, 1 mg po hs. Dosage may be slowly increased to the recommended dosage range of 1 - 5 mg once daily po.
Terbinafine Hydrochloride	LAMISIL	Antifungal	Cream: 1%	Interdigital *Tinea pedis:* Apply to affected and surrounding areas bid for at least 1 week. *Tinea cruris* or *T. corporis:* Apply to affected and surrounding areas once daily or bid for at least 1 week.
Terbutaline Sulfate	BRETHINE, BRICANYL	Bronchodilator	Tab: 2.5, 5 mg	**12-15 yrs:** 2.5 mg tid (q 6 h) po. **Over 15 yrs:** 5 mg tid (q 6 h) po.
			Inj: 1 mg/mL	0.25 mg SC; may repeat once in 15 - 30 min.
	BRETHAIRE		Aerosol: 0.2 mg/spray	2 inhalations separated by a 60-sec interval q 4 - 6 h.

Terconazole	TERAZOL 3	Antifungal	**Vaginal Cream:** 0.8% **Vaginal Suppos:** 80 mg	1 applicatorful intravaginally hs for 3 days. Insert 1 vaginally hs for 3 days.
	TERAZOL 7		**Vaginal Cream:** 0.4%	1 applicatorful intravaginally hs for 7 days.
Terfenadine	SELDANE	Antihistamine	**Tab:** 60 mg	60 mg bid po.
Testolactone	TESLAC	Antineoplastic	**Tab:** 50 mg	250 mg qid po.
Testosterone		Androgen, Antineoplastic	**Inj (per mL):** 25, 50, 100 mg (aqueous suspension)	**Replacement Therapy:** 25 - 50 mg 2 - 3 times a week by deep IM injection. **Breast Cancer:** 50 - 100 mg 3 times a week by deep IM injection.
	TESTODERM	Androgen	**Transdermal: rate = 4,** 6 mg/24 hr	**Replacement Therapy:** Start with a 6 mg/day system applied daily on clean, dry scrotal skin for up to 8 weeks; if scrotal area is inadequate, use a 4 mg/day system.
Testosterone Cypionate	DEPO-TESTOSTERONE	Androgen, Antineoplastic	**Inj (per mL):** 100, 200 mg (in oil)	**Male Hypogonadism:** 50 - 400 mg q 2 - 4 weeks IM. **Breast Cancer:** 200 - 400 mg q 2 - 4 weeks IM.
Testosterone Enanthate	DELATESTRYL	Androgen, Antineoplastic	**Inj:** 200 mg/mL (in oil)	Same dosages as for DEPO-TESTOSTERONE above.
Testosterone Propionate		Androgen, Antineoplastic	**Inj:** 100 mg/mL (in oil)	Same dosages as for Testosterone above.
Tetracaine	PONTOCAINE	Local Anesthetic	**Oint:** 0.5%	Apply to the affected area prn.
Tetracaine Hydrochloride	PONTOCAINE	Local Anesthetic	**Cream:** 1%	Apply to the affected area prn.
	PONTOCAINE HCL PONTOCAINE EYE		**Ophth Solution:** 0.5% **Ophth Oint:** 0.5%	1 - 2 drops into eye(s). Apply 0.5 - 1 inch to lower conjunctival fornix.

153

GENERIC NAME	COMMON TRADE NAMES	THERAPEUTIC CATEGORY	PREPARATIONS	COMMON ADULT DOSAGE
Tetracycline Hydrochloride	ACHROMYCIN	Antibacterial	Ophth Susp: 10 mg/mL (1%) Ophth Oint: 10 mg/g (1%)	2 drops in the affected eye(s) bid to qid. Apply to the affected eye(s) q 2 h.
	ACHROMYCIN V	Antibacterial	Cpsl: 250, 500 mg	**Usual Dosage:** 1 - 2 g po divided into 2 or 4 equal doses. **Brucellosis:** 500 mg qid po for 3 weeks with streptomycin.
	SUMYCIN		Cpsl & Tab: 250, 500 mg Syrup: 125 mg/5 mL	**Syphilis:** 30 - 40 g po in equally divided doses over a period of 10 - 15 days. **Gonorrhea:** Initially, 1.5 g po followed by 500 mg q 6 h for 4 days (total dose of 9 g). **Uncomplicated Urethral, Endocervical or Rectal Infections due to Chlamydia trachomatis:** 500 mg qid po for at least 7 days.
	TOPICYCLINE		**Powd for Solution:** 150 mg [with 70 mL of liquid]	Apply generously bid to the entire affected area until the skin is wet.
Tetrahydrozoline Hydrochloride	TYZINE	Nasal Decongestant	Nasal Solution: 0.1%	2 - 4 drops in each nostril q 4 - 6 h.
	VISINE	Ocular Decongestant	Ophth Solution: 0.05%	1 - 2 drops in affected eye(s) up to qid.
Theophylline, Anhydrous	AEROLATE	Bronchodilator	Cpsl: 65, 130, 260 mg	1 cpsl q 12 h po; in severe attacks, 1 cpsl q 8 h po. Usually 260 mg are used in adults.
	ELIXOPHYLLIN		Elixir: 80 mg/15 mL (20% alcohol) Cpsl: 100, 200 mg	See Oral Theophylline Doses Table, p. 216.
	RESPBID		Sustained-Rel Tab: 250, 500 mg	See Oral Theophylline Doses Table, p. 217.
	SLO-BID		Extended-Rel Cpsl: 50, 75, 100, 125, 200, 300 mg	See Oral Theophylline Doses Table, p. 217.

	SLO-PHYLLIN	**Syrup:** 80 mg/15 mL **Tab:** 100, 200 mg **Extended-Rel Cpsl:** 60, 125, 250 mg	See Oral Theophylline Doses Table, p. 216. See Oral Theophylline Doses Table, p. 217.
	THEO-24	**Extended-Rel. Cpsl:** 100, 200, 300, 400 mg	See Oral Theophylline Doses Table, p. 218.
	THEO-DUR	**Extended-Rel. Tab:** 100, 200, 300, 450 mg	See Oral Theophylline Doses Table, p. 217.
	THEO-DUR SPRINKLE	**Sustained-Action Cpsl:** 50, 75, 125, 200 mg	See Oral Theophylline Doses Table, p. 217.
	THEOLAIR	**Liquid:** 80 mg/15 mL **Tab:** 125, 250 mg	See Oral Theophylline Doses Table, p. 216.
	THEOLAIR-SR	**Sustained-Rel Tab:** 200, 250, 300, 500 mg	See Oral Theophylline Doses Table, p. 217.
	T-PHYL	**Controlled-Rel Tab:** 200 mg	See Oral Theophylline Doses Table, p. 217.
Thiabendazole	MINTEZOL	**Susp:** 500 mg/5 mL **Chewable Tab:** 500 mg	**Strongyloidiasis, Intestinal Roundworms and Cutaneous Larva Migrans:** 2 doses/day (as below) po for 2 successive days. **Trichinosis:** 2 doses/day (as below) po for 2 - 4 successive days. **Visceral Larva Migrans:** 2 doses/day (as below) po for 7 successive days. Each Dose: 10 mg/lb.
Thiethylperazine Maleate	NORZINE, TORECAN	**Tab:** 10 mg **Inj:** 10 mg/2 mL **Rectal Suppos:** 10 mg	10 mg once daily to tid po. 10 mg once daily to tid IM. Insert 1 rectally once daily to tid.
Thioguanine		**Tab:** 40 mg	Initially, 2 mg/kg daily po. If no improvement occurs after 4 weeks, the dosage may be increased to 3 mg/kg/day.

GENERIC NAME	COMMON TRADE NAMES	THERAPEUTIC CATEGORY	PREPARATIONS	COMMON ADULT DOSAGE
Thioridazine	MELLARIL-S	Antipsychotic	**Susp (per 5 mL):** 25, 100 mg	Initially 50 - 100 mg tid po, with a gradual increment to a maximum of 800 mg daily if necessary. The maintenance dosage varies from 200 - 800 mg daily, divided into 2 or 4 doses.
Thioridazine Hydrochloride	MELLARIL	Antipsychotic	**Liquid Conc (per mL):** 30, (3% alcohol), 100 mg (4.2% (alcohol) **Tab:** 10, 15, 25, 50, 100, 150, 200 mg	Same dosage as for MELLARIL-S above.
Thiothixene	NAVANE	Antipsychotic	**Cpsl:** 1, 2, 5, 10, 20 mg	**Mild Psychoses:** Initially 2 mg tid po; dosage may be increased to 15 mg/day if needed. **More Severe Psychoses:** Initially 5 mg bid po; the usual optimal dosage is 20 - 30 mg daily. Dosage may be increased to 60 mg/day.
Thiothixene Hydrochloride	NAVANE	Antipsychotic	**Liquid Conc:** 5 mg/mL (7% alcohol) **Inj (per mL):** 2, 5 mg	Same dosages as for NAVANE Capsules above. 4 mg bid to qid IM.
Thyroid Dessicated	ARMOUR THYROID	Thyroid Hormone	**Tab:** 15, 30, 60, 90, 120, 180, 240, 300 mg	Initial: 30 mg daily po, with increments of 15 mg q 2 - 3 weeks. Maintenance: Usually 60 - 120 mg daily po.
Ticarcillin Disodium	TICAR	Antibacterial	**Powd for Inj:** 1, 3, 6 g	**Urinary Tract Infections:** **Uncomplicated:** 1 g IM or direct IV q 6 h. **Complicated:** 150 - 200 mg/kg/day by IV infusion in divided doses q 4 or 6 h. **Most Other Infections:** 200 - 300 mg/kg/day by IV infusion in divided doses q 4 or 6 h.
Ticlopidine Hydrochloride	TICLID	Platelet Aggregation Inhibitor	**Tab:** 250 mg	250 mg bid po, taken with food.

Timolol Maleate	BLOCADREN	Antihypertensive, Post-MI Drug, Antimigraine Agent	**Tab:** 5, 10, 20 mg	**Hypertension:** Initially 10 mg bid po. The usual maintenance dosage is 20 - 40 mg daily. **Myocardial Infarction:** 10 mg bid po. **Migraine Headache:** 10 mg bid po. The 20 mg daily dosage may be given as a single dose during maintenance therapy.
Tioconazole	TIMOPTIC TIMOPTIC-XE	Anti-Glaucoma Agent	**Ophth Solution:** 0.25, 0.5% **Ophth Gel:** 0.25, 0.5%	1 drop into affected eye(s) bid. Apply to affected eye(s) once daily.
	VAGISTAT-1	Antifungal	**Vaginal Oint:** 6.5%	Insert 1 applicatorful intravaginally hs.
Tobramycin	TOBREX	Antibacterial	**Ophth Oint:** 3 mg/g (0.3%)	**Mild to Moderate Infections:** Apply 1/2 inch ribbon into the affected eye(s) q 4 h. **Severe Infections:** Apply 1/2 inch ribbon into the affected eye(s) q 3 - 4 h until improvement occurs; reduce dosage prior to discontinuation.
			Ophth Solution: 3 mg/mL (0.3%)	**Mild to Moderate Infections:** 1 - 2 drops into the affected eye(s) q 4 h. **Severe Infections:** 2 drops into the affected eye(s) hourly until improvement occurs; reduce dosage prior to discontinuation.
Tobramycin Sulfate	NEBCIN	Antibacterial	**Inj (per mL):** 10, 40 mg **Powd for Inj:** 30 mg	**Serious Infections:** 3 mg/kg/day IM or IV in 3 equal doses q 8 h. **Life-Threatening Infections:** Up to 5 mg/kg/day may be given IM or IV in 3 or 4 equal doses.
Tocainide Hydrochloride	TONOCARD	Antiarrhythmic	**Tab:** 400, 600 mg	Initially 400 mg q 8 h po. The usual dosage is 1200 - 1800 mg/day in 3 divided doses.
Tolazamide	TOLINASE	Hypoglycemic	**Tab:** 100, 250, 500 mg	**Initial:** 100 - 250 mg daily po, administered with breakfast or the first main meal. Dosage adjustment are made in increment of 100 to 250 mg at weekly intervals. **Maintenance:** Usually 250 - 500 mg daily po.

GENERIC NAME	COMMON TRADE NAMES	THERAPEUTIC CATEGORY	PREPARATIONS	COMMON ADULT DOSAGE
Tolbutamide	ORINASE	Hypoglycemic	Tab: 250, 500 mg	**Initial:** 1 - 2 g daily po, as a single dose in the AM or in divided doses throughout the day. **Maintenance:** Usually 0.25 - 2 g daily po, as a single dose in the AM or in divided doses throughout the day.
Tolmetin Sodium	TOLECTIN 200 TOLECTIN DS TOLECTIN 600	Antiinflammatory	Tab: 200 mg Cpsl: 400 mg Tab: 600 mg	Initially 400 mg tid po, preferably including a dose on arising and a dose hs; adjust dosage after 1 - 2 weeks. Control is usually achieved at 600 - 1800 mg daily in divided doses (generally tid).
Tolnaftate	AFTATE	Antifungal	Gel, Powder, Aerosol Powder & Liquid Spray: 1%	Apply a thin layer over affected area morning and night for 2 - 3 weeks.
	DR. SCHOLL'S ATHLETE'S FOOT		Spray Powder & Spray Liquid: 1%	Apply liberally on entire infected area bid for 2 weeks.
	DR. SCHOLL'S TRITIN ANTIFUNGAL		Powder & Spray Powder: 1%	Apply on top and bottom of feet and between toes bid for 2 weeks.
	NP-27		Cream, Solution, Powder & Spray Powder: 1%	Apply a thin layer over affected area morning and night for 2 - 4 weeks.
	TINACTIN		Cream, Solution, Powder, Aerosol Powder & Liquid Aerosol: 1%	Apply to affected areas morning and night for 2 - 4 weeks.
	TING		Cream, Powder, Aerosol Powder & Liquid Spray: 1%	Apply a thin layer over affected area morning and night for 2 - 4 weeks.
	DESENEX		Spray Liquid: 1%	Apply to affected areas morning and night.

Torsemide	DEMADEX	Diuretic. Antihypertensive	**Tab:** 5, 10, 20, 100 mg **Inj:** 10 mg/mL	**Hypertension:** 5 mg once daily po. After 4 - 6 weeks, the dose may be increased to 10 mg once daily po. **Diuresis in:** **Congestive Heart Failure:** Initially, 10 or 20 mg once daily po or slow IV (over 2 min). If the response is inadequate, titrate dose upward by approximately doubling. Maximum dose: 200 mg. **Chronic Renal Failure:** Initially, 20 mg once daily po or IV (over 2 min). If the response is inadequate, titrate dose upward by approximately doubling. Maximum dose: 200 mg. **Hepatic Cirrhosis:** Initially, 5 or 10 mg once daily po or IV (over 2 min), together with a potassium-sparing diuretic. If the response is inadequate, titrate dose upward by approx. doubling. Maximum dose: 40 mg.
Tranexamic Acid	CYKLOKAPRON	Hemostatic	**Inj:** 100 mg/mL	10 mg/kg IV immediately before dental surgery. After surgery, give 25 mg/kg po tid - qid for 2 to 8 days. In patients unable to take oral medication, give 10 mg/kg tid to qid. 25 mg/kg po tid - qid beginning 1 day prior to dental surgery.
Tranylcypromine Sulfate	PARNATE	Antidepressant	**Tab:** 10 mg	30 mg/day po in divided doses. Adjust dosage in approximately 2 weeks in 10 mg increments at intervals of 1 - 3 weeks to a maximum of 60 mg per day.
Trazodone Hydrochloride	DESYREL	Antidepressant	**Tab:** 50, 100, 150, 300 mg	Initially 150 mg/day po in divided doses. The dose may be increased by 50 mg/day q 3 - 4 days to a maximum of 400 mg/day (for outpatients) or 600 mg/day (for more severely-depressed inpatients).

GENERIC NAME	COMMON TRADE NAMES	THERAPEUTIC CATEGORY	PREPARATIONS	COMMON ADULT DOSAGE
Tretinoin	RETIN-A	Anti-Acne Agent	Cream: 0.025, 0.05, 0.1% Gel: 0.01, 0.025% Liquid: 0.05%	Cover the entire affected area once daily hs.
Triamcinolone	ARISTOCORT	Corticosteroid	Tab: 1, 2, 4, 8 mg	Initial dose may vary from 4 to 48 mg po per day. Dose requirements are variable and must be individualized based on the disease and the patient's response.
Triamcinolone Acetonide	ARISTOCORT A	Corticosteroid	Cream: 0.025, 0.1, 0.5% Oint: 0.1%	Apply to affected area as a thin film tid - qid depending on the severity of the condition.
	KENALOG		Oint: 0.025, 0.1, 0.5%	Apply a thin film to the affected area bid - qid (of the 0.025%) or bid - tid (of the 0.1% or 0.5%). Rub in gently.
			Cream: 0.025, 0.1, 0.5%	Apply to the affected area bid - qid (of the 0.025%) or bid - tid (of the 0.1 or 0.5%). Rub in gently.
			Lotion: 0.025, 0.1%	Apply to the affected area bid - qid (of the 0.025%) or bid - tid (of the 0.1%). Rub in.
			Spray: 0.2%	Spray onto affected area tid - qid.
	AZMACORT		Aerosol: 100 μg/spray	2 inhalations tid or qid.
	NASACORT		Aerosol: 55 μg/spray	2 sprays in each nostril once a day. If needed, the dose may be doubled, either as a once a day dosage or divided up to 4 times daily.
	KENALOG-10		Inj: 10 mg/mL	**Intra-articular or Intrabursal Injection and Injection into Tendon Sheaths:** Initially, 2.5 to 5 mg (for smaller joints) and 5 - 15 mg (for larger joints). **Intradermal Injection:** Varies depending on the disease, but should be limited to 1.0 mg per injection site.

Generic	Brand	Class	Forms	Dosage
	KENALOG-40		Inj: 40 mg/mL	**IM (deep):** Usual initial dose is 60 mg. Dosage is usually adjusted from 40 - 80 mg, depending on the patient response and the duration of relief. **Intra-articular or Intrabursal Injection and Injection into Tendon Sheaths:** Initially, 2.5 to 5 mg (for smaller joints) and 5 - 15 mg (for larger joints).
Triamcinolone Diacetate	ARISTOCORT FORTE	Corticosteroid	Inj (per mL): 25, 40 mg	Initial dosage may vary from 3 - 48 mg daily, depending on the specific disease being treated. The average dose is 40 mg IM once a week or 5 - 40 mg intra-articularly or intrasynovially.
Triamcinolone Hexacetonide	ARISTOSPAN	Corticosteroid	Inj (per mL): 5, 20 mg	Initial dosage may vary from 2 - 48 mg daily, depending on the specific disease being treated. The average dose is 2 - 20 mg intra-articularly (depending on the size of the joint), repeated q 3 - 4 weeks. Up to 0.5 mg/square inch of skin may be given by intralesional or sublesional injection.
Triamterene	DYRENIUM	Diuretic	Caps: 50, 100 mg	100 mg bid po pc.
Triazolam (C-IV)	HALCION	Hypnotic	Tab: 0.125, 0.25 mg	0.25 mg hs po.
Trichlormethiazide	NAQUA	Diuretic, Antihypertensive	Tab: 2, 4 mg	**Diuresis:** 1 - 4 mg daily po. **Hypertension:** 2 - 4 mg daily po.
Trifluoperazine Hydrochloride	STELAZINE	Antipsychotic	Tab: 1, 2, 5, 10 mg Conc Liquid: 10 mg/mL Inj: 2 mg/mL	Initially, 2 - 5 mg bid po. Most show optimum response on 15 - 20 mg daily po. 1 - 2 mg by deep IM q 4 - 6 h prn.
Trifluridine	VIROPTIC	Antiviral	Ophth Solution: 1%	1 drop into affected eye(s) q 2 h while awake for a maximum of 9 drops daily until the cornea has re-epithelialized. Then use 1 drop q 4 h while awake for 7 days.

GENERIC NAME	COMMON TRADE NAMES	THERAPEUTIC CATEGORY	PREPARATIONS	COMMON ADULT DOSAGE
Trihexyphenidyl Hydrochloride	ARTANE	Antiparkinsonian	Elixir: 2 mg/5 mL Tab: 2, 5 mg Sustained-Rel. Cpsl: 5 mg	Initially 1 mg po on the first day. The dose may be increased by 2 mg increments at intervals of 3 - 5 days to a maximum of 6 - 10 mg daily.
Trimeprazine Tartrate	TEMARIL	Antihistamine, Antipruritic	Syrup: 2.5 mg/5 mL (5.7% alcohol) Tab: 2.5 mg Sustained-Rel. Cpsl: 5 mg	2.5 mg qid po. 2.5 mg qid po. 5 mg q 12 h po.
Trimethadione	TRIDIONE	Antiepileptic	Solution: 40 mg/mL Chewable Tab: 150 mg Cpsl: 300 mg	Initially 0.9 g daily po; increase by 300 mg at weekly intervals. Usual dosage is 0.9 - 2.4 g daily po in 3 or 4 equally divided doses (i.e., 300 - 600 mg tid or qid).
Trimethaphan Camsylate	ARFONAD	Antihypertensive	Inj: 50 mg/mL	1 mg/mL (in a suitable IV diluent) by IV infusion at an initial rate of 3 - 4 mL/minute.
Trimethobenzamide Hydrochloride	TIGAN	Antiemetic	Cpsl: 100, 250 mg Rectal Suppos: 200 mg Inj: 100 mg/mL	250 mg tid or qid po. 200 mg tid or qid rectally. 200 mg tid or qid IM.
Trimethoprim	PROLOPRIM	Antibacterial	Tab: 100, 200 mg	100 mg q 12 h po for 10 days, or 200 mg q 24 h po for 10 days.
	TRIMPEX		Tab: 100 mg	Same dosage as for PROLOPRIM above.
Trimipramine Maleate	SURMONTIL	Antidepressant	Cpsl: 25, 50, 100 mg	Outpatients: Initially, 75 mg/day po in divided doses. Maintenance doses range from 50 to 150 mg/day po. Hospitalized Patients: Initially, 100 mg/day po in divided doses. May gradually increase in a few days to 200 mg/day. If no improvement occurs in 2 - 3 weeks, dose may be raised to a maximum dose of 250 - 300 mg/day.

Tripelennamine Citrate	PBZ	Antihistamine	Elixir: 37.5 mg/5 mL (12% alcohol)	5 - 10 mL (25 - 50 mg as the HCl equivalent) q 4 - 6 h po.
Tripelennamine Hydrochloride	PBZ PBZ-SR	Antihistamine	Tab: 25, 50 mg Extended-Rel. Tab: 100 mg	25 - 50 mg q 4 - 6 h po. 100 mg bid po, in the morning and in the evening.
Trolamine Salicylate	MYOFLEX	Analgesic, Topical	Cream: 10%	Apply to affected area not more than tid to qid. Affected areas may be wrapped loosely prn.
Troleandomycin	TAO	Antibacterial	Cpsl: 250 mg	250 - 500 mg qid po.
Tubocurarine Chloride		Neuromuscular Blocker	Inj: 3 mg (20 Units)/mL	**Usual Effective IV Doses (General Reference): Paresis of Limb Muscles:** 0.1 - 0.2 mg/kg. **Abdominal Relaxation:** 0.4 - 0.5 mg/kg. **Endotracheal Intubation:** 0.5 - 0.6 mg/kg. In prolonged procedures, repeat incremental doses in 40 - 60 minutes, as required.
Urea	UREAPHIL	Osmotic Diuretic	Inj: 40 g/150 mL	1 - 1.5 g/kg by slow IV infusion, at a rate not to exceed 4 mL/min (Maximum: 120 g/day).
Urokinase	ABBOKINASE	Thrombolytic	Powd for Inj: 250,000 IUnits	**Pulmonary Embolism:** A priming dose of 2,000 IUnits/lb IV (at a rate of 90 mL/h over 10 minutes), followed by an IV infusion of 2,000 IU/lb/h (at a rate of 15 mL/h) for 12 h. **Lysis of Coronary Artery Thrombosis:** After an IV bolus of heparin (2,500 - 10,000 units), infuse into occluded artery at a rate of 4 mL/min (6,000 IU/min) for periods up to 2 h.
Valproic Acid	DEPAKENE	Antiepileptic	Syrup: 250 mg/5 mL Cpsl: 250 mg	Initially 15 mg/kg/day po in 2 or 3 divided doses, increasing at 1 week intervals by 5 to 10 mg/kg/day (Maximum: 60 mg/kg/day).

163

GENERIC NAME	COMMON TRADE NAMES	THERAPEUTIC CATEGORY	PREPARATIONS	COMMON ADULT DOSAGE
Vancomycin Hydrochloride	VANCOCIN HCL	Antibacterial	**Powd for Solution:** 1, 10 g **Cpsl:** 125, 250 mg **Powd for Inj:** 500 mg; 1, 10 g	**Pseudomembranous Colitis:** 500 mg - 2 g daily po in 3 or 4 divided doses for 7 - 10 days. 2 g daily, divided either as 500 mg q 6 h or 1 g q 12 h, by IV infusion (at a rate no more than 10 mg/min) over at least 60 minutes.
Vasopressin	PITRESSIN	Posterior Pituitary Hormone	**Inj:** 20 pressor Units/mL	**Diabetes Insipidus:** 5 - 10 Units bid - tid IM or SC prn. **Abdominal Distention:** Initially, 5 Units IM; increase to 10 Units at subsequent injections if necessary. Repeat at 3 - 4 hour intervals.
Vecuronium Bromide	NORCURON	Neuromuscular Blocker	**Powd for Inj:** 10, 20 mg	Initially 0.08 - 0.1 mg/kg as an IV bolus. Maintenance doses of 0.010 - 0.015 mg/kg are recommended and are usually required within 25 - 40 minutes.
Venlafaxine	EFFEXOR	Antidepressant	**Tab:** 25, 37.5, 50, 75, 100 mg	Initially, 75 mg/day po, given in 2 or 3 divided doses, with food. Dose may be increased to 150 mg/day and then to 225 mg/day at intervals of ≥ 4 days.
Verapamil Hydrochloride	CALAN, ISOPTIN	Antianginal, Antiarrhythmic, Antihypertensive	**Tab:** 40, 80, 120 mg	**Angina:** 80 - 120 mg tid po. **Arrhythmias:** **Digitalized Patients with Chronic Atrial Fibrillation:** 240 - 320 mg/day po in 3 or 4 divided doses. **Prophylaxis of PSVT (Non-Digitalized Patients):** 240 - 480 mg/day po in 3 or 4 divided doses. **Hypertension:** 80 mg tid po. Adjust dosage up to 360 mg daily.

Generic	Brand	Category	Formulation	Dosage
	CALAN SR ISOPTIN SR	Antihypertensive	Sustained-Rel. Cplt: 120, 180, 240 mg Sustained-Rel. Tab: 120, 180, 240 mg	**Hypertension:** Initially 180 mg po in the AM with food. Adjust doses upward at weekly intervals, until therapeutic goal is reached as follows: (a) 240 mg each AM; (b) 180 mg bid, AM & PM, or 240 mg each AM and 120 mg each PM; (c) 240 mg q 12 h.
	VERELAN	Antihypertensive	Sustained-Rel. Cpsl: 120, 180, 240 mg	**Hypertension:** Initially 240 mg po in the AM with food. Adjust doses upward until the therapeutic goal is reached as follows: (a) 240 mg each AM; (b) 360 mg each AM; (c) 480 mg each AM.
	ISOPTIN	Antiarrhythmic	Inj: 2.5 mg/mL	5 - 10 mg IV (over at least 2 minutes). Repeat with 10 mg after 30 minutes if response is not adequate.
Vidarabine Monohydrate	VIRA-A	Antiviral	Inj: 200 mg/mL Ophth Oint: 3%	15 mg/kg/day by IV infusion (over 12 - 24 h) for 10 days. Apply 1/2 inch into lower conjunctival sac 5 times daily at 3 h intervals.
Vinblastine Sulfate	VELBAN	Antineoplastic	Powd for Inj: 10 mg	Dose at weekly intervals as follows: 1st dose- 3.7 mg/m^2 IV; 2nd dose- 5.5 mg/m^2 IV; 3rd dose- 7.4 mg/m^{2}IV; 4th dose- 9.25 mg/m^2 IV; 5th dose- 11.1 mg/m^2 IV. The dose should not be increased after that dose which reduces the WBC to approx. 3,000 cell/mm^2.
Vincristine Sulfate	ONCOVIN	Antineoplastic	Inj: 1 mg/mL	1.4 mg/m^2 IV (at weekly intervals).
Warfarin Sodium	COUMADIN	Anticoagulant	Tab: 1, 2, 2.5, 4, 5, 7.5, 10 mg	Must be individualized for each patient based on the prothrombin time. Initial dosage is commonly 10 mg/day for 2 - 4 days po. For maintenance, usually 2 - 10 mg daily po.

GENERIC NAME	COMMON TRADE NAMES	THERAPEUTIC CATEGORY	PREPARATIONS	COMMON ADULT DOSAGE
Xylometazoline Hydrochloride	OTRIVIN	Nasal Decongestant	Nasal Solution: 0.1% Nasal Spray: 0.1%	2 -3 drops into each nostril q 8 - 10 h. 2 - 3 sprays into each nostril q 8 - 10 h.
Zidovudine	RETROVIR	Antiviral	Syrup: 50 mg/5 mL Cpsl: 100 mg	**Symptomatic HIV Infection:** Initially, 200 mg q 4 h po around the clock. After 1 month, the dose may be reduced to 100 mg q 4 h po around the clock. **Asymptomatic HIV Infection:** 100 mg q 4 h po while awake (500 mg/day).
	RETROVIR I.V. INFUSION		Inj: 10 mg/mL	1 - 2 mg/kg infused IV over 1 hour at a constant rate; administer q 4 h around the clock (6 times daily).
Zinc Oxide		Skin Protectant	Oint: 20%	Apply topically prn.
Zolpidem Tartrate (C-IV)	AMBIEN	Hypnotic	Tab: 5, 10 mg	10 mg po hs.

C-II: Controlled Substance, Schedule II
C-III: Controlled Substance, Schedule III
C-IV: Controlled Substance, Schedule IV

166

SELECTED

COMBINATION

DRUG

PREPARATIONS

TRADE NAME	THERAPEUTIC CATEGORY	DOSAGE FORMS AND COMPOSITION	COMMON ADULT DOSAGE
A-200	Pediculicide	Shampoo: pyrethrins (0.3%), piperonyl butoxide technical (3%), related compounds (0.6%)	Apply to dry hair and scalp or other affected areas. Use enough to completely wet area being treated; massage in. Allow the product to remain for 10 min. Rinse and towel dry. Repeat in 7 - 10 days if reinfestation occurs.
ACNOMEL	Anti-Acne Agent	Cream: sulfur (8%), resorcinol (2%), alcohol (11%)	Apply a thin coating once or twice daily.
ACTIFED	Decongestant-Antihistamine	Syrup (per 5 mL): pseudoephedrine HCl (30 mg), triprolidine HCl (1.25 mg) Tab: pseudoephedrine HCl (60 mg), triproline HCl (2.5 mg)	10 mL q 4 - 6 h po. 1 tab q 4 - 6 h po.
ACTIFED PLUS	Decongestant-Antihistamine-Analgesic	Cplt & Tab: pseudoephedrine HCl (30 mg), triprolidine HCl (1.25 mg), acetaminophen (500 mg)	2 cplt (or tab) q 6 h po.
ACTIFED W/CODEINE (C-V)	Decongestant-Antihistamine-Antitussive	Syrup (per 5 mL): pseudoephedrine HCl (30 mg), triprolidine HCl (1.25 mg), codeine phosphate (10 mg), alcohol (4.3%)	10 mL q 4 - 6 h po, not to exceed 4 doses in 24 h.
ADVIL COLD & SINUS	Decongestant-Analgesic	Cplt: pseudoephedrine HCl (30 mg), ibuprofen (200 mg)	1 - 2 cplt q 4 - 6 h po, not to exceed 6 cplt in 24 h.
AFRIN SALINE MIST	Nasal Moisturizer	Nasal Spray: sodium chloride with sodium phosphate buffer	2 - 6 sprays into each nostril prn.
AGORAL	Emollient Laxative-Irritant Laxative	Liquid Emulsion (per 15 mL): mineral oil (4.2 g), phenolphthalein (200 mg)	7.5 - 15 mL po hs.

Drug	Classification	Composition	Dosage
ALDACTAZIDE	Diuretic, Antihypertensive	**Tab:** spironolactone (25 mg), hydrochlorothiazide (25 mg) **Tab:** spirololactone (50 mg), hydrochlorothiazide (50 mg)	**Diuresis:** The usual maintenance dose is 100 mg of each component daily po, as a single dose or in divided doses, but may range from 25 to 200 mg of each component daily. **Hypertension:** Usually 50 - 100 mg of each component daily po, as a single dose or in divided doses.
ALDOCLOR-150 ALDOCLOR-250	Antihypertensive	**Tab:** chlorothiazide (150 mg), methyldopa (250 mg) **Tab:** chlorothiazide (250 mg), methyldopa(250 mg)	1 tab bid or tid po. 1 tab bid or tid po.
ALDORIL-15 ALDORIL-25 ALDORIL D30 ALDORIL D50	Antihypertensive	**Tab:** hydrochlorothiazide (15 mg), methyldopa (250 mg) **Tab:** hydrochlorothiazide (25 mg), methyldopa (250 mg) **Tab:** hydrochlorothiazide (30 mg), methyldopa (500 mg) **Tab:** hydrochlorothiazide (50 mg), methyldopa (500 mg)	1 tab bid or tid po. 1 tab bid or tid po. 1 tab bid or tid po. 1 tab bid or tid po.
ALLEREST 12 HOUR	Decongestant-Antihistamine	**Cplt:** phenylpropanolamine HCl (75 mg), chlorpheniramine maleate (12 mg)	1 cplt q 12 h po.
ALLEREST HEADACHE STRENGTH	Decongestant-Antihistamine-Analgesic	**Tab:** pseudoephedrine HCl (30 mg), chlorpheniramine maleate (2 mg), acetaminophen (325 mg)	2 tab q 4 h po.
ALLEREST MAXIMUM STRENGTH	Decongestant-Antihistamine	**Tab:** pseudoephedrine HCl (30 mg), chlorpheniramine maleate (2 mg)	2 tab q 4 h po.
ALLEREST, NO DROWSINESS	Decongestant-Analgesic	**Tab:** pseudoephedrine HCl (30 mg), acetaminophen (325 mg)	2 tab q 4 h po.
ALLEREST SINUS PAIN FORMULA	Decongestant-Antihistamine-Analgesic	**Tab:** pseudoephedrine HCl (30 mg), chlorpheniramine maleate (2 mg), acetaminophen (500 mg)	2 tab q 6 h po.
AMBENYL (C-V)	Antitussive-Antihistamine	**Syrup (per 5 mL):** codeine phosphate (10 mg), bromodiphenhydramine HCl (12.5 mg), alcohol (5%)	5 - 10 mL q 4 - 6 h po.
ANEXSIA 5/500 (C-III) ANEXSIA 7.5/650 (C-III)	Analgesic	**Tab:** hydrocodone bitartrate (5 mg), acetaminophen (500 mg) **Tab:** hydrocodone bitartrate (7.5 mg), acetaminophen (650 mg)	1 - 2 tab q 4 - 6 h po, prn pain. 1 tab q 4 - 6 h po, prn pain.

TRADE NAME	THERAPEUTIC CATEGORY	DOSAGE FORMS AND COMPOSITION	COMMON ADULT DOSAGE
ANUSOL	Antihemorrhoidal	Oint: pramoxine HCl (1%), mineral oil (46.7%), zinc oxide (12.5%) Rectal Suppos: phenylephrine HCl (0.25%), hard fat (88.7%)	Apply externally to the affected area up to 5 times daily. Insert 1 rectally in the morning, at bedtime, and after each bowel movement.
APRESAZIDE 25/25 APRESAZIDE 50/50 APRESAZIDE 100/50	Antihypertensive	Cpsl: hydralazine HCl (25 mg), hydrochlorothiazide (25 mg) Cpsl: hydralazine HCl (50 mg), hydrochlorothiazide (50 mg) Cpsl: hydralazine HCl (100 mg), hydrochlorothiazide (50 mg)	1 cpsl bid po. 1 cpsl bid po. 1 cpsl bid po.
ASBRON G	Antiasthmatic	Elixir (per 5 mL): theophylline sodium glycinate (300 mg, equal to 150 mg of theophylline), guaifenesin (100 mg), alcohol (15%) Tab: theophylline sodium glycinate (300 mg, equal to 150 mg of theophylline), guaifenesin (100 mg)	Usual Dosage: 15 - 30 mL tid or qid po. Usual Dosage: 1 - 2 tab tid or qid po.
AUGMENTIN 250	Antibacterial	Powd for Susp (per 5 mL): amoxicillin (250 mg), clavulanic acid (62.5 mg) Chewable Tab: amoxicillin (250 mg), clavulanic acid (62.5 mg) Tab: amoxicillin (250 mg), clavulanic acid (125 mg)	Usual Dosage: 1 AUGMENTIN 250 tab q 8 h po. More Severe Infections and Respiratory Infections: 1 AUGMENTIN 500 tab q 8 h po.
AUGMENTIN 500		Tab: amoxicillin (500 mg), clavulanic acid (125 mg)	
AURALGAN OTIC	Analgesic (Topical)	Otic Solution (per mL): benzocaine (14 mg = 1.4%), antipyrine (54 mg = 5.4%), glycerin	Instill in ear canal until filled, then insert a cotton pledget moistened with solution into meatus. Repeat q 1 - 2 h.
AYR SALINE	Nasal Moisturizer	Nasal Solution & Spray: sodium chloride (0.65%) with monobasic potassium phosphate/sodium hydroxide buffer	2 - 4 drops or 2 sprays into each nostril prn.
AZO-GANTANOL	Urinary Anti-infective-Analgesic	Tab: sulfamethoxazole (500 mg), phenazopyridine HCl (100 mg)	Initially 4 tab po, followed by 2 tab morning and evening for up to 2 days.
AZO-GANTRISIN	Urinary Anti-infective-Analgesic	Tab: sulfisoxazole (500 mg), phenazopyridine HCl (50 mg)	Initially 4 tab po, followed by 2 tab qid po for up to 2 days.

BACTRIM	Antibacterial	**Susp (per 5 mL):** sulfamethoxazole (200 mg), trimethoprim (40 mg)
BACTRIM DS		**Tab:** sulfamethoxazole (400 mg), trimethoprim (80 mg)
		Tab: sulfamethoxazole (800 mg), trimethoprim (160 mg)

Urinary Tract Infections: 1 BACTRIM DS tab, 2 BACTRIM tab or 20 mL of Suspension q 12 h po for 10 to 14 days.

Shigellosis: 1 BACTRIM DS tab, 2 BACTRIM tab or 20 mL of Suspension q 12 h for 5 days.

Acute Exacerbations of Chronic Bronchitis: 1 BACTRIM DS tab, 2 BACTRIM tab or 20 mL of Suspension q 12 h po for 14 days.

P. carinii **Pneumonia Treatment:** 20 mg/kg trimethoprim and 100 mg/kg sulfamethoxazole per 24 h in equally divided doses q 6 h for 14 days.

P. carinii **Pneumonia Prophylax.:** 1 BACTRIM DS tab, 2 BACTRIM tab or 20 mL of Suspension q 24 h po.

Travelers' Diarrhea: 1 BACTRIM DS tab, 2 BACTRIM tab or 20 mL of Suspension q 12 h po for 5 days.

BACTRIM I.V. INFUSION	Antibacterial	**Inj (per 5 mL):** sulfamethoxazole (400 mg), trimethoprim (80 mg)

Severe Urinary Tract Infections and Shigellosis: 8 - 10 mg/kg daily (based on trimethoprim) in 2 - 4 equally divided doses q 6, 8 or 12 h by IV infusion for up to 14 days for UTI and 5 days for shigellosis.

P. carinii **Pneumonia:** 15 - 20 mg/kg daily (based on trimethoprim) in 3 - 4 equally divided doses q 6 - 8 h by IV infusion for up to 14 days.

TRADE NAME	THERAPEUTIC CATEGORY	DOSAGE FORMS AND COMPOSITION	COMMON ADULT DOSAGE
BANCAP-HC (C-III)	Analgesic	Cpsl: hydrocodone bitartrate (5 mg), acetaminophen (500 mg)	1 cpsl q 6 h po, prn pain. Maximum: 2 cpsl q 6 h po.
BENADRYL COLD	Decongestant-Antihistamine-Analgesic	Tab: pseudoephedrine HCl (30 mg), diphenhydramine HCl (12.5 mg), acetaminophen (500 mg)	2 tab q 6 h po.
BENADRYL COLD NIGHTTIME		Liquid (per 30 mL): pseudoephedrine HCl (60 mg), diphenhydramine HCl (50 mg), acetaminophen (1000 mg), alcohol (10%)	30 mL, starting hs, q 6 h po.
BENADRYL DECONGESTANT	Decongestant-Antihistamine	Elixir (per 5 mL): pseudoephedrine HCl (30 mg), diphenhydramine HCl (12.5 mg), alcohol (5%) Cpsl & Tab: pseudoephedrine HCl (60 mg), diphenhydramine HCl (25 mg)	10 mL q 4 - 6 h po. Maximum: 40 mL/day. 1 cpsl (or tab) q 4 - 6 h po. Maximum: 4 daily.
BENYLIN EXPECTORANT	Antitussive-Expectorant	Liquid (per 5 mL): dextromethorphan HBr (5 mg), guaifenesin (100 mg)	10 - 20 mL q 4 h po, not to exceed 120 mL in 24 h.
BENZAMYCIN	Anti-Acne Agent	Gel (per g): erythromycin (30 mg = 3%), benzoyl peroxide (50 mg = 5%)	Apply topically bid, AM and PM.
BICILLIN C-R	Antibacterial	Inj (per mL): penicillin G benzathine (150,000 Units), penicillin G procaine (150,000 Units) Inj (per mL): penicillin G benzathine (300,000 Units), penicillin G procaine (300,000 Units)	Streptococcal Infections: 2,400,000 Units by deep IM injection (multiple sites). Pneumococcal Infections (except Meningitis): 1,200,000 Units by deep IM injection, repeated q 2 - 3 days until the temperature is normal for 48 hours.
BICILLIN C-R 900/300		Inj (per 2 mL): penicillin G benzathine (900,000 Units), penicillin G procaine (300,000 units)	Streptococcal Infections: A single deep IM injection is usually sufficient. Pneumococcal Infections (except Meningitis): One 2 mL deep IM injection, repeated q 2 - 3 days until the temp. is normal for 48 hours.

BLEPHAMIDE	Antibacterial-Corticosteroid	**Ophth Susp:** sulfacetamide sodium (10%), prednisolone acetate (0.2%) **Ophth Oint:** sulfacetamide sodium (10%), prednisolone acetate (0.2%)	1 drop into affected eye(s) bid to qid. Apply to affected eye(s) tid - qid and once or twice at night.
BREVICON	Oral Contraceptive	**Tab:** ethinyl estradiol (35 µg), norethindrone (0.5 mg) in 21-Day and 28-Day Wallettes	21-Day regimen po or 28-Day regimen po.
BRONKAID	Antiasthmatic	**Tab:** theophylline (100 mg), ephedrine sulfate (24 mg), guaifenesin (100 mg)	1 tab q 4 h po, up to 5 tab per day.
BRONKOLIXIR	Antiasthmatic	**Elixir (per 5 mL):** theophylline (15 mg), ephedrine sulfate (12 mg), guaifenesin (50 mg), phenobarbital (4 mg), alcohol (19%)	10 mL q 3 - 4 h po, up to 4 doses per day.
BRONKOTAB	Antiasthmatic	**Tab:** theophylline (100 mg), ephedrine sulfate (24 mg), guaifenesin (100 mg), phenobarbital (8 mg)	1 tab q 3 - 4 h po, up to 5 doses per day.
BRONTEX (C-III) BRONTEX LIQUID (C-V)	Antitussive-Expectorant	**Tab:** codeine phosphate (10 mg), guaifenesin (300 mg) **Liquid (per 20 mL):** codeine phosphate (10 mg), guaifenesin (300 mg)	1 tab q 4 h po, prn. 20 mL q 4 h po, prn.
CAFERGOT	Antimigraine Agent	**Tab:** ergotamine tartrate (1 mg), caffeine (100 mg) **Rectal Suppos:** ergotamine tartrate (2 mg), caffeine (100 mg)	2 tab stat po, then 1 tab q 0.5 h if needed (maximum of 6 tab per attack). Insert 1 rectally stat, then 1 suppos. after 1 h if needed.
CALCIDRINE (C-V)	Antitussive-Expectorant	**Syrup (per 5 mL):** codeine (8.4 mg), calcium iodide (152 mg), alcohol (6%)	5 - 10 mL q 4 h po.
CAPOZIDE 25/15 CAPOZIDE 25/25 CAPOZIDE 50/15 CAPOZIDE 50/25	Antihypertensive	**Tab:** captopril (25 mg), hydrochlorothiazide (15 mg) **Tab:** captopril (25 mg), hydrochlorothiazide (25 mg) **Tab:** captopril (50 mg), hydrochlorothiazide (15 mg) **Tab:** captopril (50 mg), hydrochlorothiazide (25 mg)	1 CAPOZIDE 25/15 tab bid po, 1 h ac. Increased captopril dosage may be obtained by utilizing CAPOZIDE 50/15 bid, or higher hydrochlorothiazide dosage may be obtained by utilizing CAPOZIDE 25/25 bid. CAPOZIDE 25/15 and 50/15 may also be used tid po.

173

TRADE NAME	THERAPEUTIC CATEGORY	DOSAGE FORMS AND COMPOSITION	COMMON ADULT DOSAGE
CEROSE-DM	Decongestant-Antihistamine-Antitussive	**Liquid (per 5 mL):** phenylephrine HCl (10 mg), chlorpheniramine maleate (4 mg), dextromethorphan HBr (15 mg), alcohol (2.4%)	5 mL q 4 h po, prn.
CHERACOL (C-VI)	Antitussive-Expectorant	**Syrup (per 5 mL):** codeine phosphate (10 mg), guaifenesin (100 mg), alcohol (4.75%)	10 mL q 4 - 6 h po.
CHERACOL D	Antitussive-Expectorant	**Liquid (per 5 mL):** dextromethorphan HBr (10 mg), guaifenesin (100 mg), alcohol (4.75%)	10 mL q 4 h po.
CHLOROMYCETIN HYDROCORTISONE	Antibacterial-Corticosteroid	**Powd for Ophth Susp:** chloramphenicol (12.5 mg), hydrocortisone acetate (25 mg) in vials with diluent	2 drops in the affected eye(s) q 3 h. Continue dosing day & night for the first 48 h, after which the interval between applications may be increased. Treatment should continue for 48 h after the eye appears normal.
CHLOR-TRIMETON 4 HOUR RELIEF	Decongestant-Antihistamine	**Tab:** pseudoephedrine sulfate (60 mg), chlorpheniramine maleate (4 mg)	1 tab q 4 - 6 h po, up to 4 tabs per day.
CHLOR-TRIMETON 12 HOUR RELIEF	Decongestant-Antihistamine	**Sustained-Rel Tab:** pseudoephedrine sulfate (120 mg), chlorpheniramine maleate (8 mg)	1 tab q 12 h po.
CLARITIN-D	Decongestant-Antihistamine	**Extended-Rel Tab:** pseudoephedrine sulfate (120 mg), loratidine (5 mg)	1 tab q 12 h po on an empty stomach.
COLBENEMID	Anti-Gout Agent	**Tab:** colchicine (0.5 mg), probenecid (500 mg)	1 tab daily po for 1 week, then 1 tab bid thereafter.
COLY-MYCIN S OTIC	Antibacterial-Corticosteroid	**Otic Susp (per mL):** neomycin sulfate (4.71 mg, equivalent to 3.3 mg neomycin base), colistin sulfate (3 mg), hydrocortisone acetate (10 mg = 1%)	5 instilled drops into the affected ear(s) tid - qid.
COMBIPRES 0.1 COMBIPRES 0.2 COMBIPRES 0.3	Antihypertensive	**Tab:** clonidine HCl (0.1 mg), chlorthalidone (15 mg) **Tab:** clonidine HCl (0.2 mg), chlorthalidone (15 mg) **Tab:** clonidine HCl (0.3 mg), chlorthalidone (15 mg)	1 tab once daily or bid po. 1 tab once daily or bid po. 1 tab once daily or bid po.

COMHIST LA	Decongestant-Antihistamine	Cpsl: phenylephrine HCl (20 mg), chlorpheniramine maleate (4 mg), phenyltoloxamine citrate (50 mg)	1 cpsl q 8 - 12 h po.
COMTREX	Antitussive-Decongestant-Antihistamine-Analgesic	Cplt & Tab: dextromethorphan HBr (10 mg), pseudoephedrine HCl (30 mg), chlorpheniramine maleate (2 mg), acetaminophen (325 mg)	2 cplt (or tab) q 4 h po, not to exceed 8 cplt (or tab) in 24 h.
		Liqui-Gel Cpsl: dextromethorphan HBr (10 mg), phenylpropanolamine HCl (12.5 mg), chlorpheniramine maleate (2 mg), acetaminophen (325 mg)	2 cpsl q 4 h po, not to exceed 12 cpsl in 24 h.
		Liquid (per 30 mL): dextromethorphan HBr (20 mg), pseudoephedrine HCl (60 mg), chlorpheniramine maleate (4 mg), acetaminophen (650 mg), alcohol (20%)	30 mL q 4 h po, not to exceed 4 doses in 24 h.
COMTREX, ALLERGY-SINUS	Decongestant-Antihistamine-Analgesic	Cplt & Tab: pseudoephedrine HCl (30 mg), chlorpheniramine maleate (2 mg), acetaminophen (500 mg)	2 cplt (or tab) q 6 h po.
COMTREX COUGH FORMULA	Antitussive-Decongestant-Expectorant-Analgesic	Liquid (per 20 mL): dextromethorphan HBr (20 mg), pseudoephedrine HCl (60 mg), guaifenesin (200 mg), acetaminophen (500 mg), alcohol (20%)	20 mL q 4 h po, not to exceed 4 doses in 24 h.
COMTREX, DAY-NIGHT	Antitussive-Decongestant-Antihistamine-Analgesic	Daytime Cplt: dextromethorphan HBr (10 mg), pseudoephedrine HCl (30 mg), acetaminophen (325 mg); Nighttime Tab: Same active ingredients as above plus chlorpheniramine maleate (2 mg)	2 Daytime cplt q 4 h po and 2 Nighttime Tab hs, if needed, to be taken no sooner than 4 h after the last dose of the Daytime cplt.
COMTREX, NON-DROWSY	Antitussive-Decongestant-Analgesic	Cplt: dextromethorphan HBr (10 mg), pseudoephedrine HCl (30 mg), acetaminophen (325 mg)	2 cplt q 4 h po, not to exceed 4 doses in 24 h.
CORICIDIN	Antihistamine-Analgesic	Tab: chlorpheniramine maleate (2 mg), acetaminophen (325 mg)	2 tab q 4 h po.
CORICIDIN "D"	Decongestant-Antihistamine-Analgesic	Tab: phenylpropanolamine HCl (12.5 mg), chlorpheniramine maleate (2 mg), acetaminophen (325 mg)	2 tab q 4 h po.
CORICIDIN MAXIMUM STRENGTH SINUS HEADACHE	Decongestant-Antihistamine-Analgesic	Tab: phenylpropanolamine HCl (12.5 mg), chlorpheniramine maleate (2 mg), acetaminophen (500 mg)	2 tab q 6 h po.

TRADE NAME	THERAPEUTIC CATEGORY	DOSAGE FORMS AND COMPOSITION	COMMON ADULT DOSAGE
CORRECTOL	Irritant Laxative-Stool Softener	**Tab:** yellow phenolphthalein (65 mg), docusate sodium (100 mg)	1 - 2 tab po hs.
CORTISPORIN	Antibacterial-Corticosteroid	**Ophth Susp (per mL):** polymyxin B sulfate (10,000 Units), neomycin sulfate (equal to 3.5 mg of neomycin base), hydrocortisone (10 mg = 1%) **Ophth Oint (per g):** polymyxin B sulfate (10,000 Units), neomycin sulfate (equal to 3.5 mg of neomycin base), bacitracin zinc (400 Units), hydrocortisone (10 mg = 1%) **Otic Solution & Susp (per mL):** polymyxin B sulfate (10,000 Units), neomycin sulfate (equal to 3.5 mg of neomycin base), hydrocortisone (10 mg = 1%) **Cream (per g):** polymyxin B sulfate (10,000 Units), neomycin sulfate (equal to 3.5 mg of neomycin base), hydrocortisone acetate (5 mg = 0.5%) **Oint (per g):** polymyxin B sulfate (5,000 Units), neomycin sulfate (equal to 3.5 mg of neomycin base), bacitracin zinc (400 Units), hydrocortisone (10 mg = 1%)	1 - 2 drops into the affected eye(s) q 3 - 4 h, depending on the severity of the condition. Apply to the affected eye(s) q 3 - 4 h, depending on the severity of the condition. 4 drops instilled in the affected ear(s) tid to qid. Apply topically bid - qid. If the conditions permit, gently rub into the affected areas. Apply topically as a thin film bid to qid prn.
CORZIDE 40/5 CORZIDE 80/5	Antihypertensive	**Tab:** nadolol (40 mg), bendroflumethiazide (5 mg) **Tab:** nadolol (80 mg), bendroflumethiazide (5 mg)	1 tab daily po. 1 tab daily po.
DARVOCET-N 50 (C-IV)	Analgesic	**Tab:** propoxyphene napsylate (50 mg), acetaminophen (325 mg)	2 tab q 4 h prn pain po.
DARVOCET-N 100 (C-IV)	Analgesic	**Tab:** propoxyphene napsylate (100 mg), acetaminophen (650 mg)	1 tab q 4 h prn pain po.
DARVON COMPOUND-65 (C-IV)	Analgesic	**Cpsl:** propoxyphene HCl (65 mg), aspirin (389 mg), caffeine (32.4 mg)	1 cpsl q 4 h po, prn pain.
DECADRON W/XYLOCAINE	Corticosteroid-Local Anesthetic	**Inj (per mL):** dexamethasone sodium phosphate (4 mg), lidocaine HCl (10 mg)	Initial dose ranges from 0.1 to 0.75 mL by injection. Some patients respond to a single injection; in others, additional doses may be needed, usually at 4 - 7 day intervals.

DECONAMINE	Decongestant-Antihistamine	**Syrup (per 5 mL):** pseudoephedrine HCl (30 mg), chlorpheniramine maleate (2 mg).	5 - 10 mL tid - qid po.
		Tab: pseudoephedrine HCl (60 mg), chlorpheniramine maleate (4 mg)	1 tab tid - qid po.
DECONAMINE SR		**Sustained-Rel Cpsl:** pseudoephedrine HCl (120 mg), chlorpheniramine maleate (8 mg)	1 cpsl q 12 h po.
DEMULEN 1/35	Oral Contraceptive	**Tab:** ethinyl estradiol (35 µg), ethynodiol diacetate (1 mg) in 21-Day and 28-Day Compaks	21-Day regimen po or 28-Day regimen po.
DEMULEN 1/50		**Tab:** ethinyl estradiol (50 µg), ethynodiol diacetate (1 mg) in 21-Day and 28-Day Compaks	21-Day regimen po or 28-Day regimen po.
DESENEX	Antifungal	**Cream, Oint, Powder, & Spray Powder:** total undecylenate = 25% as undecylenic acid and zinc undecylenate **Foam:** undecylenic acid (10%), isopropyl alcohol (29.2%)	Cleanse the skin with soap and water and dry thoroughly. Apply to the affected skin areas morning and night.
DESOGEN	Oral Contraceptive	**Tab:** ethinyl estradiol (30 µg), desogestrel (0.15 mg) in 28-Day packs	28-Day regimen po.
DEXACIDIN	Antibacterial-Corticosteroid	**Ophth Oint (per g):** neomycin sulfate (equal to 3.5 mg of neomycin base), polymyxin B sulfate (10,000 Units), dexamethasone (1 mg)	Apply a small amount (about 0.5 in.) into the conjunctival sac tid - qid.
DIALOSE PLUS	Irritant Laxative-Stool Softener	**Tab:** yellow phenolphthalein (65 mg), docusate sodium (100 mg)	1 - 2 tab daily po, hs or on arising.
DIMETANE DECONGESTANT	Decongestant-Antihistamine	**Elixir (per 5 mL):** phenylephrine HCl (5 mg), brompheniramine maleate (2 mg), alcohol (2.3%)	10 mL q 4 h po.
		Cplt: phenylephrine HCl (10 mg), brompheniramine maleate (4 mg)	1 cplt q 4 h po.
DIMETANE-DC (C-V)	Antitussive-Decongestant-Antihistamine	**Syrup (per 5 mL):** codeine phosphate (10 mg), phenylpropanolamine HCl (12.5 mg), brompheniramine maleate (2 mg), alcohol (0.95%)	10 mL q 4 h po.
DIMETANE-DX	Antitussive-Decongestant-Antihistamine	**Syrup (per 5 mL):** dextromethorphan HBr (10 mg), pseudoephedrine HCl (30 mg), brompheniramine maleate (2 mg), alcohol (0.95%)	10 mL q 4 h po.

177

TRADE NAME	THERAPEUTIC CATEGORY	DOSAGE FORMS AND COMPOSITION	COMMON ADULT DOSAGE
DIMETAPP	Decongestant-Antihistamine	**Elixir (per 5 mL):** phenylpropanolamine HCl (12.5 mg), brompheniramine maleate (2 mg), alcohol (2.3%). **Tab & Liqui-Gel Cpsl:** phenylpropanolamine HCl (25 mg), brompheniramine maleate (4 mg)	10 mL q 4 h po. 1 tab (or Liqui-Gel) q 4 h po.
DIMETAPP EXTENTAB		**Sustained-Rel Tab:** phenylpropanolamine HCl (75 mg), brompheniramine maleate (12 mg)	1 tab q 12 h po.
DIMETAPP COLD AND FLU	Decongestant-Antihistamine-Analgesic	**Cplt:** phenylpropanolamine HCl (12.5 mg), brompheniramine maleate (2 mg), acetaminophen (500 mg)	2 cplt q 6 h po.
DIMETAPP DM	Decongestant-Antihistamine-Antitussive	**Elixir (per 5 mL):** phenylpropanolamine HCl (12.5 mg), brompheniramine maleate (2 mg), dextromethorphan HBr (10 mg), alcohol (2.3%)	10 mL q 4 h po.
DIURES 250 DIURES 500	Antihypertensive	**Tab:** chlorothiazide (250 mg), reserpine (0.125 mg). **Tab:** chlorothiazide (500 mg), reserpine (0.125 mg).	1 - 2 tab daily or bid po. 1 tab daily or bid po.
DOMEBORO	Astringent	**Powder (per packet):** aluminum sulfate (1191 mg), calcium acetate (938 mg) **Tablets:** aluminum sulfate (878 mg), calcium acetate (604 mg)	**As a Compress:** Dissolve 1 or 2 packets (or tablets) in 16 fl. oz. of warm water. Saturate a clean dressing in the solution, gently squeeze and apply loosely to the affected area. Remove, remoisten and reapply q 15 to 30 minutes prn. **As a Soak:** Dissolve 1 or 2 packets (or tablets) in 16 fl. oz. of warm water. Soak the affected area for 15 - 30 minutes. Repeat tid.
DONNATAL	Antispasmodic, Anticholinergic	**Cpsl & Tab:** atropine sulfate (0.0194 mg), scopolamine HBr (0.0065 mg), hyoscyamine sulfate (0.1037 mg), phenobarbital (16.2 mg) **Elixir (per 5 mL):** atropine sulfate (0.0194 mg), scopolamine HBr (0.0065 mg), hyoscyamine sulfate (0.1037 mg), phenobarbital (16.2 mg), alcohol (23%)	1 - 2 cpsl (or tab) tid or qid po. 5 - 10 mL tid or qid po.

DONNATAL EXTENTABS	Antispasmodic, Anticholinergic	**Extended-Rel Tab:** atropine sulfate (0.0582 mg), scopolamine HBr (0.0195 mg), hyoscyamine sulfate (0.3111 mg), phenobarbital (48.6 mg)	1 tab q 8 - 12 h po.
DOXIDAN	Irritant Laxative-Stool Softener	**Cpsl:** yellow phenolphthalein (65 mg), docusate calcium (60 mg)	1 - 2 cpsl daily po, for up to 1 week.
DRIXORAL	Decongestant-Antihistamine	**Syrup (per 5 mL):** pseudoephedrine sulfate (30 mg), dexbrompheniramine maleate (2 mg)	10 mL q 4 - 6 h po.
DRIXORAL COLD & ALLERGY	Decongestant-Antihistamine	**Sustained-Rel Tab:** pseudoephedrine sulfate (120 mg), dexbrompheniramine maleate (6 mg)	1 tab q 12 h po.
DRIXORAL COLD & FLU	Decongestant-Antihistamine-Analgesic	**Sustained-Rel Tab:** pseudoephedrine sulfate (60 mg), dexbrompheniramine maleate (3 mg), acetaminophen (500 mg)	2 tab q 12 h po.
DRIXORAL SINUS	Decongestant-Antihistamine-Analgesic	**Sustained-Rel Tab:** pseudoephedrine sulfate (60 mg), dexbrompheniramine maleate (3 mg), acetaminophen (500 mg)	2 tab q 12 h po.
DUO-MEDIHALER	Antiasthmatic	**Aerosol:** isoproterenol HCl (160 μg), phenylephrine bitartrate (240 μg)/spray	**Acute:** 1 inhalation; if not relieved in 2 - 5 minutes, repeat once. **Maintenance:** 1 - 2 inhalations 4 - 6 times daily.
DURATUSS	Decongestant-Expectorant	**Sustained-Rel Tab:** pseudoephedrine HCl (120 mg), guaifenesin (600 mg)	1 tab q 12 h po.
DURATUSS HD (C-III)	Antitussive-Decongestant-Expectorant	**Elixir (per 5 mL):** hydrocodone bitartrate (2.5 mg), pseudoephedrine HCl (30 mg), guaifenesin (100 mg), alcohol (5%)	10 mL q 4 - 6 h po.
DYAZIDE	Diuretic, Antihypertensive	**Cpsl:** triamterene (37.5 mg), hydrochlorothiazide (25 mg)	1 - 2 cpsl once daily po.

179

TRADE NAME	THERAPEUTIC CATEGORY	DOSAGE FORMS AND COMPOSITION	COMMON ADULT DOSAGE
ELIXOPHYLLIN-GG	Antiasthmatic	**Liquid (per 15 mL):** theophylline anhydrous (100 mg), guaifenesin (100 mg)	Dose based on theophylline; see Oral Theophylline Doses Table, p. 216. **Initial:** 6 mg/kg po; then reduce to 3 mg/kg q 6 h for 2 doses. **Maintenance:** 3 mg/kg q 8 h po.
ELIXOPHYLLIN-KI	Antiasthmatic	**Elixir (per 15 mL):** theophylline anhydrous (80 mg), potassium iodide (130 mg), alcohol (10%)	Dose based on theophylline; see Oral Theophylline Doses Table, p. 216. **Initial:** 6 mg/kg po; then reduce to 3 mg/kg q 6 h for 2 doses. **Maintenance:** 3 mg/kg q 8 h po.
EMETROL	Antiemetic	**Solution (per 5 mL):** dextrose (1.87 g), levulose (1.87 g), phosphoric acid (21.5 mg)	15 - 30 mL po. Repeat q 15 min. until distress subsides.
EMPIRIN W/CODEINE #3 (C-III) #4 (C-III)	Analgesic	**Tab:** aspirin (325 mg), codeine phosphate (30 mg) **Tab:** aspirin (325 mg), codeine phosphate (60 mg)	1 - 2 tab q 4 h po, prn. 1 tab q 4 h po, prn.
ENLON-PLUS	Cholinomimetic- Anticholinergic	**Inj (per mL):** edrophonium chloride (10 mg), atropine sulfate (0.14 mg)	Dosages range from 0.05 - 1 mL/kg IV given slowly over 45 to 60 seconds at a point of at least 5% recovery of twitch response to neuromuscular stimulation (95% block). The dosage delivered is 0.5 to 1 mg/kg edrophonium and 7 to 14 μg/kg atropine. A total dosage of 1 mg/kg of edrophonium should rarely be exceeded.

180

ENOVID 5 mg ENOVID 10 mg	Estrogen-Progestin	**Tab:** mestranol (75 μg), norethynodrel (5 mg) **Tab:** mestranol (150 μg), norethynodrel (9.85 mg)	**Hypermenorrhea:** 1 tab daily po from Day 5 through Day 24 of the menstrual cycle. **Endometriosis:** 1 tab daily po for 2 weeks, beginning on Day 5 of the menstrual cycle. Increase by 1 tab at 2 week intervals, up to 20 mg/day.
ENTEX	Decongestant-Expectorant	**Cpsl:** phenylpropanolamine HCl (45 mg), phenylephrine HCl (5 mg), guaifenesin (200 mg) **Liquid (per 5 mL):** phenylpropanolamine HCl (20 mg), phenylephrine HCl (5 mg), guaifenesin (100 mg), alcohol (5%)	1 cpsl qid (q 6 h) po with food or fluid. 10 mL qid (q 6 h) po.
ENTEX LA		**Long-Acting Tab:** phenylpropanolamine HCl (75 mg), guaifenesin (400 mg)	1 tab bid (q 12 h) po.
E-PILO-1	Anti-Glaucoma Agent	**Ophth Solution:** epinephrine bitartrate (1%), pilocarpine HCl (1%)	1 - 2 drops into affected eye(s) up to qid.
E-PILO-2		**Ophth Solution:** epinephrine bitartrate (1%), pilocarpine HCl (2%)	1 - 2 drops into affected eye(s) up to qid.
E-PILO-3		**Ophth Solution:** epinephrine bitartrate (1%), pilocarpine HCl (3%)	1 - 2 drops into affected eye(s) up to qid.
E-PILO-4		**Ophth Solution:** epinephrine bitartrate (1%), pilocarpine HCl (4%)	1 - 2 drops into affected eye(s) up to qid.
E-PILO-6		**Ophth Solution:** epinephrine bitartrate (1%), pilocarpine HCl (6%)	1 - 2 drops into affected eye(s) up to qid.
EQUAGESIC (C-IV)	Analgesic- Antianxiety Agent	**Tab:** aspirin (325 mg), meprobamate (200 mg)	1 - 2 tab tid po, prn pain.
ESGIC	Analgesic	**Cpsl & Tab:** acetaminophen (325 mg), butalbital (50 mg), caffeine (40 mg)	1 - 2 cpsl (or tab) q 4 h po, prn pain.
ESGIC-PLUS	Analgesic	**Tab:** acetaminophen (500 mg), butalbital (50 mg), caffeine (40 mg)	1 tab q 4 h po, prn pain.
ESIMIL	Antihypertensive	**Tab:** guanethidine monosulfate (10 mg), hydrochlorothiazide (25 mg)	2 tab daily po. Dosage may be increased at weekly intervals.

181

TRADE NAME	THERAPEUTIC CATEGORY	DOSAGE FORMS AND COMPOSITION	COMMON ADULT DOSAGE
ETRAFON ETRAFON 2-10 ETRAFON-FORTE	Antipsychotic-Antidepressant	**Tab:** perphenazine (2 mg), amitriptyline HCl (25 mg) **Tab:** perphenazine (2 mg), amitriptyline HCl (10 mg) **Tab:** perphenazine (4 mg), amitriptyline HCl (25 mg)	1 tab tid or qid po. 1 tab tid or qid po. 1 tab tid or qid po.
EXTENDRYL	Decongestant-Antihistamine-Anticholinergic	**Syrup (per 5 mL):** phenylephrine HCl (10 mg), chlorpheniramine maleate (2 mg), methscopolamine nitrate (1.25 mg)	10 mL q 4 h po.
		Tab: phenylephrine HCl (10 mg), chlorpheniramine maleate (2 mg), methscopolamine nitrate (1.25 mg)	2 tab q 4 h po.
EXTENDRYL SR		**Sustained-Rel Cpsl:** phenylephrine HCl (20 mg), chlorpheniramine maleate (8 mg), methscopolamine nitrate (2.5 mg)	1 cpsl q 12 h po.
FANSIDAR	Antimalarial	**Tab:** sulfadoxine (500 mg), pyrimethamine (25 mg)	**Acute Attack:** 2 - 3 tab po as a single dose. **Prophylaxis:** 1 tab po once weekly or 2 tab q 2 weeks, beginning 1 - 2 days before departure to an endemic area; continue for 4 - 6 weeks after return.
FEDAHIST EXPECTORANT	Decongestant-Expectorant	**Syrup (per 5 mL):** pseudoephedrine HCl (20 mg), guaifenesin (200 mg)	10 mL q 4 - 6 h po, up to 40 mL per day.
FEDAHIST GYROCAPS	Decongestant-Antihistamine	**Timed-Rel Cpsl:** pseudoephedrine HCl (65 mg), chlorpheniramine maleate (10 mg)	1 cpsl q 12 h po.
FEDAHIST TIMECAPS	Decongestant-Antihistamine	**Timed-Rel Cpsl:** pseudoephedrine HCl (120, chlorpheniramine maleate (8 mg)	1 cpsl q 12 h po.
FERANCEE	Hematinic	**Chewable Tab:** ferrous fumarate (200 mg), vitamin C (150 mg from ascorbic acid and sodium ascorbate)	2 tab daily po.
FERANCEE-HP	Hematinic	**Tab:** ferrous fumarate (330 mg), vitamin C (600 mg from ascorbic acid and sodium ascorbate)	1 tab daily po. pc.
FERO-FOLIC-500	Hematinic	**Controlled-Rel Tab:** ferrous sulfate (525 mg), folic acid, (800 μg), sodium ascorbate (500 mg)	1 tab daily po.

FERO-GRAD-500	Hematinic	**Controlled-Rel Tab:** ferrous sulfate (525 mg), sodium ascorbate (500 mg)	1 tab daily po.
FERRO-SEQUELS	Hematinic-Stool Softener	**Timed-Rel Tab:** ferrous fumarate (150 mg), docusate sodium (100 mg)	1 tab once or twice daily po.
FIORICET	Analgesic	**Tab:** acetaminophen (325 mg), butalbital (50 mg), caffeine (40 mg)	1 - 2 tab q 4 h po. Maximum of 6 tabs daily.
FIORICET W/CODEINE (C-III)	Analgesic	**Cpsl:** acetaminophen (325 mg), butalbital (50 mg), caffeine (40 mg), codeine phosphate (30 mg)	1 - 2 cpsl q 4 h po. Maximum of 6 cpsls daily.
FIORINAL (C-III)	Analgesic	**Cpsl & Tab:** aspirin (325 mg), caffeine (40 mg), butalbital (50 mg)	1 - 2 cpsl (or tab) q 4 h po. Maximum of 6 daily.
FIORINAL W/CODEINE (C-III)	Analgesic	**Cpsl:** aspirin (325 mg), caffeine (40 mg), butalbital (50 mg), codeine phosphate (30 mg)	1 - 2 cpsl q 4 h po. Maximum of 6 caps daily.
FML-S	Antibacterial-Corticosteroid	**Ophth Susp:** sulfacetamide sodium (10%), fluorometholone (0.1%)	1 drop in affected eye(s) qid.
HALEY'S M-O	Emollient Laxative-Saline Laxative	**Liquid (per 5 mL):** mineral oil (1.25 mL), magnesium hydroxide (304 mg)	15 - 30 mL po in the morning and hs.
HUMIBID DM	Antitussive-Expectorant	**Sustained-Rel. Tab:** dextromethorphan HBr (30 mg), guaifenesin (600 mg)	1 or 2 tablets q 12 h po.
HUMIBID DM SPRINKLE	Antitussive-Expectorant	**Sustained-Rel. Cpsl:** dextromethorphan HBr (15 mg), guaifenesin (300 mg)	2 or 4 capsules q 12 h po.
HYCODAN (C-III)	Antitussive-Anticholinergic	**Syrup (per 5 mL):** hydrocodone bitartrate (5 mg), homatropine methylbromide (1.5 mg) **Tab:** hydrocodone bitartrate (5 mg), homatropine methylbromide (1.5 mg)	5 mL q 4 - 6 h po. 1 tab q 4 - 6 h po.
HYCOMINE (C-III)	Antitussive-Decongestant	**Syrup (per 5 mL):** hydrocodone bitartrate (5 mg), phenylpropanolamine HCl (25 mg)	5 mL q 4 h po.

TRADE NAME	THERAPEUTIC CATEGORY	DOSAGE FORMS AND COMPOSITION	COMMON ADULT DOSAGE
HYCOMINE COMPOUND (C-III)	Antitussive-Decongestant-Antihistamine-Analgesic	**Tab:** hydrocodone bitartrate (5 mg), phenylephrine HCl (10 mg), chlorpheniramine maleate (2 mg), acetaminophen (250 mg), caffeine (30 mg)	1 tab qid po.
HYCOTUSS EXPECTORANT (C-III)	Antitussive-Expectorant	**Syrup (per 5 mL):** hydrocodone bitartrate (5 mg), guaifenesin (100 mg), alcohol (10%)	5 mL q 4 h po, pc & hs.
HYDROCET (C-III)	Analgesic	**Cpsl:** hydrocodone bitartrate (5 mg), acetaminophen (500 mg)	1 - 2 cpsl q 4 - 6 h po, prn pain.
HYDROPRES 25 HYDROPRES 50	Antihypertensive	**Tab:** hydrochlorothiazide (25 mg), reserpine (0.125 mg) **Tab:** hydrochlorothiazide (50 mg), reserpine (0.125 mg)	1 - 2 tab daily po. 1 tab daily po.
INDERIDE-40/25 INDERIDE-80/25	Antihypertensive	**Tab:** propranolol HCl (40 mg), hydrochlorothiazide (25 mg) **Tab:** propranolol HCl (80 mg), hydrochlorothiazide (25 mg)	1 tab bid po. 1 tab bid po.
INDERIDE LA 80/50 INDERIDE LA 120/50 INDERIDE LA 160/50	Antihypertensive	**Cpsl:** propranolol HCl (80 mg), hydrochlorothiazide (50 mg) **Cpsl:** propranolol HCl (120 mg), hydrochlorothiazide (50 mg) **Cpsl:** propranolol HCl (160 mg), hydrochlorothiazide (50 mg)	1 cpsl daily po. 1 cpsl daily po. 1 cpsl daily po.
ISOCLOR (C-V)	Decongestant-Expectorant-Antitussive	**Liquid (per 5 mL):** pseudoephedrine HCl (30 mg), guaifenesin (100 mg), codeine phosphate (10 mg), alcohol (5%)	10 mL tid - qid po.
JENEST-28	Oral Contraceptive	**Tab:** ethinyl estradiol (35 μg), norethindrone (0.5 mg) in 28-Day Cyclic Tablet Dispensers	28-Day regimen po.
KINESED	Antispasmodic, Anticholinergic	**Chewable Tab:** atropine sulfate (0.12 mg), scopolamine HBr (0.007 mg), phenobarbital (16 mg)	1 - 2 tab tid - qid po with liquids.
LEVLEN	Oral Contraceptive	**Tab:** ethinyl estradiol (30 μg), levonorgestrel (0.15 mg) in 21-Day and 28-Day Slidecases	21-Day regimen po or 28-Day regimen po.
LIBRAX	Anticholinergic-Antianxiety	**Cpsl:** clidinium bromide (2.5 mg), chlordiazepoxide HCl (5 mg)	1 - 2 cpsl qid po, ac & hs.
LIMBITROL (C-IV) LIMBITROL DS (C-IV)	Antianxiety Agent-Antidepressant	**Tab:** chlordiazepoxide (5 mg), amitriptyline HCl (12.5 mg) **Tab:** chlordiazepoxide (10 mg), amitriptyline HCl (25 mg)	1 tab tid or qid po. 1 tab tid or qid po.

184

LOESTRIN 21 1/20	Oral Contraceptive	**Tab:** ethinyl estradiol (20 μg), norethindrone acetate (1 mg) in 21-Day Petipacs	21-Day regimen po.
LOESTRIN 21 1.5/30	Oral Contraceptive	**Tab:** ethinyl estradiol (30 μg), norethindrone acetate (1.5 mg) in 21-Day Petipacs	21-Day regimen po.
LOESTRIN FE 1/20	Oral Contraceptive	**Tab:** 21 tabs: ethinyl estradiol (20 μg), norethindrone acetate (1 mg) + 7 tabs: ferrous fumarate (75 mg) in 28-Day Petipacs	28-Day regimen po.
LOESTRIN FE 1.5/30	Oral Contraceptive	**Tab:** 21 tabs: ethinyl estradiol (30 μg), norethindrone acetate (1.5 mg) + 7 tabs: ferrous fumarate (75 mg) in 28-Day Petipacs	28-Day regimen po.
LOMOTIL (C-V)	Antidiarrheal	**Liquid (per 5 mL):** diphenoxylate HCl (2.5 mg), atropine sulfate (0.025 mg), alcohol (15%) **Tab:** diphenoxylate HCl (2.5 mg), atropine sulfate (0.025 mg)	10 mL po qid until control of diarrhea is achieved. 2 tab qid po until control of diarrhea is achieved.
LO/OVRAL	Oral Contraceptive	**Tab:** ethinyl estradiol (30 μg), norgestrel (0.3 mg) in 21-Day and 28-Day Pilpaks	21-Day regimen po or 28-Day regimen po.
LOPRESSOR HCT 50/25	Antihypertensive	**Tab:** metoprolol tartrate (50 mg), hydrochlorothiazide (25 mg)	2 tab daily po as a single dose or in divided doses.
LOPRESSOR HCT 100/25		**Tab:** metoprolol tartrate (100 mg), hydrochlorothiazide (25 mg)	1 - 2 tab daily po as a single dose or in divided doses.
LOPRESSOR HCT 100/50		**Tab:** metoprolol tartrate (100 mg), hydrochlorothiazide (50 mg)	1 tab daily po as a single dose or in divided doses.
LORTAB (C-III)	Analgesic	**Elixir (per 5 mL):** hydrocodone bitartrate (2.5 mg), acetaminophen (120 mg), alcohol (7%)	15 mL q 4 h po, prn pain.
LORTAB 2.5/500 (C-III)		**Tab:** hydrocodone bitartrate (2.5 mg), acetaminophen (500 mg)	1 - 2 tab q 4 - 6 h po, prn pain.
LORTAB 5/500 (C-III)		**Tab:** hydrocodone bitartrate (5 mg), acetaminophen (500 mg)	1 - 2 tab q 4 - 6 h po, prn pain.
LORTAB 7.5/500 (C-III)		**Tab:** hydrocodone bitartrate (7.5 mg), acetaminophen (500 mg)	1 tab daily q 4 - 6 h po, prn pain.
LORTAB ASA (C-III)	Analgesic	**Tab:** hydrocodone bitartrate (5 mg), aspirin (500 mg)	1 - 2 tab q 4 - 6 h po, prn pain.
LOTRISONE	Antifungal-Corticosteroid	**Cream:** clotrimazole (1%), betamethasone dipropionate (0.05%)	Massage into affected skin areas bid for up to 4 weeks.

185

TRADE NAME	THERAPEUTIC CATEGORY	DOSAGE FORMS AND COMPOSITION	COMMON ADULT DOSAGE
LUFYLLIN-EPG	Antiasthmatic	Elixir (per 10 mL): dyphylline (100 mg), guaifenesin (200 mg), ephedrine HCl (16 mg), phenobarbital (16 mg), alcohol (5.5%) Tab: dyphylline (100 mg), guaifenesin (200 mg), ephedrine HCl (16 mg), phenobarbital (16 mg)	10 - 20 mL q 6 h po. 1 - 2 tab q 6 h po.
LUFYLLIN-GG	Antiasthmatic	Elixir (per 15 mL): dyphylline (100 mg), guaifenesin (100 mg), alcohol (17%) Tab: dyphylline (200 mg), guaifenesin (200 mg)	30 mL qid po. 1 tab qid po.
MANTADIL	Corticosteroid-Antihistamine	Cream: hydrocortisone acetate (0.5%), chlorcyclizine HCl (2%)	Apply topically bid - qid. Rub in well if the condition permits.
MARAX	Antiasthmatic	Tab: theophylline (130 mg), ephedrine sulfate (25 mg), hydroxyzine HCl (10 mg)	1 tab bid - qid po. Some patients are adequately controlled with 1/2 - 1 tab hs.
MAXITROL	Antibacterial-Corticosteroid	Ophth Suspension (per mL): polymyxin B sulfate (10,000 Units), neomycin sulfate (equal to 3.5 mg of neomycin base), dexamethasone (0.1%) Ophth Oint (per g): polymyxin B sulfate (10,000 Units), neomycin sulfate (equal to 3.5 mg of neomycin base), dexamethasone (0.1%)	1 or 2 drops into the affected eye(s) q 1 h in severe disease; in mild cases, 1 - 2 drops 4 to 6 times daily. Apply a small amount into the conjunctival sac tid to qid.
MAXZIDE MAXZIDE-25 MG	Antihypertensive, Diuretic	Tab: triamterene (75 mg), hydrochlorothiazide (50 mg) Tab: triamterene (37.5 mg), hydrochlorothiazide (25 mg)	1 tab daily po. 1 - 2 tabs daily po.
MEDI-FLU	Decongestant-Antihistamine-Antitussive-Analgesic	Cplt: pseudoephedrine HCl (30 mg), chlorpheniramine maleate (2 mg), dextromethorphan HBr (15 mg), acetaminophen (500 mg) Liquid (per 15 mL): pseudoephedrine HCl (30 mg), chlorpheniramine maleate (2 mg), dextromethorphan HBr (15 mg), acetaminophen (500 mg), alcohol (19%)	2 cplt q 6 h po. 30 mL q 6 h po.
MEDI-FLU WITHOUT DROWSINESS	Decongestant-Antitussive-Analgesic	Cplt: pseudoephedrine HCl (30 mg), dextromethorphan HBr (15 mg), acetaminophen (500 mg)	2 cplt q 4 h po.

MENRIUM 5-2	Estrogen-Antianxiety Agent	**Tab:** esterified estrogens (0.2 mg), chlordiazepoxide (5 mg)	1 tab tid po in 21-day courses, skip 1 week.
MENRIUM 5-4		**Tab:** esterified estrogens (0.4 mg), chlordiazepoxide (5 mg)	1 tab tid po in 21-day courses, skip 1 week.
MENRIUM 10-4		**Tab:** esterified estrogens (0.4 mg), chlordiazepoxide (10 mg)	1 tab tid po in 21-day courses, skip 1 week.
METIMYD	Antibacterial-Corticosteroid	**Ophth Susp:** sulfacetamide sodium (10%), prednisolone acetate (0.5%)	2 - 3 drops into the affected eye(s) q 1 - 2 h during the day and hs.
		Ophth Oint: sulfacetamide sodium (10%), prednisolone acetate (0.5%)	Apply to affected eye(s) tid or qid and hs.
MIDRIN	Analgesic, Antimigraine Agent	**Cpsl:** isometheptene mucate (65 mg), dichloralphenazone (100 mg), acetaminophen (325 mg)	**Tension Headache:** 1 - 2 cpsl q 4 h po, up to 8 cpsl daily. **Migraine Headache:** 2 cpsl stat, then 1 cpsl q h po until relieved, up to 5 cpsl within a 12-hour period.
MINIZIDE 1 MINIZIDE 2 MINIZIDE 5	Antihypertensive	**Cpsl:** prazosin HCl (1 mg), polythiazide (0.5 mg) **Cpsl:** prazosin HCl (2 mg), polythiazide (0.5 mg) **Cpsl:** prazosin HCl (5 mg), polythiazide (0.5 mg)	1 cpsl bid - tid po, the strength depending upon individual requirement after titration.
MODICON	Oral Contraceptive	**Tab:** ethinyl estradiol (35 μg), norethindrone (0.5 mg) in 21-Day and 28-Day Dialpaks	21-Day regimen po or 28-Day regimen po.
MODURETIC	Diuretic	**Tab:** amiloride HCl (5 mg), hydrochlorothiazide (50 mg)	Initially 1 tab daily po. Dosage may be raised to 2 tab daily as a single dose or in divided doses.
MOTOFEN (C-IV)	Antidiarrheal	**Tab:** difenoxin HCl (1 mg), atropine sulfate (0.025 mg)	2 tab po (1st dose), then 1 tab after each loose stool or 1 tab q 3 - 4 h prn. Maximum: 8 tab per 24 hours.
MYCITRACIN PLUS PAIN RELIEVER	Antibacterial-Local Anesthetic	**Oint (per g):** polymyxin B sulfate (5,000 Units), neomycin sulfate (equal to 3.5 mg of neomycin), bacitracin (500 Units), lidocaine (40 mg)	Apply a small amount to the affected area 1 - 3 times daily.

187

TRADE NAME	THERAPEUTIC CATEGORY	DOSAGE FORMS AND COMPOSITION	COMMON ADULT DOSAGE
MYCITRACIN TRIPLE ANTIBIOTIC	Antibacterial	**Oint (per g):** polymyxin B sulfate (5,000 Units), neomycin sulfate (equal to 3.5 mg of neomycin), bacitracin (500 Units)	Apply a small amount to the affected areas bid to the affected area 1 - 3 times daily.
MYCOLOG-II	Corticosteroid-Antifungal	**Cream & Oint (per g):** triamcinolone acetonide (1.0 mg), nystatin (100,000 Units)	Apply to the affected areas bid in the morning and evening.
NALDECON	Decongestant-Antihistamine	**Syrup (per 5 mL):** phenylpropanolamine HCl (20 mg), phenylephrine HCl (5 mg), chlorpheniramine maleate (2.5 mg), phenyltoloxamine citrate (7.5 mg) **Sustained-Action Tab:** phenylpropanolamine HCl (40 mg), phenylephrine HCl (10 mg), chlorpheniramine maleate (5 mg), phenyltoloxamine citrate (15 mg)	5 mL q 3 - 4 h po, not to exceed 4 doses in 24 h. 1 tab tid on arising, in mid-afternoon, and at bedtime po.
NALDECON-CX (C-V)	Antitussive-Decongestant-Expectorant	**Liquid (per 5 mL):** codeine phosphate (10 mg), phenyl-propanolamine HCl (12.5 mg), guaifenesin (200 mg)	10 mL q 4 h po.
NALDECON-DX ADULT	Antitussive-Decongestant-Expectorant	**Liquid (per 5 mL):** dextromethorphan HBr (10 mg), phenyl-propanolamine HCl (12.5 mg), guaifenesin (200 mg), alcohol (0.06%)	10 mL q 4 h po.
NALDECON SENIOR DX	Antitussive-Expectorant	**Liquid (per 5 mL):** dextromethorphan HBr (10 mg), guaifenesin (200 mg)	10 mL q 4 h po.
NAPHCON-A	Ocular Decongestant-Antihistamine	**Ophth Solution:** naphazoline HCl (0.025%), pheniramine maleate (0.3%)	1 - 2 drops in each eye q 3 - 4 h.
NASAL	Nasal Moisturizer	**Nasal Solution & Spray:** sodium chloride (0.65%), buffered with monobasic and dibasic sodium phosphate	2 - 6 drops or spray twice in each nostril prn.
NELOVA 0.5/35E	Oral Contraceptive	**Tab:** norethindrone (0.5 mg), ethinyl estradiol (35 μg) in 28-Day Compaks	28-Day regimen po.
NELOVA 1/35E	Oral Contraceptive	**Tab:** norethindrone (1.0 mg), ethinyl estradiol (35 μg) in 28-Day Compaks	28-Day regimen po.
NELOVA 1/50M	Oral Contraceptive	**Tab:** norethindrone (1.0 mg), mestranol (50 μg) in 28-Day Compaks	28-Day regimen po.

NELOVA 10/11	Oral Contraceptive	**Tab:** 10 tabs: norethindrone (0.5 mg), ethinyl estradiol (35 μg); 11 tabs: norethindrone (1 mg), ethinyl estradiol (35 μg); + 7 placebos in 28-Day Compaks	28-Day regimen po.
NEO-CORTEF	Antibacterial-Corticosteroid	Cream & Oint: neomycin sulfate (0.5%), hydrocortisone acetate (1%)	Apply topically bid - qid.
NEO-DECADRON	Antibacterial-Corticosteroid	Ophth Solution: neomycin sulfate (equal to 0.35% of neomycin base), dexamethasone sodium phosphate (0.1%)	1 - 2 drops into eye(s) every h during the day and q 2 h at night. When a favorable response occurs, reduce the dosage to 1 drop q 4 h.
		Ophth Oint: neomycin sulfate (equal to 0.35% of neomycin base), dexamethasone sodium phosphate (0.05%)	Apply a thin coating to eye(s) tid - qid. When a favorable response occurs, reduce the dosage to bid.
		Topical Cream: neomycin sulfate (equal to 0.35% of base), dexamethasone sodium phosphate (0.1%)	Apply topically to the affected area as a thin film tid - qid.
NEO-MEDROL	Antibacterial-Corticosteroid	Topical: neomycin sulfate (0.5%), methylprednisolone acetate (0.25%)	Apply topically bid - tid.
NEOSPORIN	Antibacterial	Ophth Solution (per mL): polymyxin B sulfate (10,000 Units), neomycin sulfate (equal to 1.75 mg of neomycin base), gramicidin (0.025 mg)	1 - 2 drops in the affected eye(s) bid - qid for 7 - 10 days.
		Ophth Oint (per g): polymyxin B sulfate (10,000 Units), neomycin sulfate (equal to 3.5 mg of neomycin base), bacitracin zinc (400 Units)	Apply to eye(s) q 3 - 4 h for 7 - 10 days.
		Oint (per g): polymyxin B sulfate (5,000 Units), neomycin sulfate (equal to 3.5 mg of neomycin base), bacitracin zinc (400 Units)	Apply topically 1 - 3 times daily.
NEOSPORIN PLUS MAXIMUM STRENGTH	Antibacterial-Local Anesthetic	Cream (per g): polymyxin B sulfate (10,000 Units), neomycin sulfate (equal to 3.5 mg of neomycin base), lidocaine (40 mg)	Apply topically 1 - 3 times daily.
		Oint (per g): polymyxin B sulfate (10,000 Units), neomycin sulfate (equal to 3.5 mg of neomycin base), bacitracin zinc (500 Units), lidocaine (40 mg)	Apply topically 1 - 3 times daily.
NEO-SYNALAR	Antibacterial-Corticosteroid	Cream: neomycin sulfate (0.5%; equal to 0.35% of neomycin base), fluocinolone acetonide (0.025%)	Apply to the affected areas as a thin film bid - qid.

189

TRADE NAME	THERAPEUTIC CATEGORY	DOSAGE FORMS AND COMPOSITION	COMMON ADULT DOSAGE
NOLAMINE	Decongestant-Antihistamine	**Timed-Rel. Tab:** phenylpropanolamine HCl (50 mg), chlorpheniramine maleate (4 mg), phenindamine tartrate (24 mg)	1 tab q 8 h po. In mild cases, 1 tab q 10 - 12 h po.
NORDETTE	Oral Contraceptive	**Tab:** ethinyl estradiol (30 μg), levonorgestrel (0.15 mg) in 21-Day and 28-Day Pilpaks	21-Day regimen po or 28-Day regimen po.
NORETHIN 1/35E	Oral Contraceptive	**Tab:** ethinyl estradiol (35 μg), norethindrone (1 mg) in 21-Day and 28-Day Compaks	21-Day regimen po or 28-Day regimen po.
NORETHIN 1/50M	Oral Contraceptive	**Tab:** mestranol (50 μg), norethindrone (1 mg) in 21-Day and 28-Day Compaks	21-Day regimen po or 28-Day regimen po.
NORGESIC	Skeletal Muscle Relaxant-Analgesic	**Tab:** orphenadrine citrate (25 mg), aspirin (385 mg), caffeine (30 mg)	1 - 2 tab tid or qid po.
NORGESIC FORTE		**Tab:** orphenadrine citrate (50 mg), aspirin (770 mg), caffeine (60 mg)	1/2 - 1 tab tid or qid po.
NORINYL 1 + 35	Oral Contraceptive	**Tab:** ethinyl estradiol (35 μg), norethindrone (1 mg) in 21-Day and 28-Day Wallettes	21-Day regimen po or 28-Day regimen po.
NORINYL 1 + 50	Oral Contraceptive	**Tab:** mestranol (50 μg), norethindrone (1 mg) in 21-Day and 28-Day Wallettes	21-Day regimen po or 28-Day regimen po.
NOVAFED A	Decongestant-Antihistamine	**Controlled-Rel Cpsl:** pseudoephedrine HCl (120 mg), chlorpheniramine maleate (8 mg)	1 cpsl q 12 h po.
NOVAHISTINE	Decongestant-Antihistamine	**Elixir (per 5 mL):** phenylephrine HCl (5 mg), chlorpheniramine maleate (2 mg), alcohol (5%)	10 mL q 4 h po.
NOVAHISTINE DH (C-V)	Decongestant-Antihistamine-Antitussive	**Liquid (per 5 mL):** pseudoephedrine HCl (30 mg), chlorpheniramine maleate (2 mg), codeine phosphate (10 mg), alcohol (5%)	10 mL q 4 - 6 h po.
NOVAHISTINE DMX	Antitussive-Decongestant-Expectorant	**Liquid (per 5 mL):** dextromethorphan HBr (10 mg), pseudoephedrine HCl (30 mg), guaifenesin (100 mg), alcohol (10%)	10 mL q 4 h po. Maximum: 4 doses/day.

NOVAHISTINE EXPECTORANT (C-V)	Decongestant-Expectorant-Antitussive	**Liquid (per 5 mL):** pseudoephedrine HCl (30 mg), guaifenesin (100 mg), codeine phosphate (10 mg), alcohol (7.5%)	10 mL q 4 h po.
NUCOFED (C-III)	Decongestant-Antitussive	**Syrup (per 5 mL):** pseudoephedrine HCl (60 mg), codeine phosphate (20 mg)	5 mL q 6 h po.
		Cpsl: pseudoephedrine HCl (60 mg), codeine phosphate (20 mg)	1 cpsl q 6 h po.
NUCOFED EXPECTORANT (C-III)	Decongestant-Expectorant-Antitussive	**Syrup (per 5 mL):** pseudoephedrine HCl (60 mg), guaifenesin (200 mg), codeine phosphate (20 mg), alcohol (12.5%)	5 mL q 6 h po.
NUCOFED PEDIATRIC EXPECTORANT (C-III)	Decongestant-Expectorant-Antitussive	**Syrup (per 5 mL):** pseudoephedrine HCl (30 mg), guaifenesin (100 mg), codeine phosphate (10 mg), alcohol (6%)	10 mL q 6 h po.
OPHTHOCORT	Antibacterial-Corticosteroid	**Ophth Oint (per g):** chloramphenicol (10 mg), polymyxin B sulfate (10,000 Units), hydrocortisone acetate (5 mg)	Place a small amount into the affected eye(s) q 3 h, or more frequently if necessary. Continue day and night for the first 48 h, then increase the intervals between doses.
ORNADE	Decongestant-Antihistamine	**Controlled-Rel Cpsl:** phenylpropanolamine HCl (75 mg), chlorpheniramine maleate (12 mg)	1 cpsl q 12 h po.
ORNEX	Decongestant-Analgesic	**Cplt:** pseudoephedrine HCl (30 mg), acetaminophen (325 mg)	2 cplt q 4 h po, not to exceed 8 cplt in 24 h.
ORNEX, MAXIMUM STRENGTH		**Cplt:** pseudoephedrine HCl (30 mg), acetaminophen (500 mg)	2 cplt q 6 h po, not to exceed 8 cplt in 24 h.
ORTHO-CEPT	Oral Contraceptive	**Tab:** ethinyl estradiol (30 μg), desogestrel (0.15 mg) in 21-Day and 28-Day Dialpaks	21-Day regimen po or 28-Day regimen po.
ORTHO-CYCLEN	Oral Contraceptive	**Tab:** ethinyl estradiol (35 μg), norgestimate (0.25 mg) in 21-Day and 28-Day Dialpaks	21-Day regimen po or 28-Day regimen po.
ORTHO-NOVUM 1/35	Oral Contraceptive	**Tab:** ethinyl estradiol (35 μg), norethindrone (1 mg) in 21-Day and 28-Day Dialpaks	21-Day regimen po or 28-Day regimen po.

TRADE NAME	THERAPEUTIC CATEGORY	DOSAGE FORMS AND COMPOSITION	COMMON ADULT DOSAGE
ORTHO-NOVUM 1/50	Oral Contraceptive	**Tab:** mestranol (50 μg), norethindrone (1 mg) in 21-Day and 28-Day Dialpaks	21-Day regimen po or 28-Day regimen po.
ORTHO-NOVUM 7/7/7	Oral Contraceptive	**Tab:** 7 tabs: ethinyl estradiol (35 μg), norethindrone (0.5 mg); 7 tabs: ethinyl estradiol (35 μg), norethindrone (0.75 mg); 7 tabs: ethinyl estradiol (35 μg), norethindrone (1 mg) in 21-Day Dialpaks and with 7 inert tabs in 28-Day Dialpaks	21-Day regimen po or 28-Day regimen po.
ORTHO-NOVUM 10/11	Oral Contraceptive	**Tab:** 10 tabs: ethinyl estradiol (35 μg), norethindrone (0.5 mg); 11 tabs: ethinyl estradiol (35 μg), norethindrone (1 mg) in 21-Day Dialpaks and with 7 insert tabs in 28-Day Dialpaks	21-Day regimen po or 28-Day regimen po.
ORTHO TRI-CYCLEN	Oral Contraceptive	**Tab:** 7 tabs: ethinyl estradiol (35 μg), norgestimate (0.18 mg); 7 tabs: ethinyl estradiol (35 μg), norgestimate (0.215 mg); 7 tabs: ethinyl estradiol (35 μg), norgestimate (0.25 mg) in 21-Day Dialpaks and with 7 inert tabs in 28-Day Dialpaks	21-Day regimen po or 28-Day regimen po.
OTOBIOTIC	Antibacterial-Corticosteroid	**Otic Solution (per mL):** polymyxin B sulfate (10,000 Units), hydrocortisone (0.5%)	4 drops into ear(s) tid or qid.
OVCON-35	Oral Contraceptive	**Tab:** ethinyl estradiol (35 μg), norethindrone (0.4 mg) in 28-Day dispensers	28-Day regimen po.
OVCON-50	Oral Contraceptive	**Tab:** ethinyl estradiol (50 μg), norethindrone (1 mg) in 28-Day dispensers	28-Day regimen po.
OVRAL	Oral Contraceptive	**Tab:** ethinyl estradiol (50 μg), norgestrel (0.5 mg) in 21-Day and 28-Day Pilpaks	21-Day regimen po or 28-Day regimen po.
P_1E_1	Anti-Glaucoma Agent	**Ophth Solution:** pilocarpine HCl (1%), epinephrine bitartrate (1%)	1 - 2 drops into affected eye(s) up to qid.
P_2E_1		**Ophth Solution:** pilocarpine HCl (2%), epinephrine bitartrate (1%)	1 - 2 drops into affected eye(s) up to qid.
P_3E_1		**Ophth Solution:** pilocarpine HCl (3%), epinephrine bitartrate (1%)	1 - 2 drops into affected eye(s) up to qid.
P_4E_1		**Ophth Solution:** pilocarpine HCl (4%), epinephrine bitartrate (1%)	1 - 2 drops into affected eye(s) up to qid.
P_6E_1		**Ophth Solution:** pilocarpine HCl (6%), epinephrine bitartrate (1%)	1 - 2 drops into affected eye(s) up to qid.

PAZO	Antihemorrhoidal	Oint: camphor (2%), ephedrine sulfate (0.2%), zinc oxide (5%) Rectal Suppos: ephedrine sulfate (3.86 mg), zinc oxide (96.5 mg)	Apply to affected areas up to qid. Insert 1 rectally up to qid.
PEDIOTIC	Antibacterial-Corticosteroid	Otic Susp (per mL): polymyxin B sulfate (10,000 Units), neomycin sulfate (equal to 3.5 mg of neomycin base), hydrocortisone (10 mg = 1%)	4 drops into the affected ear(s) tid to qid.
PERCOCET (C-II)	Analgesic	Tab: oxycodone HCl (5 mg), acetaminophen (325 mg)	1 tab q 6 h po, prn pain.
PERCODAN (C-II)	Analgesic	Tab: oxycodone HCl (4.5 mg), oxycodone terephthalate (0.38 mg), aspirin (325 mg)	1 tab q 6 h po, prn pain.
PERCODAN-DEMI (C-II)	Analgesic	Tab: oxycodone HCl (2.25 mg), oxycodone terephthalate (0.19 mg), aspirin (325 mg)	1 - 2 tab q 6 h po, prn pain.
PERCOGESIC	Antihistamine-Analgesic	Tab: phenyltoloxamine citrate (30 mg), acetaminophen (325 mg)	1 - 2 tab q 4 h po, up to 8 tab per day.
PERDIEM	Bulk Laxative-Irritant Laxative	Granules (per rounded teaspoonful): psyllium hydrophilic mucilloid (3.25 g), senna (0.74 g)	In the evening and/or before breakfast, 1 - 2 rounded teaspoonfuls in at least 8 oz. of cool beverage po.
PERI-COLACE	Irritant Laxative-Stool Softener	Cpsl: casanthranol (30 mg), docusate sodium (100 mg) Syrup (per 15 mL): casanthranol (30 mg), docusate sodium (60 mg), alcohol (10%)	1 - 2 cpsl hs po. 15 - 30 mL hs po.
PHENAPHEN-650 W/CODEINE (C-III)	Analgesic	Tab: acetaminophen (650 mg), codeine phosphate (30 mg)	1 - 2 tab q 4 h po, prn pain.
PHENERGAN VC	Antihistamine-Decongestant	Syrup (per 5 mL): promethazine HCl (6.25 mg), phenylephrine HCl (5 mg), alcohol (7%)	5 mL q 4 - 6 h po.
PHENERGAN VC W/ CODEINE (C-V)	Antihistamine-Decongestant-Antitussive	Syrup (per 5 mL): promethazine HCl (6.25 mg), phenylephrine HCl (5 mg), codeine phosphate (10 mg), alcohol (7%)	5 mL q 4 - 6 h po, not to exceed 30 mL in 24 h.
PHENERGAN W/CODEINE (C-V)	Antihistamine-Antitussive	Syrup (per 5 mL): promethazine HCl (6.25 mg), codeine phosphate (10 mg), alcohol (7%)	5 mL q 4 - 6 h po, not to exceed 30 mL in 24 h.

193

TRADE NAME	THERAPEUTIC CATEGORY	DOSAGE FORMS AND COMPOSITION	COMMON ADULT DOSAGE
PHENERGAN W/ DEXTROMETHORPHAN	Antihistamine-Antitussive	**Syrup (per 5 mL):** promethazine HCl (6.25 mg), dextromethorphan HBr (15 mg), alcohol (7%)	5 mL q 4 - 6 h po, not to exceed 30 mL in 24 h.
PHRENILIN PHRENILIN FORTE	Analgesic	**Tab:** acetaminophen (325 mg), butalbital (50 mg) **Cpsl:** acetaminophen (650 mg), butalbital (50 mg)	1 - 2 tab q 4 h po, prn. 1 cpsl q 4 h po, prn.
PMB 200 PMB 400	Estrogen-Antianxiety Agent	**Tab:** conjugated estrogens (0.45 mg), meprobamate (200 mg) **Tab:** conjugated estrogens (0.45 mg), meprobamate (400 mg)	1 tab tid po administered cyclically (3 weeks on and 1 week off).
POLYCILLIN-PRB	Antibacterial	**Powd for Susp:** ampicillin trihydrate (equal to 3.5 g of ampicillin), probenecid (1 g)	Administer the entire contents as a single dose po.
POLY-PRED	Antibacterial-Corticosteroid	**Ophth Suspension (per mL):** neomycin sulfate (equal to 3.5 mg of neomycin base), polymyxin B sulfate (10,000 Units), prednisolone acetate (0.5%)	1 or 2 drops q 3 - 4 h into affected eye(s). Acute infections may require dosing q 30 minutes, initially.
POLYSPORIN	Antibacterial	**Ophth Oint (per g):** polymyxin B sulfate (10,000 Units), bacitracin zinc (500 Units) **Powder & Oint (per g):** polymyxin B sulfate (10,000 Units), bacitracin zinc (500 units)	Apply to eye(s) q 3 - 4 h. Apply topically 1 - 3 times daily.
POLYTRIM	Antibacterial	**Ophth Solution (per mL):** trimethoprim sulfate (equal to 1 mg of trimethoprim base), polymyxin B sulfate (10,000 Units)	1 drop into affected eye(s) q 3 h (maximum of 6 doses per day) for 7 - 10 days.
PRED-G	Antibacterial-Corticosteroid	**Ophth Suspension:** gentamicin sulfate (0.3%), prednisolone acetate (1.0%) **Ophth Oint:** gentamicin sulfate (0.3%), prednisolone acetate (0.6%)	1 drop into affected eye(s) bid to qid. During the initial 24 to 48 h, dosage may be raised up to 1 drop every hour. Apply a small amount (1/2 in.) to the conjunctival sac 1 - 3 times daily.

PREPARATION H   Antihemorrhoidal

Cream & Oint (per 30 g): live yeast cell derivative skin respiratory factor (2,000 Units), shark liver oil (3.0%)

Rectal Suppos: live yeast cell derivative skin respiratory factor (2,000 Units), shark liver oil (3.0%)

Apply to rectal area from 3 - 5 times daily, especially at night, in the morning and after each bowel movement.
Insert 1 rectally from 3 - 5 times daily, especially at night, in the morning and after each bowel movement.

PRIMATENE   Antiasthmatic

Tab: theophylline anhydrous (130 mg), ephedrine HCl (24 mg)

1 - 2 tab initially po, then 1 tab q 4 h po.

PRIMAXIN I.M.   Antibacterial

Powd for Inj: imipenem (500 mg), cilastatin sodium (500 mg)
Powd for Inj: imipenem (750 mg), cilastatin sodium (750 mg)

Lower Respiratory Tract, Skin & Skin Structure, and Gynecologic Infections: 500 or 750 mg (of imipenem) q 12 h IM.
Intra-Abdominal Infections: 750 mg q 12 h IM.

PRIMAXIN I.V.   Antibacterial

Powd for Inj: imipenem (250 mg), cilastatin sodium (250 mg)
Powd for Inj: imipenem (500 mg), cilastatin sodium (500 mg)

Administer by IV infusion. Each 250 or 500 mg dose (of imipenem) should be given over 20 - 30 min. Each 1000 mg dose should be infused over 40 - 60 min.
Infections:
Mild: 250 - 500 mg q 6 h.
Moderate: 500 - 1000 mg q 6 to 8 h.
Severe, Life-Threatening: 500 mg q 6 h to 1000 mg q 6 to 8 h.
Urinary Tract (Uncomplicated): 250 mg q 6 h.
Urinary Tract (Complicated): 500 mg q 6 h.

PRINZIDE 10-12.5   Antihypertensive
PRINZIDE 20-12.5
PRINZIDE 20-25

Tab: lisinopril (10 mg), hydrochlorothiazide (12.5 mg)
Tab: lisinopril (20 mg), hydrochlorothiazide (12.5 mg)
Tab: lisinopril (20 mg), hydrochlorothiazide (25 mg)

1 - 2 tab once daily po.
1 - 2 tab once daily po.
1 - 2 tab once daily po.

195

TRADE NAME	THERAPEUTIC CATEGORY	DOSAGE FORMS AND COMPOSITION	COMMON ADULT DOSAGE
PROCTOCREAM-HC	Local Anesthetic-Corticosteroid	Cream: pramoxine HCl (1%), hydrocortisone acetate (1%)	Apply to the affected area as a thin film tid - qid.
PROCTOFOAM-HC	Local Anesthetic-Corticosteroid	Aerosol: pramoxine HCl (1%), hydrocortisone acetate (1%)	Apply to the affected area tid to qid.
QUADRINAL	Antiasthmatic	Tab: theophylline calcium salicylate (130 mg; equivalent to 65 mg of theophylline base), ephedrine HCl (24 mg), potassium iodide (320 mg), phenobarbital (24 mg)	1 tab tid - qid po; if needed, an additional tab hs for nighttime relief.
QUELIDRINE	Decongestant-Expectorant-Antitussive-Antihistamine	Syrup (per 5 mL): ephedrine HCl (5 mg), phenylephrine HCl (5 mg), ammonium chloride (40 mg), ipecac fluidextract (0.005 mL), dextromethorphan HBr (10 mg), chlorpheniramine maleate (2 mg), alcohol (2%)	5 mL. 1 to 4 times daily po.
QUIBRON QUIBRON-300	Antiasthmatic	Cpsl: theophylline (150 mg), guaifenesin (90 mg) Cpsl: theophylline (300 mg), guaifenesin (180 mg)	Dose based on theophylline; see Oral Theophylline Doses Table, p. 216.
R & C	Pediculicide	Shampoo: pyrethrins (0.30%), piperonyl butoxide technical (3%)	Apply to dry hair and scalp or other affected areas. Use enough to completely wet area being treated; massage in. Allow the product to remain for 10 min. Rinse and towel dry. Repeat in 7 - 10 days if reinfestation occurs.
RID	Pediculicide	Shampoo: pyrethrins (0.33%), piperonyl butoxide technical (4%), related compounds (0.8%)	Same dosage and directions as for R & C Shampoo above.
RIFAMATE	Tuberculostatic	Cpsl: rifampin (300 mg), isoniazid (150 mg)	2 cpsl daily po, 1 hour before or 2 hours after a meal.

196

RIFATER	Tuberculostatic	**Tab:** rifampin (120 mg), isoniazid (50 mg), pyrazinamide (300 mg)	**Over 15 yrs and:** ≤ 44 kg: 4 tab po once daily. 44-54 kg: 5 tab po once daily. ≥ 55 kg: 6 tab po once daily. Give on an empty stomach with a full glass of water.
ROBAXISAL	Skeletal Muscle Relaxant-Analgesic	**Tab:** methocarbamol (400 mg), aspirin (325 mg)	2 tab qid po. 3 tab qid po may be used in severe conditions for 1 - 3 days in patients who are able to tolerate salicylates.
ROBITUSSIN A-C (C-V)	Antitussive-Expectorant	**Syrup (per 5 mL):** codeine phosphate (10 mg), guaifenesin (100 mg), alcohol (3.5%)	10 mL q 4 h po.
ROBITUSSIN-CF	Antitussive-Decongestant-Expectorant	**Syrup (per 5 mL):** dextromethorphan HBr (10 mg), phenylpropanolamine HCl (12.5 mg), guaifenesin (100 mg), alcohol (4.75%)	10 mL q 4 h po.
ROBITUSSIN-DAC (C-V)	Antitussive-Decongestant-Expectorant	**Syrup (per 5 mL):** codeine phosphate (10 mg), pseudoephedrine HCl (30 mg), guaifenesin (100 mg), alcohol (1.9%)	10 mL q 4 h po.
ROBITUSSIN-DM	Antitussive-Expectorant	**Syrup (per 5 mL):** dextromethorphan HBr (10 mg), guaifenesin (100 mg)	10 mL q 4 h po.
ROBITUSSIN-PE	Antitussive-Decongestant	**Syrup (per 5 mL):** dextromethorphan HBr (10 mg), pseudoephedrine HCl (30 mg)	10 mL q 6 h po.
ROBITUSSIN MAXIMUM STRENGTH COUGH & COLD LIQUID	Decongestant-Antihistamine-Antitussive-Analgesic	**Liquid (per 30 mL):** phenylephrine HCl (10 mg), pyrilamine maleate (50 mg), dextromethorphan HBr (30 mg), acetaminophen (650 mg)	30 mL q 6 h po (if confined to bed or at home) or 30 mL hs. Do not take for more than 10 days.
ROBITUSSIN-PE	Decongestant-Expectorant	**Syrup (per 5 mL):** pseudoephedrine HCl (30 mg), guaifenesin (100 mg), alcohol (1.4%)	10 mL q 4 h po. Maximum: 4 doses/day.

197

TRADE NAME	THERAPEUTIC CATEGORY	DOSAGE FORMS AND COMPOSITION	COMMON ADULT DOSAGE
RONDEC	Decongestant-Antihistamine	**Syrup (per 5 mL)**: pseudoephedrine HCl (60 mg), carbinoxamine maleate (4 mg)	5 mL qid po.
		Tab: pseudoephedrine HCl (60 mg), carbinoxamine maleate (4 mg)	1 tab qid po.
RONDEC-TR		**Timed-Rel. Tab**: pseudoephedrine HCl (120 mg), carbinoxamine maleate (8 mg)	1 tab bid po.
RONDEC-DM	Decongestant-Antihistamine-Antitussive	**Syrup (per 5 mL)**: pseudoephedrine HCl (60 mg), carbinoxamine maleate (4 mg), dextromethorphan HBr (15 mg)	5 mL qid po.
RYNA	Decongestant-Antihistamine	**Liquid (per 5 mL)**: pseudoephedrine HCl (30 mg), chlorpheniramine maleate (2 mg)	10 mL q 6 h po.
RYNA-C (C-V)	Antitussive-Decongestant-Antihistamine	**Liquid (per 5 mL)**: codeine phosphate (10 mg), pseudoephedrine HCl (30 mg), chlorpheniramine maleate (2 mg)	10 mL q 6 h po.
RYNA-CX (C-V)	Antitussive-Decongestant-Expectorant	**Liquid (per 5 mL)**: codeine phosphate (10 mg), pseudoephedrine HCl (30 mg), guaifenesin (100 mg)	10 mL q 6 h po.
RYNATAN	Decongestant-Antihistamine	**Tab**: phenylephrine tannate (25 mg), pyrilamine tannate (25 mg), chlorpheniramine tannate (8 mg)	1 - 2 tab q 12 h po.
RYNATUSS	Decongestant-Antihistamine-Antitussive	**Tab**: phenylephrine tannate (10 mg), ephedrine tannate (10 mg), chlorpheniramine tannate (5 mg), carbetapentane tannate (60 mg)	1 - 2 tab q 12 h po.
SELDANE-D	Decongestant-Antihistamine	**Extended-Rel Tab**: pseudoephedrine HCl (120 mg), terfenadine (60 mg)	1 tab po, morning and night.
SEMPREX-D	Decongestant-Antihistamine	**Cpsl**: pseudoephedrine HCl (60 mg), acrivastine (8 mg)	1 cpsl qid po.

198

Drug	Category	Formulation	Dosage
SEPTRA	Antibacterial	Susp (per 5 mL): sulfamethoxazole (200 mg), trimethoprim (40 mg). Tab: sulfamethoxazole (400 mg), trimethoprim (80 mg)	**Urinary Tract Infections:** 1 SEPTRA DS tab, 2 SEPTRA tab or 20 mL of Suspension q 12 h po for 10 - 14 days. **Shigellosis:** 1 SEPTRA DS tab, 2 SEPTRA tab or 20 mL of Suspension for 5 days. **Acute Exacerbations of Chronic Bronchitis:** 1 SEPTRA DS tab, 2 SEPTRA tab or 20 mL of Susp. q 12 h po for 14 days. *P. carinii* **Pneumonia Treatment:** 20 mg/kg trimethoprim and 100 mg/kg sulfamethoxazole per 24 h in equally divided doses q 6 h for 14 days. *P. carinii* **Pneumonia Prophylax.:** 1 SEPTRA DS tab, 2 SEPTRA tab or 20 mL of Suspension q 24 h po. **Travelers' Diarrhea:** 1 SEPTRA DS tab, 2 SEPTRA tab or 20 mL of Suspension q 12 h po for 5 days.
SEPTRA DS		Tab: sulfamethoxazole (800 mg), trimethoprim (160 mg)	
SEPTRA I.V. INFUSION	Antibacterial	Inj (per 5 mL): sulfamethoxazole (400 mg), trimethoprim (80 mg).	**Severe Urinary Tract Infections and Shigellosis:** 8 - 10 mg/kg daily (based on trimethoprim) in 2 - 4 equally divided doses q 6, 8 or 12 h by IV infusion for up to 14 days for UTI and 5 days for shigellosis. *P. carinii* **Pneumonia:** 15 - 20 mg/kg daily (based on trimethoprim) in 3 - 4 equally divided doses q 6 - 8 h by IV infusion for up to 14 days.
SER-AP-ES	Antihypertensive	Tab: reserpine (0.1 mg), hydralazine HCl (25 mg), hydrochlorothiazide (15 mg)	1 -2 tab tid po.

TRADE NAME	THERAPEUTIC CATEGORY	DOSAGE FORMS AND COMPOSITION	COMMON ADULT DOSAGE
SINEMET 10-100	Antiparkinsonian	**Tab:** carbidopa (10 mg), levodopa (100 mg)	**Initial:** 1 tab tid - qid po. The dosage may be increased by 1 tab every day or every other day until 8 tab/day (2 tab qid) is reached. **Maintenance:** At least 70 - 100 mg of carbidopa/day should be provided.
SINEMET 25-100	Antiparkinsonian	**Tab:** carbidopa (25 mg), levodopa (100 mg)	**Initial:** 1 tab tid po. The dosage may be increased by 1 tab every day or every other day until 8 tab/day (2 tab qid) is reached. **Maintenance:** At least 70 - 100 mg of carbidopa/day should be provided. When a greater proportion of carbidopa is required, 1 SINEMET 25-100 tab may be substituted for each tab of SINEMET 10-100.
SINEMET 25-250	Antiparkinsonian	**Tab:** carbidopa (25 mg), levodopa (250 mg)	**Maintenance Only:** At least 70 - 100 mg of carbidopa/day should be provided. When a large proportion of carbidopa is required, SINEMET 25-250 may be substituted for either of the above two products.
SINE-OFF MAXIMUM STRENGTH ALLERGY/SINUS	Decongestant-Antihistamine-Analgesic	**Cplt:** pseudoephedrine HCl (30 mg), chlorpheniramine maleate (2 mg), acetaminophen (500 mg)	2 cplt q 6 h po.
SINE-OFF MAXIMUM STRENGTH NO DROWSINESS FORMULA	Decongestant-Analgesic	**Cplt:** pseudoephedrine HCl (30 mg), acetaminophen (500 mg)	2 cplt q 6 h po.

Product	Category	Composition	Dosage
SINE-OFF SINUS MEDICINE	Decongestant-Antihistamine-Analgesic	**Tab:** phenylpropanolamine HCl (12.5 mg), chlorpheniramine maleate (2 mg), aspirin (325 mg)	2 tab q 4 h po, up to 8 tab per day
SINUTAB SINUS ALLERGY MEDICATION, MAXIMUM STRENGTH	Decongestant-Antihistamine-Analgesic	**Cplt & Tab:** pseudoephedrine HCl (30 mg), chlorpheniramine maleate (2 mg), acetaminophen (500 mg)	2 tab (or cplt) q 6 h po.
SINUTAB SINUS MEDICAT.., MAXIMUM STRENGTH WITHOUT DROWSINESS	Decongestant-Analgesic	**Cplt:** pseudoephedrine HCl (30 mg), acetaminophen (500 mg)	2 cplt q 6 h po.
SINUTAB SINUS MEDICAT.., REGULAR STRENGTH WITHOUT DROWSINESS	Decongestant-Analgesic	**Tab:** pseudoephedrine HCl (30 mg), acetaminophen (325 mg)	2 tab q 4 h po.
SLO-PHYLLIN GG	Antiasthmatic	**Syrup (per 15 mL):** theophylline anhydrous (150 mg), guaifenesin (90 mg) **Cpsl:** theophylline anhydrous (150 mg), guaifenesin (90 mg)	Dose based on theophylline; see Oral Theophylline Doses Table, p. 216. Initially 16 mg/kg/day po, up to 400 mg/day in 3 - 4 divided doses q 6 - 8 h. At 3 day intervals, increase if needed in 25% increments as tolerated.
SOMA COMPOUND	Skeletal Muscle Relaxant-Analgesic	**Tab:** carisoprodol (200 mg), aspirin (325 mg)	1 - 2 tab qid po.
SOMA COMPOUND W/ CODEINE (C-III)	Skeletal Muscle Relaxant-Analgesic	**Tab:** carisoprodol (200 mg), aspirin (325 mg), codeine phosphate (16 mg)	1 - 2 tab qid po.
SUDAFED COUGH SYRUP	Antitussive-Decongestant-Expectorant	**Syrup (per 5 mL):** dextromethorphan HBr (5 mg), pseudoephedrine HCl (15 mg), guaifenesin (100 mg), alcohol (2.4%)	20 mL q 4 h po, up to 80 mL per day.
SUDAFED PLUS	Decongestant-Antihistamine	**Liquid (per 5 mL):** pseudoephedrine HCl (30 mg), chlorpheniramine maleate (2 mg) **Tab:** pseudoephedrine HCl (60 mg), chlorpheniramine maleate (4 mg)	10 mL q 4 - 6 h po, up to 40 mL per day. 1 tab q 4 - 6 h po, up to 4 tab per day.

TRADE NAME	THERAPEUTIC CATEGORY	DOSAGE FORMS AND COMPOSITION	COMMON ADULT DOSAGE
SUDAFED SINUS	Decongestant-Analgesic	**Cplt & Tab:** pseudoephedrine HCl (30 mg), acetaminophen (500 mg)	2 cplt (or tab) q 6 h po.
SULFACET-R	Anti-Acne Agent	**Lotion:** sulfacetamide sodium (10%), sulfur (5%)	Apply a thin film to affected areas 1 to 3 times daily.
SULTRIN	Antibacterial	**Vaginal Tab:** sulfathiazole (172.5 mg), sulfacetamide (143.75 mg), sulfabenzamide (184 mg) with urea **Vaginal Cream:** sulfathiazole (3.42%), sulfacetamide (2.86%), sulfabenzamide (3.7%), urea (0.64%)	1 tab intravaginally hs and in the morning for 10 days. 1 applicatorful intravaginally bid for 4 - 6 days.
SYNALGOS-DC (C-III)	Analgesic	**Cpsl:** dihydrocodeine bitartrate (16 mg), aspirin (356.4 mg), caffeine (30 mg)	2 cpsl q 4 h po, prn pain.
TALACEN (C-IV)	Analgesic	**Tab:** pentazocine HCl (equal to 25 mg pentazocine base), acetaminophen (650 mg)	1 tab q 4 h po, prn pain.
TALWIN COMPOUND (C-IV)	Analgesic	**Cplt:** pentazocine HCl (equal to 12.5 mg pentazocine base), aspirin (325 mg)	2 cplt tid or qid po, prn pain.
TALWIN NX	Analgesic	**Tab:** pentazocine HCl (equal to 50 mg pentazocine base), naloxone HCl (0.5 mg)	1 tab q 3 - 4 h po.
TAVIST-D	Decongestant-Antihistamine	**Tab:** phenylpropanolamine HCl (75 mg), clemastine fumarate (1.34 mg)	1 tab q 12 h po.
TENORETIC 50 TENORETIC 100	Antihypertensive	**Tab:** atenolol (50 mg), chlorthalidone (25 mg) **Tab:** atenolol (100 mg), chlorthalidone(25 mg)	1 tab daily po. 1 tab daily po.
TERRA-CORTRIL	Antibacterial-Corticosteroid	**Ophth Suspension (per mL):** oxytetracycline (5 mg), hydrocortisone acetate (15 mg)	1 or 2 drops into the affected eye(s) tid.
THEO-ORGANIDIN	Antiasthmatic	**Elixir (per 15 mL):** theophylline (120 mg), iodinated glycerol (30 mg), alcohol (15%)	**Acute Attack:** 45 mL po. **Maintenance:** 15 - 30 mL tid (q 6 - 8 h) po.

202

THYROLAR 1/4	Thyroid Hormone	**Tab:** levothyroxine sodium (12.5 μg), liothyronine sodium (3.1 μg)	**Initial:** Usually 50 μg of levo-thyroxine po or its isocaloric equivalent (THYROLAR 1/2), with increments of 25 μg q 2 to 3 weeks.
THYROLAR 1/2		**Tab:** levothyroxine sodium (25 μg), liothyronine sodium (6.25 μg)	**Initial:** Usually 50 μg of levo-thyroxine po or its isocaloric equivalent (THYROLAR 1/2), with increments of 25 μg q 2 to 3 weeks.
THYROLAR 1		**Tab:** levothyroxine sodium (50 μg), liothyronine sodium (12.5 μg)	**Maintenance:** Usually 100 - 200 μg/day po (THYROLAR 1 or THYROLAR 2).
THYROLAR 2		**Tab:** levothyroxine sodium (100 μg), liothyronine sodium (25 μg)	
THYROLAR 3		**Tab:** levothyroxine sodium (150 μg), liothyronine sodium (37.5 μg)	
TIMENTIN	Antibacterial	**Powd for Inj:** 3.1 g (3 g ticarcillin, 0.1 g clavulanic acid) **Powd for Inj:** 3.2 g (3 g ticarcillin, 0.2 g clavulanic acid)	**Systemic and Urinary Tract Infections:** 3.1 g (combo) q 4 to 6 h by IV infusion. **Gynecologic Infections:** **Moderate:** 200 mg/kg/day in divided doses q 6 h by IV infusion. **Severe:** 300 mg/kg/day in divided doses q 4 h by IV infusion. **Urinary Tract Infections:** 3.2 g (combo) q 8 h by IV infusion.
TIMOLIDE 10-25	Antihypertensive	**Tab:** timolol maleate (10 mg), hydrochlorothiazide (25 mg)	1 tab bid po or 2 tab once daily.
TOBRADEX	Antibacterial-Corticosteroid	**Ophth Suspension:** tobramycin (0.3%), dexamethasone (0.1%) **Ophth Oint:** tobramycin (0.3%), dexamethasone (0.1%)	1 or 2 drops into affected eye(s) q 4 - 6 h. During the initial 24 to 48 h, the dosage may be increased to 1 or 2 drops q 2 h. Apply a small amount (1/2 in.) to the conjunctival sac tid or qid.
TRIAMINIC-12	Decongestant-Antihistamine	**Sustained-Rel Tab:** phenylpropanolamine HCl (75 mg), chlorpheniramine maleate (12 mg)	1 tab q 12 h po.
TRIAMINIC ALLERGY	Decongestant-Antihistamine	**Tab:** phenylpropanolamine HCl (25 mg), chlorpheniramine maleate (4 mg)	1 tab q 4 h po.

TRADE NAME	THERAPEUTIC CATEGORY	DOSAGE FORMS AND COMPOSITION	COMMON ADULT DOSAGE
TRIAMINIC COLD TABLETS	Decongestant-Antihistamine	**Tab:** phenylpropanolamine HCl (12.5 mg), chlorpheniramine maleate (2 mg)	2 tab q 4 h po.
TRIAMINIC-DM	Decongestant-Antitussive	**Syrup (per 5 mL):** phenylpropanolamine HCl (6.25 mg), dextromethorphan HBr (5 mg)	20 mL q 4 h po.
TRIAMINIC EXPECTORANT	Decongestant-Expectorant	**Liquid (per 5 mL):** phenylpropanolamine HCl (6.25 mg), guaifenesin (50 mg)	20 mL q 4 h po.
TRIAMINIC EXPECTORANT DH (C-III)	Decongestant-Expectorant-Antitussive-Antihistamine	**Liquid (per 5 mL):** phenylpropanolamine HCl (12.5 mg), guaifenesin (100 mg), hydrocodone bitartrate (1.67 mg), pyrilamine maleate (6.25 mg), pheniramine maleate (6.25 mg), alcohol (5%)	10 mL q 4 h po.
TRIAMINIC EXPECTORANT W/CODEINE (C-V)	Decongestant-Expectorant-Antitussive	**Liquid (per 5 mL):** phenylpropanolamine HCl (12.5 mg), guaifenesin (100 mg), codeine phosphate (10 mg), alcohol (5%)	10 mL q 4 h po.
TRIAMINIC NITE LIGHT	Decongestant-Antihistamine-Antitussive	**Liquid (per 5 mL):** pseudoephedrine HCl (15 mg), chlorpheniramine maleate (1 mg), dextromethorphan HBr (7.5 mg)	20 mL q 6 h po.
TRIAMINIC SORE THROAT FORMULA	Decongestant-Antitussive-Analgesic	**Liquid (per 5 mL):** pseudoephedrine HCl (15 mg), dextromethorphan HBr (7.5 mg), acetaminophen (160 mg)	20 mL q 6 h po.
TRIAMINIC SYRUP	Decongestant-Antihistamine	**Syrup (per 5 mL):** phenylpropanolamine HCl (6.25 mg), chlorpheniramine maleate (1 mg)	20 mL q 4 h po.
TRIAMINICIN	Decongestant-Antihistamine-Analgesic	**Tab:** phenylpropanolamine HCl (25 mg), chlorpheniramine maleate (4 mg), acetaminophen (650 mg)	1 tab q 4 h po.
TRIAMINICOL MULTI-SYMPTOM COLD TABLETS	Decongestant-Antihistamine-Expectorant	**Tab:** phenylpropanolamine HCl (12.5 mg), chlorpheniramine maleate (2 mg), dextromethorphan HBr (10 mg)	2 tab q 4 h po.
TRIAMINICOL MULTI-SYMPTOM RELIEF	Decongestant-Antihistamine-Expectorant	**Syrup (per 5 mL):** phenylpropanolamine HCl (6.25 mg), chlorpheniramine maleate (1 mg), dextromethorphan HBr (5 mg)	20 mL q 4 h po.

TRIAVIL 2-10 TRIAVIL 2-25 TRIAVIL 4-10 TRIAVIL 4-25 TRIAVIL 4-50	Antipsychotic-Antidepressant	Tab: perphenazine (2 mg), amitriptyline HCl (10 mg) Tab: perphenazine (2 mg), amitriptyline HCl (25 mg) Tab: perphenazine (4 mg), amitriptyline HCl (10 mg) Tab: perphenazine (4 mg), amitriptyline HCl (25 mg) Tab: perphenazine (4 mg), amitriptyline HCl (50 mg)	**Psychoneuroses:** 1 tab TRIAVIL 2-25 or TRIAVIL 4-25 tid - qid po or 1 tab of TRIAVIL 4-50 bid po. **Schizophrenia:** 2 tab of TRIAVIL 4-25 tid po and, if needed, hs.
TRIDESILON OTIC	Antibacterial-, Antifungal-Corticosteroid	Otic Solution: acetic acid (2%), desonide (0.05%)	3 - 4 drops into the affected ear(s) tid - qid.
TRI-LEVLEN	Oral Contraceptive	Tab: 6 tabs: ethinyl estradiol (30 μg), levonorgestrel (0.05 mg); 5 tabs: ethinyl estradiol (40 μg), levonorgestrel (0.075 mg); 10 tabs: ethinyl estradiol (30 μg), levonorgestrel (0.125 mg) in 21-Day Compacts and with 7 inert tabs in 28-Day Compacts	21-Day regimen po or 28-Day regimen po.
TRILISATE	Non-Opioid Analgesic, Antipyretic, Antiinflammatory	Tab: choline magnesium salicylate (500 mg as: choline salicylate (293 mg) and magnesium salicylate (362 mg)) Tab: choline magnesium salicylate (750 mg as: choline salicylate (440 mg) and magnesium salicylate (544 mg)) Tab: choline magnesium salicylate (1000 mg as: choline salicylate (587 mg) and magnesium salicylate (725 mg)) Liquid (per 5 mL): choline magnesium salicylate (500 mg as: choline salicylate (293 mg) and magnesium salicylate (362 mg))	**Pain & Fever:** 1000 - 1500 mg bid po. **Inflammation:** 1500 mg bid po or 3000 mg once daily hs po.
TRINALIN REPETABS	Decongestant-Antihistamine	Long-Acting Tab: pseudoephedrine sulfate (120 mg), azatadine maleate (1 mg)	1 tab bid po.
TRIND	Decongestant-Antihistamine	Liquid (per 5 mL): phenylpropanolamine HCl (12.5 mg), chlorpheniramine maleate (2 mg), alcohol (5%)	10 mL q 4 h po.
TRI-NORINYL	Oral Contraceptive	Tab: 7 tabs: ethinyl estradiol (35 μg), norethindrone (0.5 mg); 9 tabs: ethinyl estradiol (35 μg), norethindrone (1 mg); 5 tabs: ethinyl estradiol (35 μg), norethindrone (0.5 mg) in 21-Day Wallettes and with 7 inert tabs in 29-Day Wallettes	21-Day regimen po or 28-Day regimen po.

TRADE NAME	THERAPEUTIC CATEGORY	DOSAGE FORMS AND COMPOSITION	COMMON ADULT DOSAGE
TRIPHASIL	Oral Contraceptive	**Tab:** 6 tabs: ethinyl estradiol (30 μg), levonorgestrel (0.05 mg); 5 tabs: ethinyl estradiol (40 μg), levonorgestrel (0.075 mg); 10 tabs: ethinyl estradiol (30 μg), levonorgestrel (0.125 mg) in 21-Day Pilpaks and with 7 inert tabs in 28-Day Pilpaks	21-Day regimen po or 28-Day regimen po.
TUINAL 100 MG (C-II)	Hypnotic	**Cpsl:** amobarbital sodium (50 mg), secobarbital sodium (50 mg)	1 cpsl po hs.
TUINAL 200 MG (C-II)		**Cpsl:** amobarbital sodium (100 mg), secobarbital sodium (100 mg)	1 cpsl po hs.
TUSSAR-2 (C-V)	Decongestant-Expectorant-Antitussive	**Liquid (per 5 mL):** pseudoephedrine HCl (30 mg), guaifenesin (100 mg), codeine phosphate (10 mg), alcohol (2.5%)	10 mL q 4 h po. Maximum: 40 mL/day.
TUSSAR DM	Decongestant-Antihistamine-Antitussive	**Liquid (per 5 mL):** pseudoephedrine HCl (30 mg), chlorpheniramine maleate (2 mg), dextromethorphan HBr (15 mg)	10 mL q 6 h po.
TUSSAR SF (C-V)	Decongestant-Expectorant-Antitussive	**Liquid (per 5 mL):** pseudoephedrine HCl (30 mg), guaifenesin (100 mg), codeine phosphate (10 mg), alcohol (2.5%)	10 mL q 4 h po. Maximum: 40 mL/day.
TUSSIONEX (C-III)	Antihistamine-Antitussive	**Extended-Release Susp (per 5 mL):** chlorpheniramine polistirex (8 mg), hydrocodone polistirex (10 mg)	5 mL q 12 h po.
TUSSI-ORGANIDIN NR (C-V)	Antitussive-Expectorant	**Liquid (per 5 mL):** codeine phosphate (10 mg), guaifenesin (100 mg)	10 mL q 4 h po.
TUSSI-ORGANIDIN DM NR	Antitussive-Expectorant	**Liquid (per 5 mL):** dextromethorphan HBr (10 mg), guaifenesin (100 mg)	10 mL q 4 h po.
TUSS-ORNADE	Decongestant-Antitussive	**Liquid (per 5 mL):** phenylpropanolamine HCl (12.5 mg), caramiphen edisylate (6.7 mg), alcohol (5%)	10 mL q 4 h po.
		Cpsl: phenylpropanolamine HCl (75 mg), caramiphen edisylate (40 mg)	1 cpsl q 12 h po.
TYLENOL W/CODEINE (C-V)	Analgesic	**Elixir (per 5 mL):** acetaminophen (120 mg), codeine phosphate (12 mg), alcohol (7%)	15 mL q 4 h po, prn pain.

TYLENOL W/CODEINE #2 (C-III) #3 (C-III) #4 (C-III)	Analgesic	Tab: acetaminophen (300 mg), codeine phosphate (15 mg). Tab: acetaminophen (300 mg), codeine phosphate (30 mg). Tab: acetaminophen (300 mg), codeine phosphate (60 mg).	2 - 3 tab q 4 h po, prn pain. 1 - 2 tab q 4 h po, prn pain. 1 tab q 4 h po, prn pain.
TYLOX (C-II)	Analgesic	Cpsl: oxycodone HCl (5 mg), acetaminophen (500 mg).	1 cpsl q 6 h po, prn pain.
UNASYN	Antibacterial	Powd for Inj: 1.5 g (1 g ampicillin sodium, 0.5 g sulbactam sodium) Powd for Inj: 3.0 g (2 g ampicillin sodium, 1 g sulbactam sodium)	1.5 - 3.0 g q 6 h by deep IM inj, by slow IV injection (over at least 10 - 15 min), or by IV infusion (diluted with 50 - 100 mL of a compatible diluent and given over 15 - 30 mins).
UNISOM WITH PAIN RELIEF	Analgesic-Sedative	Tab: acetaminophen (650 mg), diphenhydramine HCl (50 mg)	1 tab po, 30 minutes before retiring.
URISED	Urinary Analgesic	Tab: methenamine (40.8 mg), phenyl salicylate (18.1 mg), methylene blue (5.4 mg), benzoic acid (4.5 mg), atropine sulfate (0.03 mg), hyoscyamine (0.03 mg)	2 tab qid po.
UROBIOTIC-250	Urinary Anti-Infective-Analgesic	Cpsl: oxytetracycline HCl (equal to 250 mg of oxytetracycline base), sulfamethizole (250 mg), phenazopyridine HCl (50 mg)	1 cpsl qid po. In refractory cases, 2 cpsl qid po.
VANOXIDE-HC	Anti-Acne Agent	Lotion (per g): benzoyl peroxide (50 mg), hydrocortisone acetate (5 mg)	Gently massage a thin film into affected skin areas 1 to 3 times daily.
VASERETIC 10-25	Antihypertensive	Tab: enalapril maleate (10 mg), hydrochlorothiazide (25 mg)	1 - 2 tab once daily po.
VASOCIDIN	Antibacterial-Corticosteroid	Ophth Solution: sulfacetamide sodium (10%), prednisolone acetate (0.25%) Ophth Oint: sulfacetamide sodium (10%), prednisolone acetate (0.5%)	2 drops into affected eye(s) q 4 h. Prolong dosing interval as the condition improves. Apply to affected eye(s) tid or qid during the day and 1 - 2 times at night.

TRADE NAME	THERAPEUTIC CATEGORY	DOSAGE FORMS AND COMPOSITION	COMMON ADULT DOSAGE
VICODIN (C-III) VICODIN ES (C-III)	Analgesic	**Tab:** hydrocodone bitartrate (5 mg), acetaminophen (500 mg) **Tab:** hydrocodone bitartrate (7.5 mg), acetaminophen (750 mg)	1 - 2 tab q 4 - 6 h po, prn pain. 1 tab q 4 - 6 h po, prn pain.
VIOFORM-HYDROCORTISONE	Antifungal-Corticosteroid	**Cream & Oint:** clioquinol (3%), hydrocortisone (1%)	Apply a thin layer to affected areas tid - qid.
VIOFORM-HYDROCORTISONE MILD		**Cream:** clioquinol (3%), hydrocortisone (0.5%)	Apply a thin layer to affected areas tid - qid.
VOSOL HC	Antibacterial-Corticosteroid	**Otic Solution:** acetic acid (2%), hydrocortisone (1%)	Carefully remove all cerumen & debris. Insert a wick saturated with the solution into the ear canal. Keep in for at least 24 h and keep moist by adding 3 to 5 drops of solution q 4 - 6 h.
WIGRAINE	Antimigraine Agent	**Rectal Suppos:** ergotamine tartrate (2 mg), caffeine (100 mg) **Tab:** ergotamine tartrate (1 mg), caffeine (100 mg)	Insert 1 rectally at the first sign of a migraine attack. Maximum: 2 suppositories for an individual attack. 2 tab po at the first sign of a migraine attack; followed by 1 tab q 30 minutes, prn, up to 6 tabs per attack. Maximum of 10 tabs per week.
WYGESIC (C-IV)	Analgesic	**Tab:** propoxyphene HCl (65 mg), acetaminophen (650 mg)	1 tab q 4 h po, prn pain.
ZESTORETIC 10-12.5 ZESTORETIC 20-12.5 ZESTORETIC 20-25	Antihypertensive	**Tab:** lisinopril (10 mg), hydrochlorothiazide (12.5 mg) **Tab:** lisinopril (20 mg), hydrochlorothiazide (12.5 mg) **Tab:** lisinopril (20 mg), hydrochlorothiazide (25 mg)	1 - 2 tab once daily po. 1 - 2 tab once daily po. 1 - 2 tab once daily po.
ZIAC	Antihypertensive	**Tab:** bisoprolol fumarate (2.5 mg), hydrochlorothiazide (6.25 mg) **Tab:** bisoprolol fumarate (5 mg), hydrochlorothiazide (6.25 mg) **Tab:** bisoprolol fumarate (10 mg), hydrochlorothiazide (6.25 mg)	Initially, one 2.5/6.25 mg tab once daily po. Adjust dosage at 14 day intervals. Maximum: two 10/ 6.25 mg tabs once daily po.

ZOSYN   Antibacterial   **Powd for Inj:** 2.25 g (2 g piperacillin, 0.25 g tazobactam)   12 g/1.5 g daily by IV infusion
                                             Powd for Inj: 3.375 g (3 g piperacillin, 0.375 g tazobactam)   (over 30 minutes), given as
                                             Powd for Inj: 4.5 g (4 g piperacillin, 0.5 g tazobactam)   3.375 g q 6 h.

ZYDONE (C-III)   Analgesic   **Cpsl:** hydrocodone bitartrate (5 mg), acetaminophen (500 mg)   1 - 2 cpsl q 4 - 6 h po, prn pain.

C-II: Controlled Substance, Schedule II
C-III: Controlled Substance, Schedule III
C-IV: Controlled Substance, Schedule IV
C-V: Controlled Substance, Schedule V

Notes

SPECIAL

DOSAGE

TABLES

DIGOXIN DOSES

I. RAPID DIGITALIZATION WITH A LOADING DOSE -

In most patients with heart failure and normal sinus rhythm, a therapeutic effect with minimum risk of toxicity should occur with peak body digoxin stores of 8 to 12 µg/kg. For adequate control of ventricular rate in patients with atrial flutter or fibrillation, larger digoxin body stores (10 to 15 µg/kg) are often required. In patients with renal insufficiency, the projected peak body stores of digoxin should be conservative (6 to 10 µg/kg) due to altered distribution and elimination.

The loading dose should be based on the projected peak body stores and administered in several portions; approximately half the total is usually given as the first dose.

FOR ORAL DOSING -

Preparation	In previously undigitalized patients, a single initial oral dose of the following produces a detectable effect in 0.5 to 2 hours that becomes maximal in 2 to 6 hours	The following additional doses may be given cautiously at 6 to 8 hour intervals until clinical evidence of an adequate effect is noted	The usual amount of each preparation that a 70 kg patient requires to achieve 8 to 15 µg/kg peak body stores is
LANOXIN Tablets	0.5 - 0.75 mg po	0.125 - 0.375 mg po	0.75 - 1.25 mg po
LANOXIN ELIXIR PEDIATRIC	0.5 - 0.75 mg po	0.125 - 0.375 mg po	0.75 - 1.25 mg po
LANOXICAPS Capsules	0.4 - 0.6 mg po	0.1 - 0.3 mg po	0.6 - 1.0 mg po

FOR INTRAVENOUS DOSING -

Preparation	In previously undigitalized patients, a single initial intravenous dose of the following produces a detectable effect in 5 to 30 minutes that becomes maximal in 1 to 4 hours	The following additional doses may be given cautiously at 4 to 8 hour intervals until clinical evidence of an adequate effect is noted	The usual amount of LANOXIN Injection that a 70 kg patient requires to achieve 8 to 15 µg/kg peak body stores is
LANOXIN Injection	0.4 - 0.6 mg IV	0.1 - 0.3 mg IV	0.6 - 1.0 mg IV

The maintenance dose should be based upon the percentage of the peak body stores lost each day through elimination. The following formula has wide clinical use:

$$\text{Maintenance Dose} = \text{Peak Body Stores (i.e., Loading Dose)} \times \text{\% Daily Loss}/100$$

where: $\text{\% Daily Loss} = 14 + \text{Creatinine Clearance (corrected to 70 kg body weight or 1.73 m}^2 \text{ surface area)}/5$

A common practice involves the use of LANOXIN Injection to achieve rapid digitalization, with conversion to LANOXIN Tablets, LANOXIN ELIXIR PEDIATRIC, or LANOXICAPS Capsules for maintenance therapy. If patients are switched from an IV to an oral digoxin preparation, allowances must be made for difference in bioavailability when calculating maintenance doses (see Inset Table below).

PRODUCT	ABSOLUTE BIOAVAILABILITY	EQUIVALENT DOSES (IN MG)		
LANOXIN Tablets	60 to 80%	0.125	0.25	0.5
LANOXIN ELIXIR PEDIATRIC	70 to 85%	0.125	0.25	0.5
LANOXIN Injection / IM	70 to 85%	0.125	0.25	0.5
LANOXIN Injection / IV	100%	0.1	0.2	0.4
LANOXICAPS Capsules	90 to 100%	0.1	0.2	0.4

213

II. GRADUAL DIGITALIZATION WITH A MAINTENANCE DOSE -

The following Table provides average **LANOXIN Tablet** daily maintenance dose requirements for patients with heart failure based upon lean body weight and renal function:

USUAL LANOXIN DAILY MAINTENANCE DOSE REQUIREMENTS (in mg) FOR ESTIMATED PEAK BODY STORES OF 10 μg/kg							
	Lean Body Weight (kg / lbs)						
	50 / 110	60 / 132	70 / 154	80 / 176	90 / 198	100 / 220	Number of Days Before Steady-State is Achieved
Corrected Creatinine Clearance (mL/min per 70 kg) 0	0.063	0.125	0.125	0.125	0.188	0.188	22
10	0.125	0.125	0.125	0.188	0.188	0.188	19
20	0.125	0.125	0.188	0.188	0.188	0.250	16
30	0.125	0.188	0.188	0.188	0.250	0.250	14
40	0.125	0.188	0.188	0.250	0.250	0.250	13
50	0.188	0.188	0.250	0.250	0.250	0.250	12
60	0.188	0.188	0.250	0.250	0.250	0.250	11
70	0.188	0.250	0.250	0.250	0.250	0.375	10
80	0.188	0.250	0.250	0.250	0.375	0.375	9
90	0.188	0.250	0.250	0.250	0.375	0.500	8
100	0.250	0.250	0.250	0.375	0.375	0.500	7

214

The following Table provides average **LANOXICAP Capsule** daily maintenance dose requirements for patients with heart failure based upon lean body weight and renal function:

USUAL LANOXICAP DAILY MAINTENANCE DOSE REQUIREMENTS (in mg) FOR ESTIMATED PEAK BODY STORES OF 10 μg/kg

Corrected Creatinine Clearance (mL/min per 70 kg)	Lean Body Weight (kg / lbs)							
	50 / 110	60 / 132	70 / 154	80 / 176	90 / 198	100 / 220		Number of Days Before Steady-State is Achieved
0	0.050	0.100	0.100	0.100	0.150	0.150	22	
10	0.100	0.100	0.100	0.150	0.150	0.150	19	
20	0.100	0.100	0.150	0.150	0.150	0.200	16	
30	0.100	0.150	0.150	0.150	0.200	0.200	14	
40	0.100	0.150	0.150	0.200	0.200	0.250	13	
50	0.150	0.150	0.200	0.200	0.250	0.250	12	
60	0.150	0.150	0.200	0.200	0.250	0.300	11	
70	0.150	0.200	0.200	0.250	0.250	0.300	10	
80	0.150	0.200	0.200	0.250	0.300	0.300	9	
90	0.150	0.200	0.250	0.250	0.300	0.350	8	
100	0.200	0.200	0.250	0.300	0.300	0.350	7	

ORAL THEOPHYLLINE DOSES

I. **IMMEDIATE-RELEASE PREPARATIONS (e.g., ELIXOPHYLLIN Elixir and Capsules, ELIXOPHYLLIN-GG Liquid, ELIXOPHYLLIN-KI Elixir, QUIBRON and QUIBRON-300 Capsules, SLO-PHYLLIN Syrup and Tablets, SLO-PHYLLIN GG Capsules and Syrup, and THEOLAIR Liquid and Tablets) -**

Acute Symptoms of Bronchospasm Requiring Rapid Attainment of Theophylline Serum Levels for Bronchodilation -

Otherwise healthy nonsmoking adults: 5 mg/kg po (oral loading dose); then, 3 mg/kg q 8 h po (maintenance doses).

Older patients and those with cor pulmonale: 5 mg/kg po (oral loading dose); then, 2 mg/kg q 8 h po (maintenance doses).

Patients with congestive heart failure: 5 mg/kg po (oral loading dose); then, 1 - 2 mg/kg q 12 h po (maintenance doses).

Chronic Therapy -

Initial Dose: 16 mg/kg/24 h or 400 mg/24 h (whichever is less) in divided doses q 6 - 8 h po.

Increasing Dose: The initial dosage may be increased in approximately 25% increments at 3 day intervals, as long as the drug is tolerated, until the clinical response is satisfactory, or the maximum dose is reached.

Maximum Dose: 13 mg/kg/day po or 900 mg/day, whichever is less

CHECK SERUM CONCENTRATION BETWEEN 1 AND 2 HOURS AFTER A DOSE WHEN NONE HAVE BEEN MISSED OR ADDED FOR AT LEAST 3 DAYS. If serum theophylline concentration is between 10 and 20 μg/mL, maintain dose, if tolerated. RECHECK THEOPHYLLINE CONCENTRATION AT 6- TO 12-MONTH INTERVALS.

216

II. SUSTAINED-RELEASE PREPARATIONS -

A. RESPBID Sustained-Release Tablets, SLO-BID Extended-Release Capsules, SLO-PHYLLIN Extended-Release Capsules, THEO-DUR SPRINKLE Sustained-Action Capsules, THEOLAIR-SR Sustained-Release Tablets and T-PHYL Controlled-Release Tablets -

Initial Therapy: 16 mg/kg/24 h or 400 mg/24 h (whichever is less) in 2 or 3 divided doses at 8 or 12 h intervals po.

Maintenance Therapy: The initial dosage may be increased in approximately 25% increments at 3-day intervals, as long as the drug is tolerated, until the clinical response is satisfactory, or the maximum dose is reached.

Maximum Dose: 13 mg/kg/day po or 900 mg/day, whichever is less

CHECK SERUM CONCENTRATION BETWEEN 5 AND 10 HOURS AFTER A DOSE WHEN NONE HAVE BEEN MISSED OR ADDED FOR AT LEAST 3 DAYS. If serum theophylline concentration is between 10 and 20 μg/mL, maintain dose, if tolerated. RECHECK THEOPHYLLINE CONCENTRATION AT 6- TO 12-MONTH INTERVALS.

B. THEO-DUR Extended-Release Tablets -

Initial Therapy: 200 mg q 12 h po

Maintenance Therapy: The dose may be increased in approximately 25% increments at 3 day intervals, as long as the drug is tolerated, until the clinical response is satisfactory, or the maximum dose is reached.

Maximum Doses: 35 - 70 kg: 300 mg q 12 h po.   Over 70 kg: 450 mg q 12 h po.

CHECK SERUM CONCENTRATION AT APPROXIMATELY 8 HOURS AFTER A DOSE WHEN NONE HAVE BEEN MISSED OR ADDED FOR AT LEAST 3 DAYS. If serum theophylline concentration is between 10 and 20 μg/mL, maintain dose, if tolerated. RECHECK THEOPHYLLINE CONCENTRATION AT 6- TO 12-MONTH INTERVALS.

C. **THEO-24 Extended-Release Capsules** -

Initial Therapy: 200 mg q 12 h po

Maintenance Therapy: If serum levels cannot be measured and the response is unsatisfactory, after 3 days the dose may be increased by
100 mg increments. Reevaluated after 3 days.

Maximum Dose: 13 mg/kg/day po   or 900 mg/day, whichever is less

CHECK PEAK SERUM CONCENTRATION (12 HOURS AFTER THE MORNING DOSE) AND TROUGH LEVEL (24 HOURS AFTER THE MORNING DOSE)
WHEN NO DOSES HAVE BEEN MISSED OR ADDED FOR AT LEAST 3 DAYS. If serum theophylline concentration is between 10 and 20 μg/mL,
maintain dose, if tolerated. RECHECK THEOPHYLLINE CONCENTRATION AT 6- TO 12-MONTH INTERVALS.

ORAL AMINOPHYLLINE DOSES

1.2 mg of aminophylline anhydrous = 1.0 mg of theophylline anhydrous

Acute Symptoms of Bronchospasm Requiring Rapid Attainment of Theophylline Serum Levels for Bronchodilation -

Otherwise healthy nonsmoking adults: 5.8 mg/kg po (oral loading dose); then, 3.5 mg/kg q 8 h po (maintenance doses).

Older patients and those with cor pulmonale: 5.8 mg/kg po (oral loading dose); then, 2.3 mg/kg q 8 h po (maintenance doses).

Patients with congestive heart failure: 5.8 mg/kg po (oral loading dose); then, 1.2 - 2.3 mg/kg q 12 h po (maintenance doses).

Chronic Therapy (Slow Clinical Titration is Generally Preferred) -

Initial Dose: 19 mg/kg/24 h or 480 mg/24 h (whichever is less) in divided doses q 6 - 8 h po.

Increasing Dose: The doses may be increased in approximately 25% increments at 3 day intervals, as long as the drug is tolerated, until the clinical response is satisfactory, or the maximum dose is reached.

Maximum Doses: 15.2 mg/kg/day po   or 1000 mg/day, whichever is less

IV AMINOPHYLLINE DOSES[a]

PATIENT GROUP	IV LOADING DOSE:[b]	DOSE FOR NEXT 12 HOURS:	DOSE BEYOND 12 HOURS:	MAXIMUM DAILY DOSE:
Otherwise Healthy Nonsmoking Adults	6 mg/kg (5 mg/kg)	0.7 mg/kg/hr (0.58 mg/kg/hr)	0.5 mg/kg/hr (0.42 mg/kg/hr)	Variable; monitor blood levels and maintain below 20 μg/mL
Older Patients and Those with Cor Pulmonale	6 mg/kg (5 mg/kg)	0.6 mg/kg/hr (0.5 mg/kg/hr)	0.3 mg/kg/hr (0.25 mg/kg/hr)	Variable; monitor blood levels and maintain below 20 μg/mL
Patients with CHF or Liver Disease	6 mg/kg (5 mg/kg)	0.5 mg/kg/hr (0.42 mg/kg/hr)	0.1 - 0.2 mg/kg/hr (0.08 - 0.16 mg/kg/hr)	Variable; monitor blood levels and maintain below 20 μg/mL

[a] Anhydrous theophylline equivalent in parentheses

[b] Administer slowly, no faster than 25 mg/minute

MISCELLANEOUS

TABLES

COMPARISON OF VARIOUS TYPES OF INSULIN

GENERIC NAME	TRADE NAME	SOURCE OF INSULIN (SPECIES)	ONSET OF ACTION (HOURS)	PEAK ACTIVITY (HOURS)	DURATION OF ACTION (HOURS)	HOW SUPPLIED
Insulin Injection (Regular)			0.5 - 1	2.5 - 5	6 - 8	
	REGULAR ILETIN I	Beef and Pork				Inj: 100 units/mL
	REGULAR INSULIN	Pork				Inj: 100 units/mL
	PORK REGULAR ILETIN II	Purified Pork				Inj: 100 units/mL
	REGULAR PURIFIED PORK INSULIN INJECTION	Purified Pork				Inj: 100 units/mL
	HUMULIN R	Human[a]				Inj: 100 units/mL
	NOVOLIN R	Human[b]				Inj: 100 units/mL
	VELOSULIN HUMAN	Human[b]				Inj: 100 units/mL
	NOVOLIN R PENFILL	Human[b]				Inj: 100 units/mL

222

Isophane Insulin Suspension (NPH)		1 - 2	8 - 10	18 - 26	
	NPH ILETIN I	Beef and Pork			Inj: 100 units/mL
	NPH INSULIN	Beef			Inj: 100 units/mL
	NPH-N	Purified Pork			Inj: 100 units/mL
	PORK NPH ILETIN II	Purified Pork			Inj: 100 units/mL
	HUMULIN N	Human[a]			Inj: 100 units/mL
	NOVOLIN N	Human[b]			Inj: 100 units/mL
	NOVOLIN N PENFILL	Human[b]			Inj: 100 units/mL
Insulin Zinc Suspension (Lente)		2	8 - 10	18 - 26	
	LENTE ILETIN I	Beef and Pork			Inj: 100 units/mL
	LENTE INSULIN	Beef			Inj: 100 units/mL
	LENTE ILETIN II	Purified Pork			Inj: 100 units/mL
	LENTE L	Purified Pork			Inj: 100 units/mL
	HUMULIN L	Human[b]			Inj: 100 units/mL
	NOVOLIN L	Human[b]			Inj: 100 units/mL

GENERIC NAME	TRADE NAME	SOURCE OF INSULIN (SPECIES)	ONSET OF ACTION (HOURS)	PEAK ACTIVITY (HOURS)	DURATION OF ACTION (HOURS)	HOW SUPPLIED
Extended Insulin Zinc Suspension (Ultralente)	ULTRALENTE U	Beef	4 - 8	16 - 18	30 - 36	Inj: 100 units/mL
	HUMULIN U ULTRALENTE	Human[a]				Inj: 100 units/mL
70% Isophane Insulin Suspension + 30% Regular Insulin Injection	HUMULIN 70/30	Human[a]	0.5	2 - 12	up to 24	Inj: 100 units/mL
	NOVOLIN 70/30	Human[b]				Inj: 100 units/mL
	NOVOLIN 70/30 PENFILL	Human[b]				Inj: 100 units/mL
50% Isophane Insulin Suspension + 50% Regular Insulin Injection	HUMULIN 50/50	Human[a]	0.5	2 - 5	up to 24	Inj: 100 units/mL

[a] Produced from bacteria using recombinant DNA technology.

[b] Produced semi-synthetically by enzymatic conversion of pork insulin.

224

COMPARISON OF H$_2$-RECEPTOR ANTAGONISTS

	Cimetidine (TAGAMET)	Ranitidine HCl (ZANTAC)	Famotidine (PEPCID)	Nizatidine (AXID)
PHARMACOKINETICS				
Oral Bioavailability (%)	60 - 70	50 - 60	40 - 45	90 - 95
Time to Peak Blood Levels (hours)	0.75 - 1.5	1 - 3	1 - 3	0.5 - 3
Plasma Protein Binding (%)	15 - 25	15	15 - 20	35
Liver Biotransformation (%)	30 - 40	10	30 - 35	15 - 20
Major Route of Elimination	Kidney	Kidney	Kidney	Kidney
Elimination Half-life (hours)	2	2.5 - 3	2.5 - 3.5	1 - 2
PHARMACODYNAMICS				
Antisecretory Activity	800 mg hs po inhibited acid output by 85% for 8 hours	150 mg hs po inhibited acid output by 92% for 13 hours	20 mg hs po inhibited acid output by 86% for 10 hours	300 mg hs po inhibited acid output by 90% for 10 hours
Incidence of Adverse Reactions	Low	Low	Low	Low
Inhibition of Microsomal Enzyme Systems (i.e., P-450)	Can be significant	Minimal effect	Minimal effect	Minimal effect
Antiandrogenic Effects	Weak	No effect	No effect	No effect
Elevation of Prolactin Secretion	Transient (after IV use)	Less than with cimetidine	Minimal effect	No effect

225

COMPARISON OF SELECTED CALCIUM CHANNEL BLOCKERS

	Verapamil (CALAN, ISOPTIN)	Diltiazem (CARDIZEM)	Nifedipine (PROCARDIA)	Nicardipine (CARDENE)	Felodipine (PLENDIL)
PHARMACOKINETICS					
Oral Absorption (%)	90	80 - 90	90	98	98
Absolute Bioavailability (%)	20 - 35	40 - 65	45 - 70	35	20
Oral Onset of Action (minutes)	30	30 - 60	20	20	120 - 300
Time to Peak Plasma Levels (hours)	1 - 2	2 - 3	0.5	0.5 - 2	2.5 - 5
Plasma Protein Binding (%)	80 - 90	70 - 80	83 - 92	95 - 98	97 - 99
Active Metabolite	Yes	Yes	No	No	Yes
Half-life (hours; single dose)	3 - 7	3.5 - 6	2 - 5	2 - 4	11 - 16
PHARMACODYNAMICS					
Depressed SA Automaticity	High	Moderate	Low	Low	Low
Depressed A-V Conduction	Very High	High	Low	Low	Low
Negative Inotropic Effect	High	Moderate	Moderate	Low	Low
Change in Heart Rate	Variable	Slightly Depressed	Increased	Increased	Increased
Coronary Vasodilation	Moderate	High	High	High	High
Peripheral Vasodilation	High	Moderate	Very High	Very High	Very High
THERAPEUTIC USES					
	1. Angina 2. Hypertension 3. Arrhythmias	1. Angina 2. Hypertension 3. Arrhythmias	1. Angina 2. Hypertension	1. Angina 2. Hypertension	1. Hypertension

226

COMPARISON OF SOME PENICILLINS

DRUG	ROUTE(S) OF ADMINISTRATION	ELIMINATION HALF-LIFE (MINUTES)	SODIUM CONTENT OF INJECTABLES (MEQ/GM)	BACTERIAL SPECTRUM OF ACTIVITY
NATURAL PENICILLINS				
Penicillin G Potassium	IM, IV	30 - 45	0.5	Gram + (except penicillinase-producing *Staphylococci*)
Penicillin V Potassium (PEN-VEE K)	PO	30 - 45	-----	Similar to Penicillin G
PENICILLINASE RESISTANT				
Cloxacillin Sodium (TEGOPEN)	PO	25 - 65	-----	Gram + including *Staphylococci*
Dicloxacillin Sodium (DYNAPEN)	PO	50 - 60	-----	Similar to Cloxacillin
Methicillin Sodium (STAPHCILLIN)	IM, IV	30 - 45	3.0	Similar to Cloxacillin
Nafcillin Disodium (UNIPEN)	PO, IM, IV	30 - 55	2.9	Similar to Cloxacillin
Oxacillin Sodium (PROSTAPHLIN)	PO, IM, IV	25 - 30	2.8	Similar to Cloxacillin
AMINOPENICILLINS				
Amoxicillin (AMOXIL, POLYMOX, TRIMOX, WYMOX)	PO	55 - 60	-----	Gram + (except penicillinase-producing *Staphylococci*); most common Gram − (except *Pseudomonas*)
Ampicillin Sodium (OMNIPEN, PRINCIPEN)	PO, IM, IV	50 - 60	3.0	Similar to Amoxicillin
EXTENDED SPECTRUM PENICILLINS				
Carbenicillin Indanyl Disodium (GEOCILLIN)	PO	55 - 60	-----	Gram + (except penicillinase-producing *Staphylococci*); Gram − including *Pseudomonas*
Mezlocillin Sodium (MEZLIN)	IM, IV	55 - 60	1.85	Similar to Carbenicillin, plus *Klebsiella*
Piperacillin Sodium (PIPRACIL)	IM, IV	45 - 75	1.85	Similar to Mezlocillin
Ticarcillin Disodium (TICAR)	IM, IV	60 - 80	4.8 - 5.2	Similar to Carbenicillin

COMPARISON OF SOME CEPHALOSPORINS

DRUG	ROUTE(S) OF ADMINISTRATION	ELIMINATION HALF-LIFE (MINUTES)	SODIUM CONTENT (MEQ/GM)	BACTERIAL SPECTRUM OF ACTIVITY
FIRST GENERATION				
Cephalothin Sodium (KEFLIN NEUTRAL)	IM, IV	25 - 60	2.8	Most Gram + and Gram − (except *Proteus, Serratia* and *Pseudomonas*)
Cefadroxil Monohydrate (DURICEF, ULTRACEF)	PO	70 - 80	-----	Similar to Cephalothin
Cefazolin Sodium (ANCEF)	IM, IV	90 - 130	2.0	Similar to Cephalothin
Cephalexin (KEFLEX)	PO	30 - 70	-----	Similar to Cephalothin
Cephalexin Hydrochloride (KEFTAB)	PO	30 - 70	-----	Similar to Cephalothin
Cephradine (VELOSEF)	PO	45 - 120	6.0	Similar to Cephalothin
Cephapirin Sodium (CEFADYL)	IM, IV	25 - 35	2.4	Similar to Cephalothin
SECOND GENERATION				
Cefaclor (CECLOR)	PO	30 - 45	-----	Similar to Cephalothin; more activity against *Bacteroides*
Cefamandole Nafate (MANDOL)	IM, IV	30 - 60	3.3	Similar to Cefaclor; increased Gram − activity (e.g., *Proteus* and *Enterobacter*)
Cefonocid Sodium (MONOCID)	IM, IV	210 - 300	3.7	Similar to Cephalothin
Cefmetazole Sodium (ZEFAZONE)	IV	70 - 75	2.0	Similar to Cefamandole; more activity against Gram − organisms and *Bacteroides*
Cefpodoxime Proxetil (VANTIN)	PO	120 - 180	-----	Similar to Cefmetazole
Cefotetan Disodium (CEFOTAN)	IM, IV	180 - 270	3.5	Similar to Cefmetazole
Cefoxitin Sodium (MEFOXIN)	IV	40 - 60	2.3	Similar to Cefmetazole
Cefprozil (CEFZIL)	PO	75 - 80	-----	Similar to Cefaclor
Cefuroxime Axetil (CEFTIN)	PO	60 - 110	-----	Similar to Cefoxitin
Cefuroxime Sodium (KEFUROX, ZINACEF)	IM, IV	60 - 110	2.4	Similar to Cefoxitin

THIRD GENERATION

Ceftriaxone Sodium (ROCEPHIN)	IM, IV	350 - 540	3.6	"Broad spectrum" but greater activity than *Cefoxitin* on *Proteus, Serratia, Clostridium* and *Neisseria gonorrheae*
Cefoperazone Sodium (CEFOBID)	IM, IV	100 - 150	1.5	Less activity than *Ceftriaxone* on *Providencia, Serratia, Bacteroides* and *Clostridium*; greater activity on *Pseudomonas*
Cefixime (SUPRAX)	PO	180 - 240	.....	Similar to Cephalothin; less activity on *Staphylococci*
Cefotaxime Sodium (CLAFORAN)	IM, IV	60	2.2	Similar to Ceftriaxone
Ceftazidime (FORTAZ, TAZIDIME)	IM, IV	120	2.3	Similar to Cefoperazone
Ceftazidime Sodium (FORTAZ)	IM, IV	120	2.3	Similar to Cefoperazone
Ceftizoxime Sodium (CEFIZOX)	IM, IV	60 - 120	2.6	Similar to Ceftriaxone

GRAPHICAL COMPARISON OF CEPHALOSPORIN HALF-LIFE

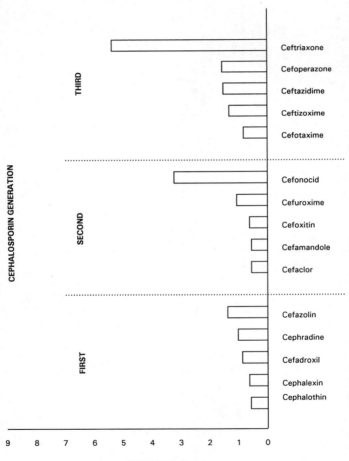

COMPARISON OF SELECTED CORTICOSTEROIDS

DRUG	EQUIVALENT DOSE (mg)[a]	RELATIVE ANTI-INFLAMMATORY POTENCY	RELATIVE MINERALOCORTICOID POTENCY
SHORT DURATION			
Cortisone	25.0	0.8	2.0
Hydrocortisone	20.0	1.0	2.0
INTERMEDIATE DURATION			
Prednisone	5.0	4.0	1.0
Prednisolone	5.0	4.0	1.0
Methylprednisolone	4.0	5.0	0.5
Triamcinolone	4.0	5.0	0
LONG DURATION			
Paramethasone	2.0	10.0	0
Dexamethasone	0.75	25.0	0
Betamethasone	0.6	30.0	0

[a] Based on oral administration.

SELECTED SUGAR-FREE, DYE-FREE AND ALCOHOL-FREE PREPARATIONS

TRADE NAME	THERAPEUTIC CATEGORY	PAGE NO.	SUGAR FREE	DYE FREE	ALCOHOL FREE
BENADRYL Elixir	Antihistamine	71			X
BENADRYL DYE-FREE Elixir	Antihistamine	71	X	X	X
BENADRYL DYE-FREE Liqui-Gel Capsules	Antihistamine	71		X	
CEROSE-DM Liquid	Decongestant-Antihistamine-Antitussive	174	X		
DECONAMINE Syrup	Decongestant-Antihistamine	177		X	X
DECONAMINE Tablets	Decongestant-Antihistamine	177		X	
DELSYM Syrup	Antitussive	67			X
DEMEROL Syrup (C-II)	Opioid Analgesic	108			X
DIMETANE-DC Syrup (C-V)	Antitussive-Decongestant-Antihistamine	177	X		
DIMETANE-DX Syrup	Antitussive-Decongestant-Antihistamine	177	X		
DIMETAPP Elixir	Decongestant-Antihistamine	178			X
DIMETAPP DM Elixir	Decongestant-Antihistamine-Antitussive	178			X
DRIXORAL Syrup	Decongestant-Antihistamine	179			X
ELIXOPHYLLIN Capsules	Bronchodilator	154		X	
ELIXOPHYLLIN-GG Liquid	Antiasthmatic	180	X	X	X

Product	Category	Page	Col 1	Col 2	Col 3
FEDAHIST EXPECTORANT Syrup	Decongestant-Expectorant	182			X
FUROXONE Liquid	Antibacterial	87	X		
GLUCOTROL Tablets	Hypoglycemic	88		X	
KAON Elixir	Potassium Supplement	137	X		
KAOPECTATE Liquid	Antidiarrheal	35			X
KLOR-CON Powder	Potassium Supplement	136	X		
KLORVESS Effervescent Powder	Potassium Supplement	136	X		
KLORVESS Effervescent Tablets	Potassium Supplement	137	X		
Lithium Citrate Syrup	Antimaniacal	103	X		
MARAX Tablets	Antiasthmatic	186		X	
NALDECON-CX Liquid (C-V)	Antitussive-Decongestant-Expectorant	188	X		X
NALDECON-DX ADULT Liquid	Antitussive-Decongestant-Expectorant	188	X		X
NALDECON SENIOR DX Liquid	Antitussive-Expectorant	188	X		X
NALDECON SENIOR EX Liquid	Expectorant	90	X		X
NICORETTE Chewing Gum	Smoking Deterrent	122	X		
NICORETTE DS Chewing Gum	Smoking Deterrent	122	X		
NOLAHIST Tablets	Antihistamine	132		X	
NOVAHISTINE Elixir	Decongestant-Antihistamine	190	X		
PEPTO-BISMOL Chewable Tablets	Antidiarrheal	41	X		

TRADE NAME	THERAPEUTIC CATEGORY	PAGE NO.	SUGAR FREE	DYE FREE	ALCOHOL FREE
PEPTO BISMOL Liquid	Antidiarrheal	41	X		
PEPTO-BISMOL MAXIMUM STRENGTH Liquid	Antidiarrheal	41	X		
RITALIN-SR Sustained-Release Tablets (C-II)	CNS Stimulant	111		X	
ROBITUSSIN A-C Syrup (C-V)	Antitussive-Expectorant	197	X		
ROBITUSSIN-DAC (C-V) Syrup	Antitussive-Decongestant-Expectorant	197	X		
RONDEC-DM	Decongestant-Antihistamine-Antitussive	198	X		X
RYNA Liquid	Decongestant-Antihistamine	198	X	X	X
RYNA-C Liquid (C-V)	Antitussive-Decongestant-Antihistamine	198	X	X	X
RYNA-CX Liquid (C-V)	Antitussive-Decongestant-Expectorant	198	X	X	X
SLO-BID Extended Release Capsules	Bronchodilator	154		X	
SLO-PHYLLIN Syrup	Bronchodilator	155	X	X	X
SLO-PHYLLIN Tablets	Bronchodilator	155		X	
SLO-PHYLLIN GG Syrup	Antiasthmatic	201		X	X
THEO-DUR Extended Release Tablets	Bronchodilator	155		X	
THEOLAIR Liquid	Bronchodilator	155			X
TRIAMINIC-DM Syrup	Antitussive-Decongestant	204			X

234

Product	Type	Page		
TRIAMINIC NITE LIGHT Liquid	Decongestant-Antihistamine-Antitussive	204		X
TRIAMINIC SYRUP	Decongestant-Antihistamine	204		X
TRIAMINICOL MULTI-SYMPTOM RELIEF Syrup	Antitussive-Decongestant-Antihistamine	204		X
TRIND Liquid	Decongestant-Antihistamine	205	X	
TUSSAR DM Liquid	Antitussive-Decongestant-Antihistamine	206		X
TUSSAR SF Liquid (C-V)	Antitussive-Expectorant-Antihistamine	206	X	
TUSSI-ORGANIDIN NR Liquid (C-V)	Antitussive-Expectorant	206	X	

C-II: Controlled Substance, Schedule II
C-V: Controlled Substance, Schedule V

Notes

PRESCRIPTION WRITING

INTRODUCTION

A **prescription** is an order for a specific medication for a specified patient at a particular time. It is the way in which a physician communicates a patient's selected drug therapy to the pharmacist and instructs the patient on how to use the prescribed medication. The prescription order may be given by a physician, dentist, veterinarian, physician assistant, or any other legally-recognized medical practitioner; the order may be written and signed or it may be oral, in which case the pharmacist is required to transcribe it into written form and obtain the prescriber's signature, if necessary, at a later time.

The transfer of the therapeutic information from prescriber to pharmacist to patient must be clear. With all of the many drug products available to the prescriber, it is easy to understand how drug strengths, dosage forms, and dosage regimens can be confused. Many drug names may also look alike (especially when written hastily) or may sound alike (when garbled over the telephone). Furthermore, numerous studies have indicated that 25% to 50% of patients do not use their prescription medication properly; the patient often fails to take the drug or uses the medication either in an incorrect dose, at an improper time, or for the wrong condition. Most errors can be traced to the prescription order or the failure of the prescriber to adequately communicate this information to the patient.

In order that these types of errors be avoided and the patient gain the maximum benefit from the prescribed drugs, it is important for the physician to understand the basic principles of prescription writing.

COMPOSITION OF THE PRESCRIPTION ORDER

A complete prescription order is composed of eight parts and follows a standardized format which facilitates its interpretation by the pharmacist. The eight major parts of a prescription order include:

1. The date prescribed
2. The name, address, and age of the patient
3. The superscription
4. The inscription
5. The subscription
6. The signa
7. The renewal information
8. The name of the prescriber

Figure 1 illustrates a sample precompounded prescription order with the eight major elements numbered for reference purposes.

1. **The Date Prescribed** - The date on which a prescription was issued is important since a patient may not always have a prescription filled on the day it was written; days, weeks, months, or on occasion, years may pass before a patient presents the prescription to the pharmacist. Medications are intended for a patient at a particular time; the date prescribed may reveal that the presented prescription was not filled when written and now, for example, months later, the patient has "symptoms which are exactly the same as the last time" and is attempting to self-diagnose and self-medicate. Furthermore, drugs controlled by special laws and regulations, e.g., the Controlled Substances Act of 1970, cannot be dispensed or renewed more than six months from the date prescribed. Therefore, the date prescribed provides an accurate record of when a prescription was originally issued to the patient.

TELEPHONE (215) 555-2474

John V. Smith, M.D.
Paula A. Doe, M.D.

3002 BROAD STREET   ANYTOWN, ANYSTATE 00000

1   DATE 2/28/95   AGE 36
    NAME Linda Bush
2   ADDRESS 1812 Coventry Lane

3   ℞

4   Bactrim DS

5   Disp #20

6   Sig. 1 tab. q 12 h
       x 10 days.

8   Dr. [signature]   Dr. _____
    Do Not Substitute   *Substitution*
                               Permissible

7   Renew: 0 (1) 2 3 4 5   DEA # _____

FIGURE 1.   A Sample Precompounded Prescription Order

238

2. **The Name, Address, and Age of the Patient** - This information serves to identify for whom the prescribed medication is intended. The full name of the patient may help to prevent a mixup of drugs within a household when, for example, a parent and child have the same name. If the patient's first name is not known or omitted, the use of the titles Mr., Mrs., Ms. or Miss is appropriate. Information regarding the patient's age should also be indicated, e.g., "adult," "child," or in the case of a young child, the exact age; this allows the pharmacist to monitor the prescribed dosage, especially since the pharmacokinetics of many drugs differ markedly in newborn, pediatric, adult, and geriatric patient populations.

3. **The Superscription** - This portion of the prescription refers to the symbol R_x, a contraction of the Latin verb *recipe*, meaning "take thou." It serves to introduce the drug(s) prescribed and the directions for use.

4. **The Inscription** - The name, strength and quantity of the desired drug is enclosed within this section of the prescription. Although drugs may be prescribed by any known name, i.e., chemical name, trivial name, nonproprietary name (more commonly referred to as the generic name) and manufacturer's proprietary (trade) name, most drugs are prescribed either by the trade name or by the generic name. Chemical and trivial names of drugs are generally not suitable for this purpose and are seldom used. When the trade name is written, the prescription must be filled with product of the specified manufacturer, unless the prescriber and patient approved substitution with another brand. If the generic name is employed, the pharmacist can select from any of the available drug preparations. When two or more drugs are written on the same prescription for compounding purposes, the name and quantity of each should be listed on a separate line directly below the preceding one. To avoid confusion, the salt of a particular medicament should be clearly indicated if more than one is available, e.g., codeine <u>sulfate</u> or codeine <u>phosphate</u>. The quantities of the ingredients may be written in either the apothecary or metric system. The latter is more popular; it is used exclusively by official pharmaceutical reference texts, and in most cases, in medical schools, hospitals, and other health agencies.

The apothecary system is an older and less popular method of measurement; however, prescriptions are still written in this system and texts may, on occasion, report drug doses in apothecary units. For example, 1 fluid-ounce (apothecary) equals approximately 30 mL (metric) and 1 pint equals 473 mL.

Regardless of which system is employed on the prescription, most patients are more comfortable with household measures, especially with liquid medications. Although the sizes of the household teaspoon and tablespoon vary considerably, the standard household teaspoon should be regarded as containing 5 mL and the tablespoon, 15 mL. Standard disposable plastic teaspoons, tablespoons and graduated two fluid-ounce cups are available in an attempt to reduce liquid dose variability, and the use of these should be encouraged.

5. **The Subscription** - Directions to the pharmacist from the prescriber comprise this section of the prescription; these state the specific dosage form to be dispensed or the desired method of preparation. The subscription is usually a short phrase or sentence such as "Dispense 30 capsules" or "Dispense 90 mL" for a precompounded prescription or "Mix and prepare 10 suppositories" for an extemporaneous preparation.

6. **The Signa** - The directions to the patient are given in this part of the prescription and are usually introduced by the latin *Signa* or *Sig.*, meaning "mark thou". These directions should be as clear and as complete as possible, so that the patient may easily follow the desired dosage schedule and receive the maximum benefit from the medication. Instructions should be provided as to the route of administration, the amount of drug to be taken, and the time and frequency of the dose. Phrases such as "take as directed" and "use as required" are not satisfactory instructions and should be avoided whenever possible.

Latin, often considered to be the language of the medical profession, was used extensively in writing prescription orders until the early part of the 20th century. Although prescription orders in the United States today are almost always written in English, many Latin words and phrases have been retained and are commonly used (as abbreviations) in the Signa. Some of the more commonly-employed Latin terms and abbreviations are given in Table 1. Thus the Signa: "Caps 1 q.i.d. p.c. + H.S. c milk" translates to: "One capsule 4 times daily after meals and at bedtime with milk".

7. **The Renewal Information** - The wishes of the prescriber with regard to refilling the medication should be indicated on every prescription, and if renewals are authorized, the number of times should be designated. Prescription orders for drugs that bear the legend: "Caution: Federal law prohibits dispensing without prescription" may not be renewed without the expressed consent of the prescriber. Prescriptions for drugs covered under Schedule III or IV of the Controlled Substances Act of 1970 may be renewed, if so authorized, not more than five times within six months of date of issue; drugs within Schedule II may not be renewed.

8. **The Name of the Prescriber** - Although in most cases the prescriber's name and address are printed on the prescription blank, the signature of the prescriber affixed to the bottom completes and validates the prescription order. For prescriptions written on hospital prescription blanks, the prescriber must print (or stamp) his/her name on the document, as well as sign it. This is a safe-guard in case a question arises concerning any aspect of the prescription order, the printed name will make it easier to identify and contact the prescriber. On oral prescriptions, the pharmacist adds the prescriber's name to the prescription; however, Federal law requires that prescriptions for Schedule II drugs be validated by the full signature of the prescriber and his/her registered Drug Enforcement Administration (DEA) number. The prescriber's registered DEA number must appear on all prescriptions for drug covered under the Controlled Substances Act (see below).

CLASSES OF PRESCRIPTION ORDERS

Prescription orders may be divided into two general classes based on the availability of the medication. A **precompounded** prescription order requests a drug or a drug mixture prepared and supplied by a pharmaceutical company; prescriptions of this class require no pharmaceutical alteration by the pharmacist. The prescription order shown in Figure 1 is a precompounded prescription. An **extemporaneous** or **compounded** prescription order is one in which the drugs, doses and dosage form, as selected by the prescriber, must be prepared by the pharmacist. Figure 2 shows an example of an extemporaneous prescription order. Most prescriptions written today are of the precompounded type; however extemporaneous prescription orders are not uncommon, especially with liquid, cream and ointment preparations.

CONTROLLED SUBSTANCES ACT

The legal aspects of prescription writing and dispensing are incorporated in various federal, state and local laws, which the medical practitioner must understand and observe; the strictest law regardless of governmental level, always takes precedence unless Federal Law is preemptive. In 1970, the Comprehensive Drug Abuse Prevention and Control Act, commonly called the Controlled Substances Act, was signed into law. This act imposes even more stringent controls on the distribution and use of all stimulant and depressant drugs and substances with the potential for abuse as designated by the Drug Enforcement Administration (DEA), U.S. Department of Justice. This act divides drugs with abuse potential into five categories or schedules as follows:

Schedule I (C-I) — Drugs in this schedule have a high potential for abuse and no currently accepted medical use in the United States. Examples of such drugs include heroin, marijuana, peyote, mescaline, some tetrahydrocannabinols, LSD, and various opioid derivatives. Substances listed in this

TABLE 1. COMMON LATIN ABBREVIATIONS

WORD OR PHRASE	ABBREVIATION	MEANING
Ad	Ad	Up to
Ana	aa	Of each
Ante cibos	a.c.	Before meals
Aqua	Aq.	Water
Aures utrae	a.u.	Each ear
Aurio dextra	a.d.	Right ear
Aurio laeva	a.l.	Left ear
Bis in die	b.i.d.	Twice a day
Capsula	Caps.	Capsule
Compositus	Comps.	Compounded
Cum	c	With
Et	Et	And
Gutta	Gtt.	A drop, drops
Hora somni	H.S.	At bedtime
Non repetatur	Non rep.	Do not repeat
Oculo utro	O.U.	Each eye
Oculus dexter	O.D.	Right eye
Oculus sinister	O.S.	Left eye
Per os	p.o.	By mouth
Post cibos	p.c.	After meals
Pro re nata	p.r.n.	When necessary
Quaque	q.	Each, every
Quantum satis	Q.S.	As much as is sufficient
Quarter in die	q.i.d.	Four times daily
Semis	ss	A half
Sine	s	Without
Statim	Stat.	Immediately
Tabella	tab	Tablet
Ter in die	t.i.d.	Three times daily
Ut dictum	Ut Dict.	As directed

TELEPHONE (215) 555-2474

John V. Smith, M.D.
Paula A. Doe, M.D.

3002 BROAD STREET   ANYTOWN, ANYSTATE 00000

DATE _2/25/95_   AGE _3_

NAME _Sarah Lewis_

ADDRESS _890 Main Blvd._

R Triamcinolone Cream
0.5 %   10 g.
Water   6 ml
Hydrophilic Oint
     q. s. ad. 30 g

Sig apply to affected
     area BID

Dr. _Paula Doe_   Dr. _____

Do Not Substitute   *Substitution*
Permissible

Renew: 0 1 2 ③ 4 5   DEA # _____

FIGURE 2.   A Sample Extemporaneous Prescription Order

242

schedule are not for prescription use; they may be obtained for chemical analysis, research, or instruction purposes by submitting an application and a protocol of the proposed use to the DEA.

Schedule II (C-II) — The drugs in this schedule have a high abuse potential with severe psychological or physical dependence liability. Schedule II controlled substances consist of certain opioid drugs, preparations containing amphetamines or methamphetamines as the single active ingredient or in combination with each other, and certain sedatives. Examples of opioids included in this schedule are opium, morphine, codeine, hydromorphone (DILAUDID), methadone (DOLOPHINE), meperidine (DEMEROL), oxycodone (PERCODAN, PERCOCET), and oxymorphone (NUMORPHAN). Also included are stimulants, e.g., cocaine, dextroamphetamine (DEXEDRINE), methamphetamine (DESOXYN), methylphenidate (RITALIN), and depressants, e.g., amobarbital (AMYTAL SODIUM), pentobarbital (NEMBUTAL SODIUM) and secobarbital.

Schedule III (C-III) — The drugs in this schedule have a potential for abuse that is less than for those drugs in Schedules I and II. The use or abuse of these drugs may lead to low or moderate physical dependence or high psychological dependence. Included in this schedule, for example, are mazindol (SANOREX), and paregoric. Analgesic mixtures containing limited amounts of codeine phosphate (e.g., TYLENOL WITH CODEINE and EMPIRIN WITH CODEINE), or hydrocodone (e.g., ANEXSIA, BANCAP-HC, and LORTAB) or cough mixtures containing hydrocodone (e.g., HYCODAN and HYCOMINE) are contained within this schedule. Also included in this schedule are certain anabolic steroids (e.g., salts of nandrolone (DURABOLIN and DECA-DURABOLIN) and oxandrolone (OXANDRIN)).

Schedule IV (C-IV) — The drugs in this category have the potential for limited physical or psychological dependence and include phenobarbital, paraldehyde, chloral hydrate, ethchlorvynol (PLACIDYL), meprobamate (EQUANIL, MILTOWN), chlordiazepoxide (LIBRIUM), diazepam (VALIUM), clorazepate (TRANXENE), flurazepam (DALMANE), oxazepam (SERAX), clonazepam (KLONOPIN), prazepam (CENTRAX), lorazepam (ATIVAN), and salts of propoxyphene (DARVON and DARVON-N). Certain other mixtures are included; for example, the antidiarrheal MOTOFEN and the analgesic DARVOCET-N.

Schedule V (C-V) — Schedule V drugs have a potential for abuse that is less than those listed in Schedule IV. These consist of preparations containing moderate quantities of certain opioids for use in pain (i.e., buprenorphine (BUPRENEX)) or as antidiarrheals (e.g., diphenoxylate (LOMOTIL), or as antitussives (such as codeine-containing cough mixtures, e.g., ROBITUSSIN A-C) may be dispensed without a prescription order, provided that specified dispensing criteria are met by the pharmacist.

Every person involved in the manufacture, importing, exporting, distribution or dispensing of any Controlled Drug must obtain an annual registration from the DEA; therefore, a physician must be registered before he/she can administer or dispense any of the drugs listed in the abuse schedules. Furthermore, the physician's DEA registration number must be indicated on every prescription order for Controlled Substances.

Notes

247

251

257

263

ORDER FORM FOR HANDBOOKS

TITLE	PRICE x QUANTITY
Handbook of Commonly Prescribed Drugs, Tenth Edition (1995), 270 pages ISBN 0-942447-15-8	$ 15.50 x _____ = $ _____.____
Handbook of Commonly Prescribed Pediatric Drugs, Fifth Edition (Expected: Summer, 1995)	$ 15.50 x _____ = $ _____.____
Handbook of Over-the-Counter Preparations, Second Edition (Expected: late Fall, 1995)	$ 15.50 x _____ = $ _____.____
Handbook of Pain Management, Fourth Edition (1994), 180 pages ISBN 0-942447-09-3	$ 15.00 x _____ = $ _____.____
Handbook of Commonly Prescribed Geriatric Drugs, First Edition (1993), 334 pages ISBN 0-942447-01-8	$ 15.00 x _____ = $ _____.____
Handbook of Common Orthopaedic Fractures, Second Edition (1992), 224 pages ISBN 0-942447-05-0	$ 14.00 x _____ = $ _____.____
Handbook of Commonly Prescribed Ocular Drugs (1991), 152 pages ISBN 0-942447-07-7	$ 13.00 x _____ = $ _____.____
	SUB-TOTAL = $ _____.____
Shipping and Handling PA Residents: Add 6% Sales Tax	= $ __4.50__
	= $ _____.____
	TOTAL = $ _____.____

For mail orders for Handbooks, please complete the reverse side of this form.

ORDER FORM FOR TEXTBOOK
IN PHARMACOLOGY

TITLE	PRICE x QUANTITY		
Basic Pharmacology in Medicine, Fourth Edition (1995), 880 pages ISBN 0-942447-04-2	$ 49.95 x _____ = $ _____._____		
	SUB-TOTAL	=	$ _____._____
Shipping and Handling		=	$ __4. 50
PA Residents: Add 6% Sales Tax		=	$ _____._____
	TOTAL	=	$ _____._____

Send mail orders for Handbooks or Textbook with checks or money orders to:

MEDICAL SURVEILLANCE INC.
P.O. Box 1629   West Chester, PA 19380

(PLEASE PRINT)

Name_____Degree_____

Organization_____

Street Address_____

City_____State_____Zip_____

Telephone Number_____

Signature_____

FOR FURTHER INFORMATION CALL COLLECT: 610 - 436-8881
FAX: 610 - 436-1803

REQUEST FOR INFORMATION

If you wish to be placed on a mailing list for information concerning new publications and updates, please fill out the form below and mail to:

MEDICAL SURVEILLANCE INC.
P.O. Box 1629   West Chester, PA 19380

(PLEASE PRINT)

Name_____

Organization_____

Street Address_____

City_____State_____

Zip Code_____

Telephone Number (Optional)_____

FOR FURTHER INFORMATION CALL: 610 - 436-8881